Simca 1300/1301 & 1500/1501 Owners Workshop Manual

by J H Haynes
Associate Member of the Guild of Motoring Writers
and Peter Strasman
MISTC

Models covered
UK: Simca 1300 Saloon. 1963 to 1966
       Simca 1301 Saloon and Estate. 1966 on
       Simca 1500 Saloon and Estate. 1963 to 1966
       Simca 1501 Saloon and Estate. 1966 on

ISBN 0 85696 199 X

HAYNES PUBLISHING GROUP
SPARKFORD YEOVIL SOMERSET ENGLAND
distributed in the USA by
HAYNES PUBLICATIONS INC
861 LAWRENCE DRIVE
NEWBURY PARK
CALIFORNIA, 91320
USA

Acknowledgements

Our thanks must go to Chrysler France through Chrysler United Kingdom for the use of certain illustrations and for technical information.

Special thanks are due to all of those people at Sparkford who helped with the preparation of this manual and to Stanley Randolph who page edited the text.

Castrol Limited supplied lubrication details.

About this manual

Its aims

This is a manual by a practical owner for a practical owner. The author, and those assisting him, learned about this range of models the only thorough way, by studying all available information and then going ahead and doing the work, under typical domestic conditions and with a typical range of tools, backed only by their experience as keen car men over a number of years.

Unlike other books of this nature, therefore, the hands in most of the photographs are those of the author, and the instructions cover every step in full detail, assuming no special knowledge on the part of the reader except how to use tools and equipment in a proper manner, firmly and positively but with due respect for precise control where this is required.

Its arrangement

The manual is divided into twelve Chapters, each covering a logical sub-division of the vehicle. The Chapters are each divided into Sections, numbered with single figures, eg 5; and the Sections into paragraphs (or sub-sections), with decimal numbers following on from the Section they are in, eg 5.1, 5.2, 5.3, etc.

It is freely illustrated, especially in those parts where there is a detailed sequence of operations to be carried out. There are two forms of illustration: figures and photographs. The figures are numbered in sequence with decimal numbers, according to their position in Chapter: eg; Fig 6.4 is the 4th drawing/illustration in Chapter 6. Photographs are numbered (either individually or in related groups) the same as the Section or sub-Section of the text where the operation they show is described.

There is an alphabetical index at the back of the manual as well as a contents list at the front.

References to the 'left' or 'right' of the vehicle are in the sense of a person in a seat facing forwards towards the engine.

Points for the reader

The accumulation of good tools normally must take place over a period of time and this is the one expense which the do-it-yourself owner must face. Cheap tools are never worth having, as they are not cheap in the long run. They rarely last, often make the work more difficult, and may even cause accidental damage which could cost more to put right than the cost of a good tool in the first place.

Certain jobs require special tools and where these are essential, the manual points out. Otherwise, alternative methods are given.

Be discreet about borrowing tools; even with great care, accidents still happen, and the replacement of a lost or damaged tool can be costly. Do not be offended, if refused: the person approached may have had an unhappy experience already!

Where appropriate, fault finding instructions are given at the end of Chapters. Accurate diagnosis of troubles depends on a careful, and above all, systematic approach, so avoid the attitude "if all else fails, read the handbook". It is better, and almost always quicker, to say: "This could be one of several things, so let's have a look at the Haynes manual before trying anything".

Whilst every care is taken to ensure that the information in this manual is correct no liability can be accepted by the authors or publishers for loss, damage or injury caused by any errors in or omissions from, the information given.

Contents

Introduction to the Simca 1300/1301 and 1500/1501

This range of vehicles was first introduced into the UK market in October 1963 as the 1300 (GL) Saloon and the 1500(L) Saloon. In September 1964 the Estate Wagon (GL) version was launched.

In October 1965, restyling and certain modifications were carried out and the 1300 Saloon was redesignated 'LS', the 1500 Saloon 'GL' and the Estate 'GLS'.

In September 1966 the smaller models were redesignated the 1301 GL Saloon and Estate and the larger models the 1501 GL and GLS Saloons and the GLS Estate.

After September 1971, all models are identified by the capacity (1301 or 1501) followed by the word 'Special'.

Mechanically all vehicles are similar but over a period of ten years, styling has been changed in detail and certain mechanical refinements carried out. These include front disc brakes, reclining front seats, floor mounted gearchange lever, servo brakes, heated rear window, improved interior heater and the provision of a twin choke carburettor on all late models.

Automatic transmission was optionally available at certain periods of production and for specified markets. The power unit fitted to all models is basically similar, the difference in capacity being achieved by a variation in the bore and stroke (See Specifications).

Simca 1301/1501 Special

Simca 1501S Estate

Buying spare parts
and vehicle identification numbers

Buying spare parts

Spare parts are available from many sources, for example: SIMCA garages, other garages and accessory shops, and motor factors. Our advice regarding spare part sources is as follows:

Officially appointed SIMCA garages - This is the best source of parts which are peculiar to your car and are otherwise not generally available (eg complete cylinder heads, internal gearbox components, badges, interior trim etc). It is also the only place at which you should buy parts if your car is still under warranty-non-SIMCA components may invalidate the warranty. To be sure of obtaining the correct parts it will always be necessary to give the storeman your car's engine and chassis number, and if possible, to take the 'old' part along for positive identification. Remember that many parts are available on a factory exchange scheme - any parts returned should always be clean! It obviously makes good sense to go straight to the specialists on your car for this type of part for they are best equipped to supply you.

Other garages and accessory shops - These are often very good places to buy materials and components needed for the maintenance of your car (eg oil filters, spark plugs, bulbs, fan belts, oils and greases, touch-up paint, filler paste etc). They also sell general accessories, usually have convenient opening hours, charge lower prices and can often be found not far from home.

Motor factors - Good factors will stock all of the more important components which wear out relatively quickly (eg clutch components, pistons, valves, exhaust systems, brake cylinders/pipes/hoses/seals/shoes and pads etc). Motor factors will often provide new or reconditioned components on a part exchange basis - this can save a considerable amount of money.

Vehicle identification numbers

When ordering spare parts, it is essential to give full details of your vehicle to the storeman. He will need to know the type, the serial number and where the engine or gearbox is concerned, the serial numbers of these units as well.

The engine number is to be found on the left-hand side of the engine block adjacent to the engine oil dipstick.

The vehicle type and serial numbers are to be found on a plate affixed to the engine compartment right-hand wing valance adjacent to the suspension upper mounting.

Location of engine number

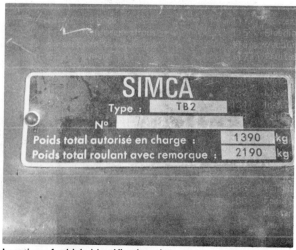

Location of vehicle identification plate

Routine maintenance

Maintenance should be regarded as essential for ensuring safety and desirable for the purpose of obtaining economy and performance from the car. By far the largest element of the maintenance routine is visual examination.

The maintenance instructions listed are those recommended by the manufacturer. They are supplemented by additional maintenance tasks which, from practical experience, need to be carried out.

The additional tasks are indicated by an asterisk (*) and are primarily of a preventative nature - they will assist in eliminating the unexpected failure of a component.

Weekly, before a long journey or at intervals of 250 miles 400 km)

1 Check the engine oil level and top up as required with Castrol GTX.
2 Check the battery electrolyte level and top-up as necessary using only distilled water. Wipe the top of the battery free from moisture and dirt.
3 Top-up the windscreen washer reservoir.
4 Check the level of coolant in the radiator and top-up if necessary to not more than one inch (25.4 mm) below the filler neck. If the engine is hot when this operation is being carried out, cover the filler cap with a cloth and unscrew the cap only ¼

turn to allow the steam to escape before completely removing the cap. Never add large quantities of cold water to a hot engine or the castings may fracture. Always maintain the strength of the antifreeze mixture by adding the correct proportion of anti-freeze to the topping-up water.
5 Check and top-up, if necessary, the brake and clutch fluid reservoirs using Castrol/Girling Universal Brake and Clutch Fluid.
 *Ensure that the reservoir breather holes are clear.
6 Check operation of all lights, direction indicators and horn.
7 Check the tyre pressures and inflate to specified levels.
8 Inspect the treads for wear and renew any tyre which has less than 1 mm of tread depth left or where the built in wear indicators are flush with the tread surface.

Every 3000 miles (4800 km) or at 3 monthly intervals

1 Drain and refill the sump with Castrol GTX. This is best carried out with the engine hot.
2 Check the fluid level in the automatic transmission (where fitted) and top-up if necessary to provide a level between the 'MINIMUM' and 'MAXIMUM' marks. This operation should be carried out with the transmission unit at normal operating temperature with the engine idling and the speed selector lever in 'P'. Withdraw the dipstick, wipe it, insert it and finally withdraw it and read off the level.

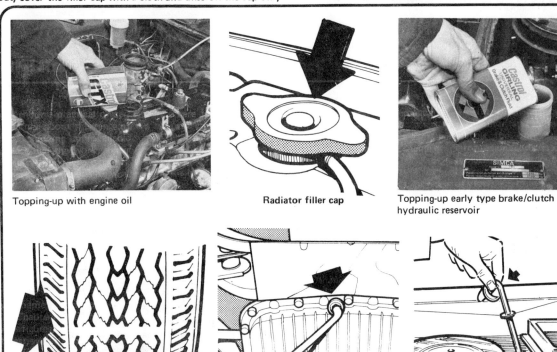

Topping-up with engine oil

Radiator filler cap

Topping-up early type brake/clutch hydraulic reservoir

Tyre tread wear indicator

Sump drain plug

Checking fluid level in automatic transmission

3* Adjust the tension of the dynamo/water pump drive belt. There should be a total deflection of ½ in (12.7 mm) at the mid point of the top run of the belt. If adjustment is required, slacken the dynamo adjustment strap and mounting bolts and prise the dynamo away from the engine until the correct tension is obtained.
4 Adjust the clutch free-movement to provide a clearance of 3/32 in (2.4 mm) between the clutch release lever and the push-rod of the clutch slave cylinder. This is carried out by first detaching the return spring and then releasing the locknut and rotating the push-rod until the correct free movement is established. Retighten the locknut.
5* Lubricate all locks and hinges with a few drops of engine oil.
6* Check that door drain holes are clear.
7* Lubricate throttle control linkage.
8* Lubricate speed selector linkage (automatic transmission).

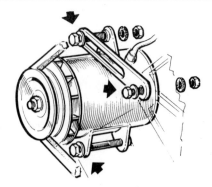

Drive belt tension adjusting bolts on dynamo

Every 6000 miles (9600 km) or at 6 monthly intervals

1 Drain the oil from the manual gearbox when warm and refill with Castrol Hypoy 90.
2 Drain the oil from the rear axle when warm and refill with Castrol Hypoy 90.
3 Top-up the steering box, if necessary with Castrol Hypoy (light) 80.
4 Clean and adjust the distributor contact breaker points (Chapter 4) lubricate the distributor and check the ignition timing.
5 Lubricate the steering and suspension joints (early models).
6 Check the steering and suspension linkage for wear by gripping one component and levering the adjacent one.
7 Lubricate the water pump.
8 Check cooling system hoses and connections for security and deterioration of rubber hose.
9 Renew the air cleaner element.
10 Disconnect the leads from the battery terminals, clean away all corrosion, refit the leads and apply petroleum jelly to the terminals.
11 *Tune the carburettor as described in Chapter 3.
12 Clean the spark plugs and adjust the gaps to that specified (0.024 in - 0.61 mm)
13 Remove the road wheels, examine tyre treads and walls for cuts or damage. Remove embedded flints and rotate the road wheels round the vehicle to even out tyre wear.
14 Check for wear in the front brake disc pads as described in Chapter 9.
15 In cold conditions, move the air cleaner lever to the 'WINTER' position. On 1301 models fit the radiator blanking panel supplied.
16 *Examine the exhaust system for leaks or severe corrosion and renew or repair as appropriate.
17 Check seat belt anchorages and condition of belts.
18 Check front wheel alignment as described in Chapter 11.
19 Check the adjustment of the kick-down control if automatic transmission fitted (Chapter 6).
20 Lubricate the propeller shaft joint with Castrol LM grease.

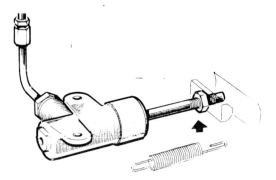

Adjusting clutch free-movement

Every 12000 miles (19300 km) or at twelve monthly intervals

1 Lubricate and adjust the front wheel bearings (Chapter 11).
2* Check the condition and security of the engine flexible mountings.
3 Clean the fuel pump filter according to type fitted.
4 Adjust the valve clearances. This operation may be carried out with the engine hot or cold. Clearances **Cold:** Inlet 0.011 in (0.30 mm). Exhaust 0.014 in. (0.35 mm)
Hot: Inlet 0.014 in (0.35 mm) Exhaust 0.016 (0.40 mm)
5 Check the wear of the rear brake shoe linings and adjust the rear brakes.
6 Inspect the brake hydraulic system for leaks corrosion of

Drain and filler/level plugs on manual gearbox

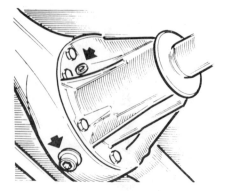

Rear axle drain and filler/level plugs

Steering box filler/level plug

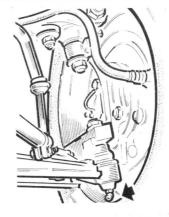

Lower suspension swivel joint grease nipple

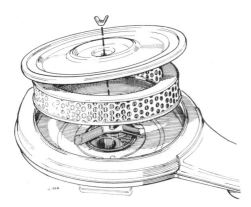

Renewing air cleaner element

Air cleaner 'Winter' and 'Summer' intake deflector control

A

Radiator blanking panel (1301 models) A to left hand side

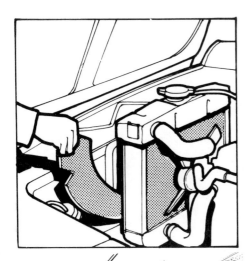

Adjusting valve clearances

Propeller shaft lubrication point

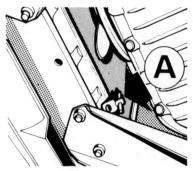

Location of radiator drain tap

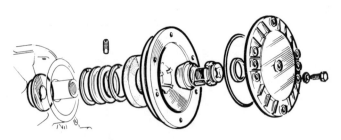

Exploded view of centrifugal type oil filter

rigid pipelines and chafing or deterioration of flexible hoses. Renew as necessary.

7   Renew the spark plugs ensuring that the new ones are in accordance with the latest recommendations of the spark plug manufacturers.

8   Drain the cooling system and refill with the correctly proportioned quantity of antifreeze mixture. The antifreeze properties of antifreeze solution may last for up to two years but the anti-corrosive inhibitors will deteriorate long before this and therefore the coolant should be renewed at annual intervals even if the mileage covered is small.

9   Check security and torque setting of all nuts and bolts.
10 Clean the centrifugal type oil filter (see Chapter 1).

Every 24000 miles (38600 km) or at two yearly intervals
1   Renew the brake vacuum servo air filter (Chapter 9).
2   Drain the brake hydraulic system, renew all seals and refill and bleed the system.
3   Drain the clutch hydraulic system, renew the seals in the master and slave cylinders and refill and bleed the system.
4   Drain the automatic transmission unit, check and adjust if necessary the front and rear brake bands and refill the unit with Castrol TQ Dexron R fluid.
5   Test the action of the shock absorbers. This can be carried out by disconnecting the upper or lower mounting and operating the unit to the full extent of its travel several times. Any lack of resistance in either direction will mean the renewal of the shock absorber.

Lubrication chart

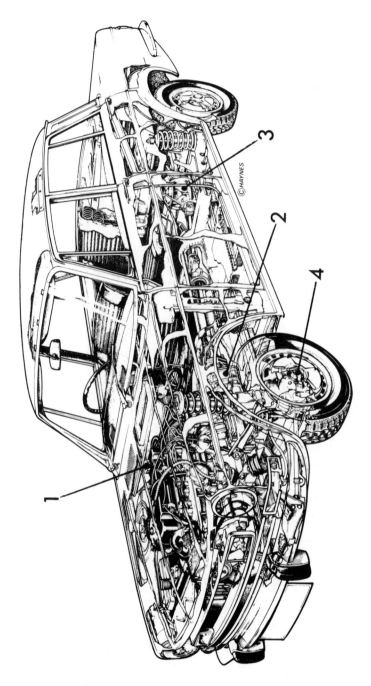

©HAYNES

Recommended lubricants and fluids

Engine (1)	...	...	...	...	...	...	...	...	Castrol GTX
Gearbox (2) : manual	...	...	...	...	...	...	...	...	Castrol Hypoy (90 EP)
automatic	...	...	...	...	...	...	...	...	Castrol TQF
Rear axle (3)	...	...	...	...	...	...	...	...	Castrol Hypoy (90 EP)
Wheel bearings (4) and chassis	...	...	...	...	...	...	...	...	Castrol LM Grease
Locks, hinges, pivots etc.		...	...	...	...	...	...	...	Castrol GTX

Note: the above are general recommendations - lubricant requirements vary from territory-to-territory. Consult the operators handbook supplied with the vehicle, if in doubt.

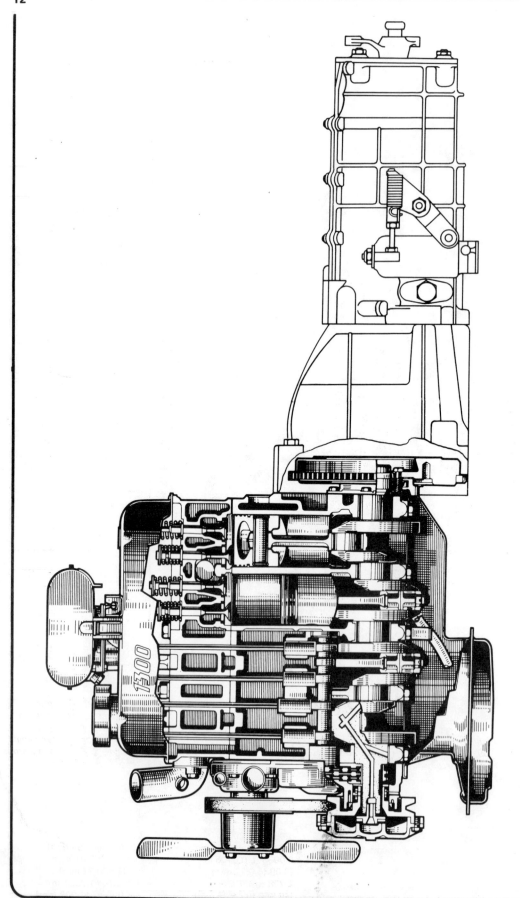

Fig 1.1 Sectional view of engine fitted to 1300 models

Chapter 1 Engine

Contents

Specifications

Engine general

	1300/1301	1500/1501
Engine type	312T (up to 1969 only)	342
Cylinder arrangement	4 in line	4 in line
Timing gear	ohv pushrod	ohv pushrod
Cylinder block material	Cast iron	Cast iron
Cylinder head material	Light alloy	Light alloy
Bore	2.913 in (74.0 mm)	2.960 in (75.21 mm)
Stroke	2.952 in (75.0 mm)	3.267 in (83.0 mm)
Piston displacement (cubic capacity)	1290 cc (78.72 cu in)	1475 cc (90.01 cu in)
Compression ratio	8.6 : 1	9.1 : 1
Maximum power output	62 bhp at 5200 rev/min	81 bhp at 5400 rev/min
Maximum torque	73.77 lb ft at 2600 rev/min	90.41 lb ft at 3500 rev/min

The following specifications show the differences between the 1300 (Type 312T) engine built up until 1969 and the 342 type engine fitted to all models after 1969. Engine specifications for 1301, 1500 and 1501 models are the same except for the differences in pistons and cylinder bores, details of which are as shown under 1300 model.

Crankshaft

	1300 (Type 312T) up to 1969	1301 (after 1969) 1500 and 1501
Material	Forged steel	Forged steel
Number of main bearings	5	5
Main journal diameter	1.886 to 1.897 in (47.875 to 47.891 mm)	2.123 to 2.124 in (53.95 to 53.97 mm)
Endfloat	0.0035 to 0.0106 in (0.09 to 0.27 mm)	0.0035 to 0.0106 in (0.09 to 0.27 mm)
Crankpin diameter	1.728 to 1.733 in (43.990 to 44.05 mm)	1.7300 to 1.7321 in (44.990 to 44.003 mm)

Main bearing type	...	...	...	...	...	...	...	...	Shell (steel/copper/lead)	Shell (steel/copper/lead)
Thickness	...	...	...	...	...	...	...	...	0.0715 to 0.0725 in (1.826 to 1.835 mm)	0.156 to 0.157 in (3.972 to 3.996 mm)
Thrust washers (type)		...	...	...	...	...	...	...	Steel/tin	Steel/tin
Thickness	...	...	...	...	...	...	...	...	0.091 to 0.093 in (2.31 to 2.36 mm)	0.091 to 0.093 in (2.31 to 2.36 mm)

Connecting rods

Material	...	...	...	...	...	...	...	...	Forged steel	Forged steel
Distance between big and small end centres				...	...	...			5.12 ± 0.003 in (130 ± 0.075 mm)	5.196 ± 0.0027 in (132 ± 0.075 mm)
Permissible weight difference between rods in same engine							...		0.175 oz (5.0 grammes)	0.10 oz (3.0 grammes)
Big end bearing type		...	...	...	...	...	...	...	Shell	Shell
Bearing thickness	...	...	...	...	...	...	...	...	0.0702 to 0.0706 in (1.783 to 1.793 mm)	0.1394 to 0.1399 in 3.542 to 3.554 mm)
Small-end bearing type		...	...	...	...	...	...	...	Bronze bush	Bronze bush
Bearing bore diameter		...	...	...	...	...	...	...	0.86614 to 0.86653 in (22.002 to 22.012 mm)	0.8691 to 0.8722 in (22.008 to 22.016 mm)

Cylinder block

									1300 (Type 312T) up to 1969	**1301 (after 1969) 1500 and 1501**
Material	...	...	...	...	...	...	...	...	Cast iron	Cast iron
Bore:										
Standard	...	...	...	...	...	...	...	...	2.9131 to 2.922 in (73.9925 to 74.0225 mm)	2.959 to 2.961 in (75.200 to 75.230 mm)
Grading: A		...	...	...	...	...	...	...	2.9131 to 2.914 in (73.9925 to 74.00 mm)	2.959 to 2.960 in (75.200 to 75.210 mm)
B			...	...	...	...	...	...	2.9140 to 2.915 in (74.0000 to 74.0075 mm)	2.960 to 2.961 in (75.210 to 75.220 mm)
C			...	...	...	...	...	...	2.915 to 2.916 in (74.0075 to 74.0150 mm)	2.961 to 2.962 in (75.220 to 75.230 mm)
D			...	...	...	...	...	...	2.916 to 2.921 in (74.0150 to 74.0225 mm)	—

Pistons

Material	...	...	...	...	...	...	...	...	Cast, light alloy	Cast, light alloy
Crown diameter	...	...	...	...	...	...	...	...	2.894 in (73.5 mm)	2.957 to 2.958 in (75.133 to 75.163 mm)
Diameter at skirt base:										
Grading: A		...	...	...	...	...	...	...	2.911 to 2.913 in (73.9475 to 73.9550 mm)	2.957 to 2.958 in (75.133 to 75.143 mm)
B			...	...	...	...	...	...	2.913 to 2.914 in (73.9550 to 73.9625 mm)	2.958 to 2.9581 in 75.143 to 75.153 mm)
C			...	...	...	...	...	...	2.914 to 2.915 in (73.9625 to 73.9700 mm)	2.9581 to 2.959 in (75.153 to 75.163 mm)
D			...	...	...	...	...	...	2.915 to 2.916 in (73.9700 to 73.9775 mm)	—

Piston rings

Quantity per piston	...	...	...	...	...	...	...	...	4	3
Compression rings:										
Quantity	...	...	...	...	...	...	...	...	2	1
Material	...	...	...	...	...	...	...	...	Cast iron	Cast iron
End-gap	...	...	...	...	...	...	...	...	0.006 to 0.014 in (0.15 to 0.35 mm)	0.011 to 0.017 in (0.30 to 0.45 mm)
Upper oil control:										
Quantity	...	...	...	...	...	...	...	...	1	2
Material	...	...	...	...	...	...	...	...	Cast iron	Cast iron
End-gap	...	...	...	...	...	...	...	...	0.006 to 0.014 in (0.15 to 0.35 mm)	0.011 to 0.017 in (0.30 to 0.45 mm)
Lower oil control:										
Quantity	...	...	...	...	...	...	...	...	1	—
Type	...	...	...	...	...	...	...	...	4 component, spring	—
End-gap	...	...	...	...	...	...	...	...	0.009 to 0.016 in (0.25 to 0.40 mm)	—

Gudgeon pins

Type	...	...	...	...	...	...	...	...	Steel, fully floating	Steel, fully floating
Outer diameter	...	...	...	...	...	...	...	...	0.867 in (22.0 mm)	0.866 in (22.0 mm)
Length	...	...	...	...	...	...	...	...	2.460 in (62.5 mm)	2.460 in (62.5 mm)

Camshaft

Type	3 bearing, cast iron	3 bearing, cast iron
Drive	Double roller chain	Double roller chain
Timing chain	46 links, pitch 0.375 in (9.525 mm)	46 links, pitch 0.375 in (9.525 mm)

Valves

Inlet:

Stem diameter	0.315 in (8.0 mm)	0.315 in (8.0 mm)
Head diameter	1.263 in (32.1 mm)	1.318 in (33.5 mm)
Overall length	4.409 in (112.0 mm)	4.409 in (112.0 mm)
Seat angle	45°	45°
Seat material	Cast iron	Cast iron
Seat outer diameter	1.303 to 1.306 in (33.1 to 33.185 mm)	1.381 to 1.382 in (35.105 to 35.125 mm)
Bore	0.79921 to 1.2204 in (20.3 to 28.5 mm)	1.102 in (28.0 mm)

Exhaust:

Stem diameter	0.315 in (8.0 mm)	0.315 in (8.0 mm)
Head diameter	1.185 in (30.1 mm)	1.181 in (30.0 mm)
Overall length	4.409 in (112.0 mm)	4.409 in (112.0 mm)
Seat angle	45°	45°
Seat material	Cast iron	Cast iron
Seat outer diameter	1.224 to 1.227 in (31.1 to 31.185 mm)	1.263 to 1.264 in (32.105 to 32.125 mm)
Bore	1.03543 to 1.04330 in (26.3 to 26.5 mm)	1.023 in (26.0 mm)

Valve guides

Material	Cast iron	Cast iron
Length	2.204 in (56.0 mm)	2.047 in (52.0 mm)
Outer diameter	0.552 in (14.0 mm)	0.552 in (14.0 mm)
Bore (after fitting)	0.315 to 0.3166 in (8.022 to 8.040 mm)	0.315 to 0.3166 in (8.022 to 8.040 mm)

Pushrods

Material	Steel	Steel
Length	9.50 in (241.5 mm)	9.743 in (247.5 mm)
Diameter	0.276 in (7.0 mm)	0.276 in (7.0 mm)

Valve springs

Free length:

Inner	2.086 in (53.0 mm)	1.850 in (47.0 mm)
Outer	—	2.286 in (58.1 mm)

Outer diameter:

Inner	1.122 in (28.5 mm)	0.822 in (20.9 mm)
Outer	—	1.227 in (31.2 mm)

Wire diameter:

Inner	0.150 in (3.8 mm)	0.098 in (2.5 mm)
Outer	—	0.149 in (3.8 mm)

Valve timing

Inlet opens	12° btdc	17° btdc
Inlet closes	60° abdc	63° abdc
Exhaust opens	52° bbdc	61° bbdc
Exhaust closes	20° atdc	19° atdc

Cam followers (tappets)

	1300 (Type 312T) up to 1969	1301 (after 1969) 1500 and 1501
Material	Cast iron	Cast iron
Length	1.968 in (50.0 mm)	1.574 in (40.0 mm)
Diameter	0.866 to 0.867 in (21.978 to 21.998 mm)	0.668 to 0.669 in (16.974 to 17.0 mm)
Running clearance	0.0007 to 0.0015 in (0.020 to 0.043 mm)	0.0008 to 0.0010 in (0.021 to 0.026 mm)

Lubrication system

Type	Sump mounted gear pump with centrifugal oil filter on front of crankshaft	Timing case mounted gear pump with centrifugal oil filter on front of crankshaft
Oil capacity	7 pints (4 litres)	8 pints (4.5 litres)
Oil pressure	50 to 64 lb in^2 at 3500 rev/min	68 to 74 lb in^2 at 3500 rev/min

Torque wrench settings

	lb ft	kg m
Cylinder head bolts (large) 1300 model	58	8.0
Cylinder head bolts (small) 1300 model	47	6.5
Cylinder head bolts (1301, 1500, 1501 models)	58	8.0
Manifold nuts	15	2.0
Rocker pillar nuts (1300 model)	22	3.0
Spark plugs	20	2.8
Rocker arm adjuster screw locknuts	9	1.2
Engine to clutch bellhousing bolts (with special washers) ...	38	5.2
Engine to clutch bellhousing bolts (without washers) ...	15	2.0
Crankshaft main bearing cap bolts (1300 model)	40	5.5
Crankshaft main bearing cap bolts (1301, 1500, 1501 models)	47	6.5
Sump bolts	7	1.0
Crankshaft rear oil seal carrier bolts	7	1.0
Oil pump bolts (1300 model)	16	2.2
Oil pump relief valve plug (1300 model)	54	7.5
Oil pump relief valve plug (1301, 1500, 1501 models)	29	4.0
Timing cover bolts	7	1.0
Water pump securing bolts	7	1.0
Engine mounting bolts	16	2.2
Centrifugal oil filter centre screw	58	8.0
Centrifugal oil filter cover bolts	7	1.0
Flywheel mounting bolts (8 mm diameter)	27	3.7
Flywheel mounting bolts (9 mm diameter)	40	5.5
Connecting rod big-end cap nuts (1300 model)	22	3.0
Connecting rod big-end cap nuts (1301, 1500, 1501 models) ...	33	4.5
Camshaft gearwheel bolts	15	2.0
Starter motor bolts	16	2.2
Flywheel cover bolts	16	2.2
Fan blade bolts	7	1.0

1 General description

Both sizes of engine covered by this manual are basically similar apart from minor differences in some small components. Originally manufactured as two individual power units, a single engine was later produced of 1475 cc capacity and the bores sleeved to provide a smaller capacity engine of 1290 cc for the model 1301.

The engine is three point mounted, the rear gearbox mounting being of rather unusual cantilever leaf spring type.

The cylinder block is of cast iron construction and the crankshaft is forged steel running in five main bearings. The pistons are made of light-alloy with floating type gudgeon pins retained by circlips.

The cylinder head is of light-alloy and incorporates the pushrod operated overhead valves. The three bearing camshaft is chain driven from the crankshaft. The distributor drive is taken from a gear on the camshaft. The inlet manifold is light-alloy and is bolted to the right-hand side of the cylinder head together with the cast-iron exhaust manifold. This arrangement provides a measure of preheating for the fuel vapour as it passes through the inlet manifold.

The lubrication system is not of connectional type but incorporates an oil pump of gear design which draws the oil from the sump and delivers it to a centrifugal type oil filter which is driven from the front end of the crankshaft. The oil (controlled by a pressure relief valve) then flows to the bearings and other moving parts of the engine. On 1300 models and 1301 models up to 1969 the oil pump is mounted within the sump but on all other models it is mounted within the timing cover.

2 Major operations with engine in vehicle

1 Although it is strongly recommended that the engine is removed for the following work to be carried out, it is possible to undertake these operations if the engine side mountings are first disconnected together with the exhaust downpipe and the cooling system drained and top and bottom radiator hoses disconnected. Hoist the engine about two inches (50.8 mm) and remove the sump bolts which are now accessible.

2 With the sump removed, the main shell bearings may be renewed, also the big-end bearings.

3 If the cylinder head is removed then the piston/connecting rod assemblies may be removed through the top of the block.

4 The oil pump may be serviced after removing it from the crankcase (1300 models and early 1301 models) or timing case (all other models).

5 The cylinder head may be removed and serviced without the need to raise the engine of course.

6 If the radiator is removed then the water pump, oil filter and timing gear may be dismantled . On 1300 models, and 1301 models up to 1969, the camshaft and cam followers may be removed.

3 Major operations requiring engine removal

1 The following operations can only be performed with the engine removed:

2 Removal and installation of the crankshaft.

3 Removal and installation of the flywheel.

4 Renewal of the crankshaft rear oil seal.

5 Removal of camshaft and cam followers (1301 (after 1969) 1500,1501 models)

4 Method of engine removal and procedure

1 The engine only can be removed on its own, leaving the gearbox (or automatic transmission) in position for subsequent removal to the rear, if required.

2 The engine together with the transmission unit cannot be removed in combined form as it would necessitate hoisting the unit out almost vertically to provide clearance for the sump and gearbox.

3 Drain the cooling system, retaining the antifreeze mixture if required for further use. Drain the engine oil.

4 Unscrew the nuts from the bonnet hinge plates. (photo)

5 With the help of an assistant, remove the bonnet. (photo)

6 Remove the air cleaner from the carburettor and cover the intake to prevent dirt or small objects droppings in. (photo)

7 Disconnect the leads from the battery terminals. (photo)

8 Lift the battery from the engine compartment. (photo)
9 Disconnect the earth strap from the dynamo adjustment strap (photo).
10 Disconnect the leads from the starter motor, oil pressure and water temperature transmitters.
11 Disconnect the leads from the dynamo and unscrew the mounting and adjustment strap bolts and remove the dynamo. (photo)
12 Disconnect the upper and lower radiator hoses. (photo)
13 Unscrew the four radiator securing screws. (photo)
14 Lift the radiator from the engine compartment. (photo)
15 Remove the bolts secure the fan blades to the mounting hub and withdraw the fan blades. (photo)
fan is of thermostatically controlled, electromagnetic type and the fan blades should be removed by unscrewing the three *outer* securing nuts only (see Chapter 2). (photo)
17 Disconnect the choke and accelerator controls at the carburettor, also the fuel inlet pipe. (photo)

18 Disconnect the crankcase breather pipe and the vacuum pipe from the carburettor and remove the carburettor from its flange. (photos)
19 Disconnect the heater hoses from their connections at the rear of the cylinder block. (photos)
20 Disconnect the fuel supply pipe from the inlet nozzle of the fuel pump and plug the pipe to prevent loss of fuel. (photo)
21 Unscrew the pinch bolts and remove the clamp ring which holds the exhaust downpipe to the exhaust manifold. (photo)
22 Remove the preheater plate from the manifold. (photo)
23 Unbolt and remove the manifold assembly. (photo)
24 Remove the starter motor securing bolts and withdraw the starter motor.
25 From underneath the vehicle, disconnect the stabiliser rod mountings and remove the rod complete. (photo)
26 Unscrew and remove the bolts which secure the clutch bellhousing to the engine. (photo)
27 Place suitable slings round the engine and attach them to the lifting hook of a hoist.

4.4 Unscrewing bonnet hinge nuts

4.5 Removing bonnet

4.6 Removing air cleaner

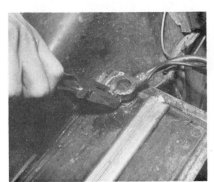

4.7 Disconnecting battery leads

4.8 Removing battery

4.9 Dynamo strap earth lead

4.11 Removing dynamo

4.12A Disconnecting radiator upper hose

4.12B Disconnecting radiator lower hose

4.13 Removing radiator securing screw

4.14 Removing radiator

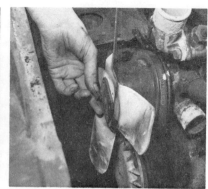

4.15 Removing fan blade bolts

4.16 Removing fan belt

4.17 Choke and accelerator cable connections

4.18A Distributor vacuum pipe and crankcase breather pipe

4.18B Removing carburettor from manifold

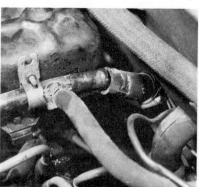

4.19A Removing heater hose from cylinder head

4.19B Disconnecting heater hose from distribution tube

4.20 Fuel inlet pipe disconnected from pump

4.21 Exhaust pipe to manifold clamp

4.22 Removing preheater plate

28 Support the weight of the gearbox on a jack; and take the weight of the engine on the hoist.

29 Unscrew the nuts from the engine flexible mountings. (photo)

30 Raise the engine an inch, or two, and pull it forward until the clutch assembly which is bolted to the flywheel is disengaged from the gearbox input shaft.

31 Hoist the engine up, and out, of the engine compartment. Take care not to damage the water outlet elbow on the rear of the cylinder block during the process (1301,1500 and 1501 models). (photo)

32 Where automatic transmission is installed, the removal procedure is similar to that just described but observe the following points:

Disconnect the downshift cable at the carburettor.

Disconnect the speed selector linkage at the transmission unit.

Unscrew and remove the four bolts which secure the driveplate to the torque converter. These bolts are accessible one at a time, by turning the engine slowly until each bolt comes into view in the lower half of the torque converter housing with the semi-circular blanking plate removed.

Disconnect the combined fluid filler and dipstick tube from the engine crankcase.

Disconnect the leads from the starter inhibitor switch which is screwed into the left-hand side of the transmission. On 1968 models only disconnect the water pipes from the Solex automatic choke carburettor.

5 Dismantling the engine - general

1 It is best to mount the engine on a dismantling stand, but if one is not available, stand the engine on a strong bench, to be at a comfortable working height. It can be dismantled on the floor if other facilities are not available.

2 During the dismantling process greatest care should be taken to keep the exposed parts free from dirt. As an aid to achieving this, thoroughly clean down the outside of the engine, removing all traces of oil and congealed dirt.

3 Use paraffin or Gunk. The latter compound will make the job much easier for, after the solvent has been applied and allowed to stand for a time, a vigorous jet of water will wash off the solvent with all the grease and dirt. If the dirt is thick and deeply embedded, work the solvent into it with a wire brush.

4 Finally wipe down the exterior of the engine with a rag and only then, when it is quite clean, should the dismantling process begin. As the engine is stripped, clean each part in a bath of paraffin or Gunk.

5 Never immerse parts with oilways (for example the crankshaft), in paraffin but to clean, wipe down carefully with a petrol dampened cloth. Oilways can be cleaned out with a piece of wire. If an air line is available, all parts can be blown dry and the oilways blown through as an added precaution.

6 Re-use of old engine gaskets is false economy and will lead to oil and water leaks, if nothing worse. Always use new gaskets throughout.

7 Do not throw the old gasket away, for it sometimes happens that an immediate replacement cannot be found and the old gasket is then very useful as a template. Hang up the old gaskets as they are removed.

8 To strip the engine it is best to work from the top down. The underside of the crankcase when supported on wood blocks acts as a firm base. When the stage is reached, where the crankshaft and connecting rods have to be removed, the engine can be turned on its side and all other work carried out with it in this position.

9 Whenever possible, replace nuts, bolts and washers finger tight from wherever they were removed. This helps avoid loss and muddle later. If they cannot be replaced lay them out in such a fashion that it is clear from whence they came.

4.23 Removing manifold

4.25 Disconnecting stabilizer rod end link

4.26 Unscrewing clutch bellhousing to engine bolt

4.29 Unscrewing flexible mounting bolt

4.31 Hoisting engine from vehicle

6.2 Removing distributor cap and leads

6.3 Removing distributor body

6.4 Removing distributor drive sleeve

6.5 Removing fuel pump

6.7 Removing crankcase breather

6.8 Unbolting water pump

6.10 Removing clutch assembly

7.2 Rocker cover clamp plate

7.3 Removing rocker cover

7.4 Lifting off the rocker gear

7.5 Removing a pushrod

8.1 Removing tappet chamber cover

6   Removing engine ancillary components

1   With the engine out of the vehicle, remove the ancillary components prior to commencing dismantling.
2   Remove the distributor cap complete with HT leads. (photo)
3   Remove the distributor from its recess (2 bolts). (Photo)
4   Remove the distributor drive sleeve from the splined shaft (1300 models only - all later models have gear pinned to distributor shaft). (photo)
5   Remove the fuel pump from the engine crankcase (2 bolts). (photo)
6   Remove the engine oil dipstick.
7   Remove the crankcase breather (2 bolts). (photo)
8   Unbolt the water pump from the front face of the engine block. (photo)
9   Remove the heater water distribution tube from the left-hand side of the rocker cover.
10 Unscrew the clutch pressure plate cover bolts. These should be unscrewed in diametrically opposite sequence a half turn at a time to prevent distortion of the plate. Remove the pressure plate and driven plate (friction disc) from the flywheel. (photo)

7   Cylinder head - removal

1   The procedure is the same whether the engine is in or out of the vehicle but the cylinder head must never be removed if it is warm. Always allow five hours to lapse after the engine has been switched off, so that the cylinder head will be quite cold before removal to prevent any possibility of distortion.
2   Unscrew the nuts from the four rocker cover bolts and remove the clamp plates.
3   Lift the rocker cover from the cylinder head. (photo)
4   Unscrew and remove the nuts from the rocker pillar studs and lift away the rocker shaft assemblies (1300 and 1301 up to head bolts also serve to retain the rocker pillars in position. (photo)
5   Withdraw each of the pushrods and retain them in the correct sequence for refitting. (photo)
6   Unscrew each of the cylinder head bolts a half turn at a time and in the *reverse* sequence to that shown in Fig 1.16 on page 37 (according to vehicle model). Remove the bolts, cylinder head and gasket. If the cylinder head is stuck, tap it gently on its sides using a hammer and a block of wood as an insulator; never attempt to prise it off using a screwdriver or other tool inserted in the gasket joint.

8   Cam followers (tappets) - removal

1   Unscrew and remove the cover plate from the tappet chamber (1300, and 1301 up to 1969). (photo)
2   Withdraw each of the cam followers and keep them in strict sequence pending refitting. (photo)
3   On all other models the camshaft must first be removed with the engine inverted (see Section 14).

9   Rocker gear - dismantling

1   The rocker arms and springs may be drawn off the rocker shafts after the circlips at both ends of each shaft have been removed.
2   Note the positions of the rocker arms so that they can be refitted in their original locations.

8.2 Withdrawing a cam follower

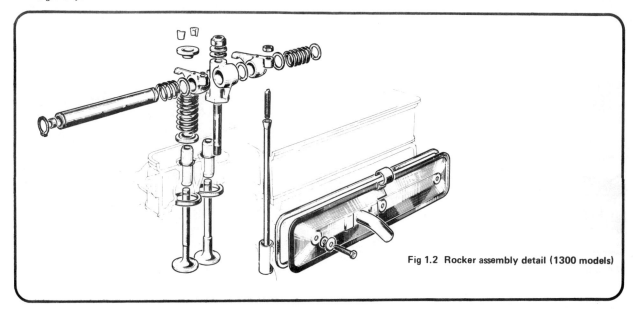

Fig 1.2 Rocker assembly detail (1300 models)

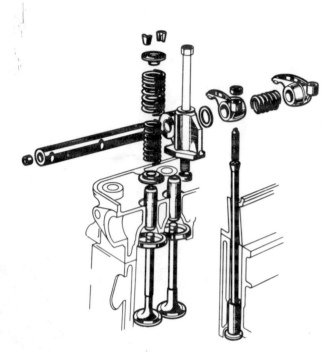

Fig 1.3 Rocker assembly detail (1301, 1500, 1501 models)

10 Valve - removal

1   Using a suitable valve spring compressor, compress each valve spring until the split collets are released and can be extracted. (photo)
2   Release the compressor and remove the spring retaining collar. (photo)
3   Remove the single valve spring (1300, and 1301 up to 1969 models) or double springs (all other models). (photo)
4   Remove the lower retaining washer. (photo)
5   The valve may now be extracted from its guide. (photo)
6   Repeat the operations on the remaining valves but keep them in their original sequence as they are removed so that they can be returned to their original guides when refitted. A piece of card or plywood with holes drilled and numbered 1 to 8 is a useful retainer.

11 Centrifugal oil filter - dismantling and cleaning

1   Unscrew and remove the bolts from the front of the oil filter cover. Two threaded holes (A) (Fig 1.4) are provided so that two bolts may be screwed into them and will have the effect of forcing off the cover. (photo)
2   If the oil filter is to be cleaned only, no further dismantling is necessary. Using a sharp instrument remove the hard scale from the interior of the filter. Refit the cover and tighten the bolts evenly to a torque not exceeding 7 lb/ft (1.0 kg/m).
3   Where further dismantling is to be carried out, bend back the tabs of the cup type locking washer (1300, and 1301 up to 1969 models only). (photo)
4   Unscrew the centre nut and remove the locking washer and deflector.
5   Withdraw the inner section of the filter body which incorporates the drive belt pulley.
6   **On all other models** the centre nut of the filter will require the

10.1 Compressing a valve spring

10.2 Removing valve spring collar

10.3 Removing a valve spring

10.4 Removing valve spring retainer

10.5 Extracting a valve from its guide

11.1 Removing oil filter cover

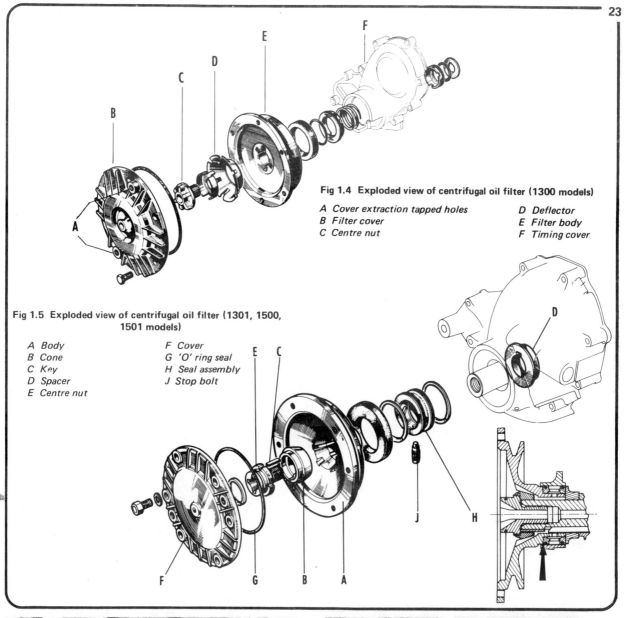

Fig 1.4 Exploded view of centrifugal oil filter (1300 models)

A Cover extraction tapped holes
B Filter cover
C Centre nut

D Deflector
E Filter body
F Timing cover

Fig 1.5 Exploded view of centrifugal oil filter (1301, 1500, 1501 models)

A Body
B Cone
C Key
D Spacer
E Centre nut

F Cover
G 'O' ring seal
H Seal assembly
J Stop bolt

11.3 Oil filter centre screw and locking washer

11.5 Withdrawing inner oil filter section and drive pulley

use of a special tool to unscrew it. Remove the locking cone and key.

12 Timing gear (1300 and 1301 up to 1969 models) - removal

1 With the centrifugal oil filter removed as described in the preceeding Section, unscrew and remove the bolts from the timing cover and lift away the cover and gasket. (photo)
2 Bend back the tabs of the locking plate and unscrew and remove the camshaft gearwheel retaining bolts. (photo)
3 Remove the spacer from the front of the crankshaft and then draw off the gearwheel and the sprocket complete with timing chain. (photo)
4 If necessary, the Woodruff key can then be removed from the crankshaft. (photo)

13 Camshaft (1300 and 1301 up to 1969 models) - removal

1 With the cam followers, centrifugal oil filter and timing gear removed as previously described, bend back the locking plate tabs and unscrew the two bolts which secure the semi-circular thrust plate to the front face of the engine block. (photo)
2 Withdraw the camshaft from the front of the engine ensuring that the lobes of the camshaft do not damage the camshaft bearings as they pass through. (photo)

14 Timing gear and camshaft (1301, 1500, 1501 models) - removal

1 The procedure is similar to that described for the 1300 model

12.1 Removing timing cover

12.2 Camshaft gearwheel bolts and locking plates

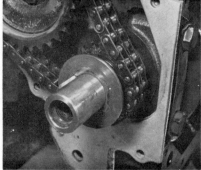
12.3 Crankshaft sprocket spacer

12.4 Crankshaft sprocket key

13.1 Camshaft thrust plate and bolts

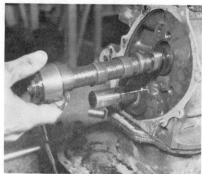
13.2 Withdrawing camshaft

15.1 Bending back a flywheel bolt locking plate tab

17.4 Removing oil pump

20.1 Extracting gudgeon pin circlip

in the previous two Sections except that the oil pump which is mounted within the timing cover must first be removed as described in Section 18 and the engine inverted to prevent the cam followers dropping out.

15 Flywheel - removal

1 Bend back the tabs on the locking plate located behind the flywheel securing bolts. (photo)
2 Mark the relative mounting position of the flywheel to the crankshaft flange.
3 Unscrew the flywheel bolts (jamming the starter ring gear if necessary to prevent the engine turning) and lift the flywheel from the crankshaft flange.

16 Sump - removal

1 Unscrew and remove the sump securing bolts and lift the sump from the crankcase flange.
2 If it is stuck tight, cut round the joint gasket with a sharp knife until it is released; do not attempt to lever it off with a screwdriver or similar object.

17 Oil pump (1300 and 1301 up to 1969 models) - removal

1 Having removed the sump, the oil pump will be found bolted to the crankcase flange.
2 The oil pump pick up tube and gauge filter are supported on a 'U' bracket bolted to a main bearing cap.
3 The oil supply tube connects with the crankcase oil gallery where the oil is first fed to the centrifugal type oil filter, in which is incorporated a pressure relief valve, and then is directed to the moving parts of the engine (see Section 23).
4 To remove the oil pump, unbolt the pump body, the intake filter bolt and the bolts from the supply tube flange. (photo)

18 Oil pump (1301,1500,1501 models) - removal

1 The oil pump and pressure relief valve are mounted within the timing cover and are accessible once the centrifugal oil filter and timing cover have been removed.
2 The driving gear of the oil pump is engaged with the front end of the camshaft by means of a stepped coupling.
3 The oil intake and gauge filter are bolted in position by means of a flange to the crankcase.

19 Pistons, connecting rods - removal

1 Flatten the tabs of the lockwashers under the big-end cap units.
2 The connecting rods are marked with their location number and this appears on the connecting rod and the big-end cap. The two numbers should be adjacent and on the camshaft side.
3 Unscrew the big-end nuts on No.1 connecting rod, remove the bearing cap and push the piston/connecting rod assembly out of the top of the bore.
4 Repeat the operation on the remaining three pistons.

20 Gudgeon pin - removal

1 Using a pair of circlip pliers, extract the circlips from both ends of the gudgeon pin. (photo)
2 Push out the pin using finger pressure only. If it is tight in the pistons, immerse the assembly in hot water for a few minutes.

21 Pistons rings - removal

1 Each piston is fitted with either two compression and two oil control rings (1300, and 1301 up to 1969 models) or one compression and two oil control.
2 The lower oil control ring is of four section spring design on the 1300, and 1301 up to 1969 model engine.
3 To remove the rings, slide them carefully off the piston taking care not to scratch the soft alloy of the piston. Never slide them off the bottom of the piston skirt. The rings will break very easily if they are twisted, or pulled out of their grooves roughly.
4 An ideal method of removing a piston ring is to lift one end and insert three old feeler blades or strips of thin tin under it.
5 Turn the feelers slowly round the piston until all three are staggered at equidistant points. The ring can now be slid up the feelers which will prevent the ring dropping into an empty groove as the ring rides over the piston lands.

22 Main bearings and crankshaft - removal

1 Flatten the tabs of the locking plates which are located beneath the main bearing cap bolts.
2 Unscrew and remove the bolts and lift off the locking plate. This will reveal the main bearing cap number. Note its position carefully and which way round it is fitted. (photo)
3 Repeat the procedure with the other four main bearings and then lift the crankshaft from the crankcase. (photo)

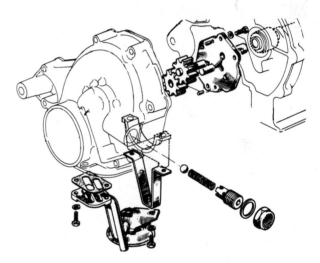

Fig 1.6 Oil pump and pressure relief valve (1301, 1500, 1501 models)

Fig 1.7 Connecting rod and cap marks

22.2 Crankshaft main bearing cap number

22.3 Lifting crankshaft from crankcase

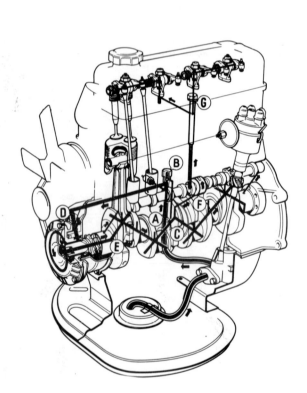

Fig 1.8 Lubrication system (1300 model)

A   Oil passage
B   Release valve
C   Oil return passage
D   Centrifugal oil filter
E   Crankshaft oil passage
F   Camshaft oil feed
G   Rocker oil feed

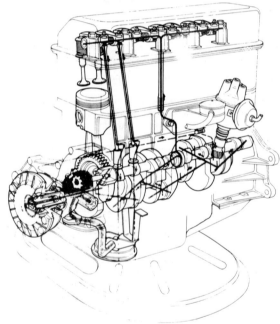

Fig 1.9 Lubrication system (1301, 1500, 1501 models)

23 Lubrication system (1300, and 1301 up to 1969 models)

1   This comprises a gear type oil pump located within the sump, a centrifugal type oil filter mounted on the front end of the crankshaft and a pressure relief valve.

2   Oil is drawn in through the intake filter and pressurised by the oil pump gears where it is then fed to the centrifugal filter and distributed to all engine working surfaces through the necessary oil galleries and drillings.

24 Lubrication system (1301,1500,1501 models)

1   This is similar to that described in the preceeding Section except that the oil pump and the pressure release valve are mounted within the timing cover.

25 Oil pump - overhaul

1 In the event of low oil pressure being observed, first check the oil level in the sump.
2 Check that the engine is in good condition mechanically, without bearing rumble or knock.
3 Check the operation of the oil pressure switch by substitution.
4 Remove the sump and check that the oil filter screen is not obstructed.
5 If all these conditions are satisfactory, the oil pump should be renewed as an assembly, the servicing of individual components not being possible.

26 Crankcase ventilation systems - maintenance

1 The crankcase ventilation system is basically similar but varies in detail according to model, year of manufacture and operating territory.
2 The system incorporates an extractor unit attached to the left-hand side of the crankcase and flexible pipes and in some versions non-return valves.

3 Check the security of the hoses and renew any that have deteriorated.
4 The non-return valves normally require no maintenance but if they do stick, soak them in paraffin and then blow dry with air from a tyre pump.

27 Engine front mountings - renewal

1 With the power unit removed from the vehicle, now is the time to examine the flexible mountings.
2 If the rubber has become very hard (or very soft through oil contamination) or if the rubber to metal bonding has parted renew the mounting.

28 Examination and renovation - general

With the engine stripped and all parts thoroughly cleaned, every component should be examined for wear. The following items should be checked and, where necessary, renewed or renovated as described later.

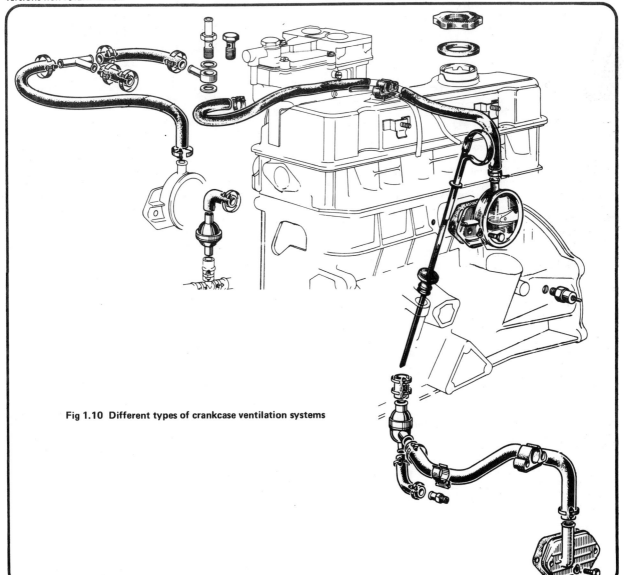

Fig 1.10 Different types of crankcase ventilation systems

29 Crankshaft - examination and renovation

Examine the crankpin and main journal surfaces for signs of scoring or scratches and check the ovality of the crankpins at different positions with a micrometer. If more than 0.001 inch (0.0254 mm) out of round, the crankpins will have to be reground. They will also have to be reground if there are any scores or scratches present. Also check the journals in the same fashion. If necessary to regrind the crankshaft and fit new bearings, an engineering works will be able to decide how much metal to grind off and be able to supply the correct undersize shells to fit.

30 Big-end and main bearings - examination and renovation

1 Big-end bearing failure is usually accompanied by a noisy knocking from the crankcase and a slight drop in oil pressure. Main bearing failure is accompanied by vibration which can be quite severe as the engine speed rises and falls, and a drop in oil pressure.
2 Bearings which have not broken up, but are badly worn will give rise to low oil pressure and some vibration. Inspect the big-ends, main bearings and thrust washers for signs of general wear, scoring, pitting and scratches. The bearings should be matt grey in colour. With lead indium bearings, should a trace of copper colour be noticed the bearings are badly worn, for the lead bearing has worn away to expose the indium underlay. Renew the bearings if they are in this condition or if there is any sign of scoring or pitting.
3 The undersizes available are designed to correspond with regrind sizes; 0.010 in bearings are correct for a crankshaft reground 0.010 in undersize. The bearings are in fact slightly more than the stated undersize as running clearances have been allowed for during their manufacture.
4 Very long engine life can sometimes be achieved by changing big end bearings at 30,000 miles (48000 km) and main bearings at 50,000 miles (80000 km), irrespective of bearing wear. Normally, crankshaft wear is infinitesimal and regular changes of bearings may ensure mileages of between 100,000 miles (160000 km) and 120,000 miles (1930000 km) before crankshaft regrinding becomes necessary. Crankshafts normally have to be reground because of scoring due to bearing failure.

31 Cylinder bores - examination and renovation

1 The cylinder bores must be examined for taper, ovality, scoring and scratches. Start by carefully examining the top of the bores, if they are worn fractionally a very slight ridge will be found on the thrust side. This marks the top of the piston travel. You will have a good indication of the bore wear prior to dismantling the engine, or removing the cylinder head. Excessive oil consumption accompanied by blue smoke from the exhaust is a sure sign of worn cylinder bores and piston rings.
2 Measure the diameter of the bore just under the ridge with a micrometer and compare it with the diameter at the bottom of the bore, which is not subject to such wear. If the difference between the two measurements is more than 0.006 inch (0.1524 mm) then it will be necessary to fit a 'ring set' or to have the cylinders rebored and fit oversize pistons and rings. If no micrometer is available remove the rings from one piston and place the piston in each bore in turn about ¾ inch (19 mm) below the top of the bore. If an 0.010 inch (0.254 mm) feeler gauge can be slid between the piston and the cylinder wall on the thrust side of the bore then remedial action must be taken. Oversize pistons are available in the following sizes:

+0.010 inch (0.254 mm)   +0.030 inch (0.762 mm)
+0.020 inch (0.508 mm)   +0.040 inch (1.016 mm)

3 These are accurately machined to just below these measurements so as to provide correct running clearances in bores bored out to the exact oversize dimensions.

4 If the bores are slightly worn but not so badly worn as to justify reboring them, special oil control rings can be fitted to the existing pistons which will restore compression and stop the engine burning oil. Several different types are available and the manufacturer's instructions concerning their fitting must be followed closely.

32 Pistons and piston rings - examination and renovation

1 If the old pistons are to be refitted carefully remove the piston rings and then thoroughly clean them. Take particular care to clean out the piston ring grooves. Do not scratch the aluminium in any way. If new rings are to be fitted to the old pistons, then the top ring should be stepped, so to clear the ridge left above the previous top ring. If a normal but oversize new ring is fitted it will hit the ridge and break, because the new ring will not have worn in the same way as the old.
2 Before fitting the rings on the pistons each should be inserted approximately 3 inches (76 mm) down the cylinder bore and the gap measured with a feeler gauge.
    On 1300, and 1301 up to 1969 models, the end-gap of the compression rings should be between 0.006 and 0.014 in (0.15 and 0.35 mm). The end gap of the upper oil control ring should be the same as that for the compression rings. The end-gap for the lower oil control ring should be between 0.010 and 0.016 in (0.25 and 0.40 mm).
    On 1301, 1500 and 1501 models, the end-gap of the compression ring should be between 0.011 and 0.017 in (0.30 and 0.45 mm). The end-gap of the upper oil control ring should be the same as that for the compression rings. The end-gap for the lower oil control ring should be between 0.009 and 0.016 in (0.25 and 0.40 mm).
3 It is essential that the gap is measured at the bottom of the ring travel, for if it is measured at the top of a worn bore and gives a perfect fit, it could easily seize at the bottom. If the ring gap is too small rub down the ends of the ring with a very fine file until the gap is correct when fitted. To keep the rings square in the bore for measurement, line each one up in turn with an old piston in the bore upside down, and use the piston to push the ring down about 3 inches (76 mm). Remove the piston and measure the piston ring gap.
4 When fitting new pistons and rings to a rebored engine the ring gap can be measured at the top of the bore as the bore will not now taper. It is not necessary to measure the side clearance in the piston ring grooves with rings fitted, as the groove dimensions are accurately machined during manufacture. When fitting new oil control rings to the pistons it may be necessary to have the grooves widened by machining to accept the new wider rings.
5 New piston rings are fitted in the reverse manner to removal (Section 21).
6 All compression rings have "TOP" marked on them. Oil control rings are unmarked and may be installed either way up on 1301, 1500 and 1501 models.

33 Camshaft and camshaft bearings - examination and renovation

1 Carefully examine the camshaft bearings for wear. If the bearings are obviously worn or pitted or the metal underlay just showing through, then they must be renewed.
2 The old bearings can be removed by driving them from the crankcase using a tubular drift. Alternatively, a length of studding may be used with the necessary nuts and washers to draw them from their seats.
3 New bearings are available which do not require reaming after installation.
4 Fit the new bearings by pressing them into position ensuring that the oil supply holes are correctly aligned.
5 The camshaft itself should show no sign of wear, but, if very

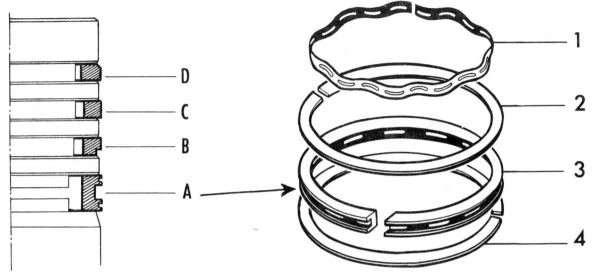

Fig 1.11 Piston ring installation diagram (1300 model)

A Lower oil control ring (1 expansion spring 2 top rail 3 ring 4 lower rail)
B Upper oil control ring C Lower compression ring D Top compression ring

Fig 1.12 Method of removal and installation of camshaft bearings

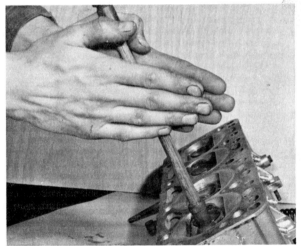

34.3 Grinding in a valve

slight scoring marks are visible they can be removed by gently rubbing down with very fine emery cloth or an oil stone. The greatest care must be taken to keep the cam profiles smooth.

34 Valves and seats - examination and renovation

1 Examine the heads of the valves for pitting or burning, especially the head of the exhaust valves. The valve seatings should be examined at the same time. If the pitting on the valve is very slight the marks can be removed by grinding the seats and valves together with coarse, and then fine, valve grinding paste Where bad pitting has occurred to the valve seats it will be necessary to recut them and fit new valves. If the valve seats are so worn that they cannot be recut then it will be necessary to fit

new valve seat inserts. These latter two jobs should be entrusted to a SIMCA garage or engineering works. In practice it is very seldom that the seats are so badly worn that they require renewal. Normally it is the valve that is too badly worn, and you can easily purchase a new set of valves and match them to the seats by valve grinding.

2 Valve grinding is easily carried out. Place the cylinder head upside down on a bench with a block of wood at each end to give clearance for the valve stems.

3 Smear a trace of coarse carborundum paste on the seat face and apply a suction grinding tool to the valve head as shown. (photo) With a semi-rotary action, grind the valve head to its seat, lifting the valve occasionally to redistribute the grinding paste. When a dull matt even surface finish is produced on both the valve seat and the valve, then wipe off the paste and repeat the process with fine carborundum paste, lifting and turning the valve to redistribute the paste as before. A light spring placed under the valve head will greatly ease this operation. When a smooth unbroken ring of light grey matt finish is produced, on

both valve and valve seat faces, the grinding operation is complete.

4   Scrape away all carbon from the valve head and the valve stem. Carefully clean away every trace of grinding compound, taking great care to leave none in the ports or in the valve guides. Clean the valve and valve seats with a paraffin soaked rag then wipe with clean rag. (If an air line is available blow clean).

35 Valve guides - examination and renovation

1   Examine the valve guides internally for wear. If the valves are a very loose fit in the guides and there is the slightest suspicion of lateral rocking, then new guides will have to be fitted.
2   Removal and refitting of valve guides requires the use of a press and heating of the alloy cylinder head to a specified temperature and it is therefore an operation best left to your SIMCA dealer.

36 Timing gear and chain - examination and renovation

1   Examine the teeth on both the crankshaft gear wheel and the camshaft gear wheel for wear. Each tooth forms an inverted 'V' with the gear wheel periphery and if worn, the side of each tooth under tension will be slightly concave in shape when compared with the other side of the tooth ie; one side of the inverted 'V' will be concave when compared with the other. If any sign of wear is present the gear wheels must be renewed.
2   Examine the links of the chain for side slackness and renew the chain if any slackness is noticeable when compared with a new chain. It is a sensible precaution to renew the chain every 30,000 miles (48,000 km) and at a lesser mileage if the engine is stripped down for a major overhaul. The actual rollers on a very badly worn chain may be slightly grooved.

37 Cam followers (tappets) - examination and removation

1   Examine the bearing surface of the tappets which run on the camshaft. Any indentation in this surface or any cracks indicate serious wear and the tappets must be renewed. Thoroughly clean them out, removing all traces of sludge. It is most unlikely that the sides of the tappets will be worn, but if they are a loose fit in their bores and can be readily rocked, they should be discarded and new tappets fitted.
2   On 1300, and 1301 (up to 1969) models the lower bearing surface of the cam follower was likely to crack due to the thin metal used. The redisigned cam followers used in 1301, 1500 and 1501 models do not suffer from this fault.

38 Connecting rods - examination and renovation

1   If a connecting rod is suspected of being twisted, it must be renewed. When renewing a connecting rod, the difference in weight between all four rods must not exceed 5 grammes; it is a good idea therefore to take one of the other rods with you when purchasing the new one.
2   Small end bushes can be reamed and oversize gudgeon pins installed if wear has occurred but new standard bushes can be fitted once the old ones have been pressed out.
3   Both these operations are best left to your SIMCA dealer having the necessary equipment.

39 Flywheel starter ring gear - examination and renovation

1   If the teeth on the flywheel starter ring gear are badly worn, or if some are missing, then it will be necessary to remove the ring. This is achieved by splitting the old ring using a cold chisel. Care must be taken not to damage the flywheel during this process.

2   To fit a new ring gear, it will be necessary to heat it gently and evenly with an oxy-acetyline flame until a temperature of approximately 350°C (662°F) is reached. (This is indicated by grey/brown surface colour). With the ring gear at this temperature, fit it to the flywheel with the front of the teeth facing the clutch fitting end of the flywheel. The ring gear should be either pressed or lightly tapped onto its register and left to cool naturally when the contraction of the metal on cooling will ensure that it is a secure and permanent fit. Great care must be taken not to overheat the ring gear, for if this happens the temper of the ring gear will be lost.
3   An alternative method is to use a high temperature oven to heat the ring.
4   Because of the need of oxy-acetylene equipment or a special oven it is not practical for refitment to take place at home. Take the flywheel and new starter ring to an engineering works willing to do the job.

40 Cylinder head and pistons - decarbonising

1   This operation can be carried out with the engine either in or out of the car. With the cylinder head off, carefully remove with a wire brush and blunt, plastic scraper, all traces of carbon deposits from the combustion spaces and the ports. The valve stems and valve guides should also be freed from any carbon deposits. Wash the combustion spaces and ports down with fuel and scrape the cylinder head surface free of any foreign matter with the side of a steel rule or similar article. Take care not to scratch the surfaces. (photo)
2   Clean the pistons and top of the cylinder bores. If the pistons are still in the cylinder bores then it is essential that great care is taken to ensure that no carbon gets into the bores for this will scratch the cylinder walls or cause damage to the piston and rings. To stop it happening first turn the crankshaft so that two of the pistons are at tdc. Place a clean non-fluffy rag into the other two bores or seal them off with paper and masking tape. The waterways and pushrod holes should be covered with a small piece of masking tape to prevent particles of carbon entering the cooling system and damaging the water pump, or entering the lubrication system and causing damage to a bearing surface.
3   There are two schools of though as to how much carbon ought to be removed from the piston union. One is that a ring of carbon should be left around the edge of the piston and on the cylinder bore wall as an aid to keep oil consumption low. Although this is probably true for engines with worn bores, on unworn engines, however, the tendency is to remove all traces of carbon.
4   If all traces of carbon are to be removed, press a little grease into the gap between the cylinder walls and the two pistons which are to be worked upon. With a blunt scraper carefully scrape away all carbon from the piston crown, taking care not to scratch the aluminium. Also scrape away the carbon from the surrounding lip of the cylinder wall. When all carbon has been removed, scrape away the grease which will now be contaminated with carbon particles, taking care not to press any into the bores. To assist prevention of carbon build up the piston crown can be polished with a metal polish such as 'Brasso' Remove the rags or masking tape from the other two cylinders and turn the crankshaft so that the two pistons which were at the bottom are now at the top. Place non-fluffy rag into the other two bores or seal them off with paper and masking tape. Do not forget the water ways and oilways as well. Proceed as previously described.

41 Timing cover - renewal of oil seals and 'O' rings

1   On 1300 and 1301 (up to 1969) models, the crankshaft oil sealing arrangement comprises a spring loaded assembly to ensure positive sealing of the centrifugal oil filter and to compensate for any crankshaft endfloat.
2   Remove the brass thrust ring from within the timing cover.

Extract the coil spring, and then drift out the second thrust ring and oil seal from the front face of the cover. (photo)

3 Renew the 'O' ring on the front brass thrust ring and drop it into position so that the cover locating 'pips' engage with the cut out of the ring. (photo)

4 Drive a new oil seal into position in the front face of the timing cover. (photo)

5 Renew the 'O' ring on the inner brass thrust ring and locate it over the coil spring so that the cut-outs of the ring also engage with the timing cover 'pips'. (photo)

6 When fitting a new oil seal always check that the rotational arrow marked on it is in accordance with the direction of rotation of the component which is being sealed, otherwise the lip scroll will not be compatible.

7 On 1301, 1500 and 1501 models, the design of the sealing components differs slightly as shown earlier in this Chapter but the principle of seal renewal applies.

42 Crankshaft rear oil seal - renewal

1 The crankshaft rear oil seal carrier is accessible after removal of the flywheel.

2 Unscrew the five retaining bolts and lift the oil seal carrier from the crankcase. (photo)

3 Drift out the old seal and press in the new one, making sure that the rotational arrow on the seal conforms with the direction of rotation of the component which it is sealing. (photo)

4 On later engines, the oil seal carrier has been modified to permit oil to drain from the channel which lies between the oil seal and the inner wall of the carrier. Older carriers should be modified when the seal is being renewed by drilling a 5.0 mm diameter hole through the **carrier inner wall as shown.** (Fig 1.13)

40.1 Suggested decarbonising kit

41.2 Removing brass thrust ring from timing cover

41.3A Installing a brass thrust ring in timing cover

41.3B Correct engagement of front brass thrust ring in timing cover

41.4 Installing a new oil seal to timing cover

41.5 Renewing 'O' ring seal on inner thrust ring of timing cover

42.2 Removing crankshaft rear oil seal carrier

42.3 Oil seal rotational direction arrow

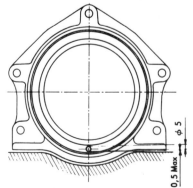
Fig 1.13 Crankshaft rear oil seal carrier modification diagram

43 Engine reassembly - general

1 To ensure maximum life with minimum trouble from a rebuilt engine, not only must everything be correctly assembled, but everything must be spotlessly clean, all the oilways must be clear, locking washers and spring washers must always be fitted where indicated and all bearing and other working surfaces must be thoroughly lubricated during assembly.

2 Before assembly begins renew any bolts or studs the threads of which are in any way damaged, and whenever possible use new spring washers and new locking plates.

3 Apart from your normal tools, a supply of clean rag; an oil can filled with engine oil (an empty plastic detergent bottle thoroughly cleaned and washed out, will invariably do just as well); a new supply of assorted spring washers; a set of new gaskets; and a torque spanner, should be collected together.

Check the cylinder block for cracks, probe the oil passages and holes with a piece of wire and clean the external surfaces.

Renew all gaskets and seals and use plenty of clean engine oil to lubricate the components as they are installed. Observe absolute cleanliness.

44 Engine reassembly - crankshaft, pistons and connecting rods

1 Locate the new shell bearings in their crankcase seats, ensuring that the retaining tongues are in alignment, also the oil feed holes. (photo)

2 Locate the semi-circular thrust washers either side of the centre main bearing web so that their lubrication grooves face outwards. Stick them in position with a little thick grease. (photo)

3 Apply engine oil liberally to the bearing surfaces and lower the crankshaft into position in the crankcase. (photo)

4 Fit the new shell bearings to the main bearing caps. (photo)

5 Refit the main bearing caps in their original sequence. (photo)

6 Fit new locking plates and the oil pump intake filter support bracket (1300, and 1301 up to 1969 models only) and screw in the main bearing bolts to the specified torque wrench setting. Do not bend up the tabs of the locking plates at this stage. (photo)

7 Using a feeler gauge, check the end-play of the crankshaft by pushing it hard, first in one direction, and then in the other. The correct endfloat should be between 0.003 and 0.010 in (0.09 and 0.27 mm) otherwise renew the thrust washers. (photo)

8 Bend up the tabs of the lockwashers after checking the torque setting of the bolts and ensuring that the crankshaft revolves smoothly.

9 Assemble the pistons to the connecting rods so that the cut-out on the piston skirt faces the front of the engine when the connecting rod numbers are facing the camshaft. (Fig 1.14)

10 Push the gudgeon pins into position (heat the piston in hot water if necessary) and fit new circlips. (photo)

11 Install the new shell bearings to the connecting rod and the bearing cap ensuring that the tag locates in the cut-out provided. (photo)

12 Insert the piston/connecting rod assembly into its original bore and compress the piston rings into their grooves using a suitable clamp. (photo)

13 Apply engine oil liberally to the piston rings and cylinder bore and then push the assembly into the engine block.

14 Engage the connecting rod with the crankshaft journal and fit the big-end cap ensuring that the rod and cap numbers are adjacent and on the side facing the camshaft. (photo)

15 Fit new locking plates and tighten the big-end cap nuts to the specified torque. Bend up the locking plate tabs and then repeat the foregoing operations on the other three piston/connecting rod assemblies. Some engines are fitted with self-locking nuts. (photo)

45 Engine reassembly - flywheel, camshaft, timing gear

1 Having renewed the crankshaft rear oil seal as described in

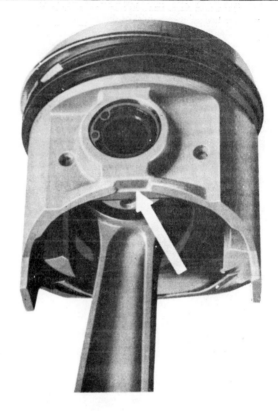

Fig 1.14 Location of piston cut-out (to face front of engine)

Section 35, bolt on the oil seal carrier and tighten the bolts to the specified torque. (photo)

2 Locate the flywheel on the crankshaft mounting flange ensuring that any marks made prior to removal are in alignment. (photo)

3 Fit new locking plates and then tighten the securing bolts to the specified torque. (photo)

4 On 1300 and 1301 (up to 1969) models lubricate the camshaft bearings with clean engine oil and insert the camshaft through the front face of the engine block. (photo)

5 On 1301, 1500 and 1501 models, the cam followers must first be installed in their correct order with the engine inverted before the camshaft is installed.

6 Locate the camshaft thrust plate, insert and fully tighten the securing bolts and bend up the tabs of the new locking plates.

7 Place a new gasket on the front face of the engine block and then position the engine plate on the locating dowels. (photo)

8 Engage the crankshaft and camshaft sprockets within the timing chain so that when the assembly is installed the crankshaft sprocket will engage with the key on the crankshaft and the camshaft sprocket bolt holes will be in correct alignment. (photo)

9 In addition, the 'O' and 'I' marks on the two sprockets must be adjacent and in alignment with an imaginary line drawn through the centres of the two sprockets. Obviously a certain amount of trial-and-error is required to achieve the correct setting of the timing gear, and the crankshaft may need turning (by means of the flywheel), also the camshaft. The camshaft mounting flange has offset bolt holes as has also the bolt locking plate to ensure correct positioning of the gearwheel. (photo)

10 Tighten the camshaft gearwheel bolts to the correct torque and bend up the tags of the locking plate. If there is a tendency for the camshaft to rotate during the bolt tightening, insert the handle of a hammer or a piece of wood between one of the crankshaft webs and the crankcase. (photo)

11 Fit another new gasket to the front face of the engine plate

44.1 Locating a main bearing shell in its seat

44.2 Locating the crankshaft thrust washers

44.3 Installing the crankshaft

44.4 Fitting shell bearing to a main bearing cap

44.5 Fitting a main bearing cap

44.6 Tightening a main bearing cap bolt

44.7 Checking crankshaft endfloat

44.10 Fitting a gudgeon pin

44.11 Fitting a shell bearing to a connecting rod

44.12 Piston fitted with a ring clamp

44.14 Fitting a big-end cap

44.15 Tightening big-end cap bolts

Fig 1.15 Oil pump drive shaft inside timing cover (1301, 1500, 1501 models)

and then bolt on the timing cover which will already have been serviced with a new oil seal and 'O' rings (see Section 41). With all models other than 1300, the oil pump drive must be engaged with the camshaft as the timing cover is pushed into position.

12 The timing cover setscrews have copper washers located beneath them, the bolts and nuts have not.

13 Tighten all securing nuts and bolts to the specified torque.

14 Install the centrifugal oil filter and tighten the centre screw to a torque of 58 lb/ft (8 kg/m).

15 Fit the oil filter front cover using a new 'O' ring seal and tightening the bolts to a torque of 7 lb/ft (1 kg/m).

46 Engine reassembly - oil pump, sump, cylinder head

1 On 1300 models refit the oil pump to the crankcase ensuring that new gaskets are used at the mounting flanges and that the intake filter is bolted to the 'U' support on the main bearing cap.

2 On all models, make sure that the sump and crankcase flange surfaces are quite clean and stick a new sump gasket in position using a little jointing compound.

3 Locate the sump in position and tighten the retaining bolts evenly and progressively to a torque of 7 lb/ft (1 kg/m). Check the security of the sump drain plug.

4 On 1300, and 1301 *up to 1969) models, insert the cam followers (well lubricated in their original locations), use a new gasket and bolt up the tappet chamber cover. (photo)

5 On all models, reassemble the valves to the cylinder head by reversing the operations described in Section 10. If the valve springs have been in use for more than 20000 miles (32000 km) it is recommended that they are renewed.

6 Scrupulously clean the mating surfaces of the cylinder head and the cylinder block.

7 Position a new gasket on the cylinder head; do not use any jointing compound. The gasket is unmarked and great care should be taken in placing it the correct way round by reference

45.1 Bolting on the crankshaft rear oil seal carrier

45.2 Flywheel located on crankshaft mounting flange

45.3 Tightening flywheel securing bolts

45.4 Inserting camshaft into its bearings

45.6 Tightening a camshaft thrust plate bolt

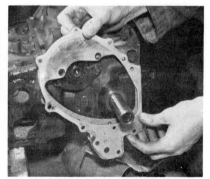
45.7 Locating a timing cover gasket on the engine front plate

45.8 Assembling the timing gears and chain

45.9 Timing gear alignment marks

45.10 Tightening the camshaft gear-wheel bolts

to the small hole at one end and the larger hole at the other end of the gasket.

8 Carefully lower the cylinder head into position and screw in the bolts finger tight. (photo)

9 On 1301, 1500 and 1501 models, some of the cylinder head bolts retain the rocker shaft pillars and the push rods and rocker gear will therefore have to be installed on these vehicles before the bolts can be finally tightened to the specified torque and in the sequence shown in Fig 1.16. (photo)

10 On 1300, and 1301 (up to 1969) models, install the push-rods, and rocker gear. (photo)

11 Fit the driven plate and clutch mechanism to the flywheel, centralising the driven plate as described in Chapter 5.

12 Using new gaskets, fit the water pump to the front face of the engine.

13 Using a new gasket (copper face to cylinder head) fit the inlet and exhaust manifold assembly. (photo)

47 Engine - installation

1 Using the hoist and sling method, carefully lower the overhauled engine into the engine compartment.

2 When it is at approximately the same level as the gearbox, push it rearwards until the input shaft of the gearbox passes through the splined hub (fully centralised see Chapter 5) of the driven plate. The engine may have to be rocked slightly to provide this engagement of the splines.

3 Lower the engine to engage one of the engine flexible mountings and then using a long screwdriver as a lever, prise the opposite mounting into engagement with its mounting bracket. (photo)

4 Tighten the mounting bolt nuts and the clutch bellhousing to crankcase bolts.

5 Where automatic transmission is fitted, the driveplate must

46.4 Fitting the tappet chamber cover

46.8 Lowering the cylinder head into position

46.9 Tightening the cylinder head bolts

46.10 Installing the rocker gear

46.13 Installing the manifold assembly

47.3 Engaging an engine flexible mounting

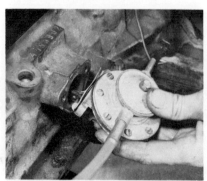
48.3 Fitting the fuel pump

48.10 Adjusting a valve clearance

48.12 Fitting rocker cover and gasket

be bolted to the torque converter and the fluid filler/dipstick tube bolted to the crankcase. Reconnect the speed selector linkage, the downshift cable and the inhibitor switch leads. On 1968 models, reconnect the coolant hoses to the Solex automatic choke carburettor.

48 Engine - final assembly and adjustments

1   With the engine installed in the vehicle, connect the exhaust downpipe to the manifold.

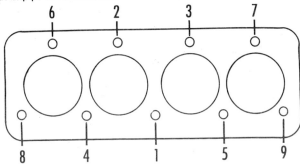

Fig 1.16 Cylinder head bolt tightening sequence diagram

(above) 1300 models (below) 1301, 1500, 1501 models

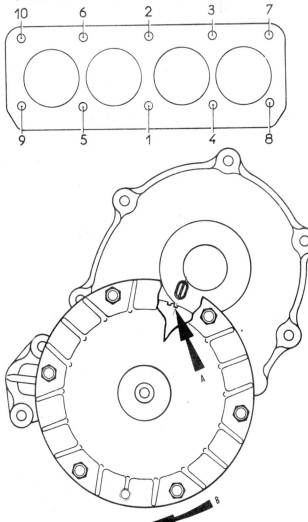

Fig 1.17 Timing marks (1300 and 1301 up to 1969 models)

A Pulley notch   B Direction of rotation

2   Refit the starter motor and then the air cleaner intake pre-heater plate.

3   Refit the fuel pump using a new mounting flange gasket and ensuring that the operating lever locates *above* the eccentric on the camshaft. (photo)

4   Install the radiator and reconnect all water and heater hoses.

5   Reconnect all pipes, wires, leads and controls which were disconnected prior to engine removal.

6   Refit the carburettor and the crankcase breather device

7   Install the distributor. On 1300, and 1301 (up to 1969) models this is carried out by turning the engine until No. 1 piston (this is the rearmost one on this engine) is at tdc on its compression stroke. This can be ascertained by placing a finger over the plug hole and feeling the compression being generated. Continue turning the engine until the first notch on the oil filter pulley groove is opposite the mark on the timing cover. Now insert the distributor driving sleeve so that when it is engaged with the driveshaft splines, its groove will be parallel to the centre line of the engine block with the smaller segment furthest from the engine. Push the distributor into its recess so that the large and small segments of its driving dog mate with those of the driving sleeve. If this operation has been carried out correctly then the rotor arm should be pointing at No.1 contact in the distributor cap. Insert and tighten the housing flange bolts and the clamp plate pinch bolt. (Fig 1.17)

8   On 1301 (after 1969) 1500 and 1501 models, the driveshaft of the distributor meshes directly with the camshaft gear. With No.1 piston (rearmost) at tdc on its compression stroke and the leading notch on the oil filter pulley groove opposite the long mark on the timing cover (ignore any shorter mark on the cover), the rotor arm of the distributor must point to No.1 contact in the distributor cap. As the distributor is pushed into its recess, the action of the meshing of the drive gears will automatically turn the rotor arm. It is therefore important to turn the rotor arm back about 30° before installing to compensate for this and ensure that when the drive gears are fully meshed then the rotor will point directly at No. 1 contact in the distributor cap. (Fig. 1.18).

9   The valve clearances must now be adjusted in the following manner. As the car is not fitted with a starting handle or a crankshaft pulley bolt, the only way to rotate the engine (without the use of the starter motor) is to engage top gear and push the car forward until the rocker arms of No.1 (rearmost) cylinder in balance (the arms are about to compress the valve springs for both the inlet and exhaust valves). This can be observed if the car is pushed and pulled slightly and the engine 'rocked'. With the engine in this situation, adjust the valve clearance of the valves on No.4 (front) cylinder. With the engine **cold** the clearances are:

1300, and 1301 (up to 1969)
inlet 0.008 in (0.203 mm)
exhaust 0.010 in (0.254 mm)
1301, 1500 and 1501
inlet 0.007 in (0.178 mm)
exhaust 0.013 in (0.330 mm)

10 Adjustment is carried out by using a feeler blade and turning the adjuster screw and locknut. (photo)

11 If the adjustment procedure just described is carried out, the following table may be utilised:

Rocker arms in balance	Rocker arms to adjust
7 inlet 8 exhaust	1 exhaust 2 inlet
5 exhaust 6 inlet	3 inlet 4 exhaust
3 inlet 4 exhaust	5 exhaust 6 inlet
1 exhaust 2 inlet	7 inlet 8 exhaust

Valves are numbered 1 to 8 from the front of the engine
Cylinders are numbered 1 to 4 from the rear of the engine

12 Fit a new rocker cover gasket and bolt down the rocker cover. (photo)

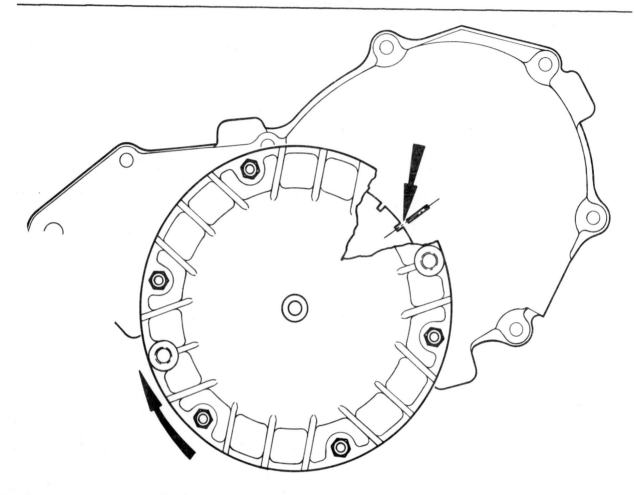

Fig 1.18 Timing marks (1301 after 1969, 1500 and 1501 models)

13 Fit the radiator fan (according to type), the dynamo and drive belt, adjusting the tension as described in Chapter 2.
14 Refit the air cleaner and the spark plugs and leads.
15 Refit the suspension stabiliser rod.
16 Fill the engine with the correct quantity of Castrol GTX.
17 Fill the cooling system with antifreeze mixture.
18 Reconnect the leads to the battery.
19 Refit the bonnet.
20 Carry out a final visual check to ensure that all leads, controls, pipes and earthing straps have been reconnected.

49 Initial start up after overhaul

1 Screw the carburettor slow running screw in about ½ turn to ensure that the engine will run at a fast tickover once it is started.
2 Pull the choke control right out and start the engine. This may take a little longer than usual as the fuel pump and the carburettor bowl will be empty and will require initial priming.
3 As soon as the engine fires, gradually push the choke control right in until the engine runs at the increased slow running speed.
4 Examine all hoses and connections for water, oil or fuel leaks while the engine is running.
5 Operate the vehicle on the road until normal operating temperature is reached and then reduce the slow running speed to the normal level and check the mixture by adjusting the volume control screw (see Chapter 3).
6 Check and adjust the ignition timing by the test lamp method or by using a stroboscope (Chapter 4).
7 After 500 miles (800 km) change the engine oil by draining it when it is hot after a run.
8 At the same time check the torque setting of the cylinder head bolts and check and adjust the valve clearances, both operations being carried out with the engine absolutely cold.
9 Check the security of all nuts and bolts which were disturbed during overhaul and engine removal.

50 Fault diagnosis - engine

Symptom	Reason/s	Remedy
Engine will not turn over when starter switch is operated	Flat battery Bad battery connections Bad connections at solenoid switch and/or starter motor Starter motor jammed Defective solenoid	Check that battery is fully charged and that all connections are clean and tight. Where a pre-engaged starter is fitted rock the car back and forth with a gear engaged. If this does not free pinion remove starter. Bridge the main terminals of the solenoid switch with a piece of heavy duty cable in order to operate the starter.
	Starter motor defective	Remove and overhaul starter motor.
Engine turns over normally but fails to start	No spark at plugs	Check ignition system according to procedures given in Chapter 4.
	No fuel reaching engine	Check fuel system according to procedures given in Chapter 3.
	Too much fuel reaching the engine (flooding)	Check the fuel system as above
Engine starts but runs unevenly and misfires	Ignition and/or fuel system faults	Check the ignition and fuel systems as though the engine had failed to start.
	Incorrect valve clearances	Check and reset clearances.
	Burnt out valves	Remove cylinder head and examine and overhaul as necessary.
	Worn out piston rings	Remove cylinder head and examine pistons and cylinder bores. Overhaul as necessary.
Lack of power	Ignition and/or fuel system faults	Check the ignition and fuel systems for correct ignition timing and carburettor settings.
	Incorrect valve clearances	Check and reset the clearances.
	Burnt out valves	Remove cylinder head and examine and overhaul as necessary.
	Worn out piston rings	Remove cylinder head and examine pistons and cylinder bores. Overhaul as necessary.
Excessive oil consumption	Oil leaks from crankshaft rear oil seal, timing cover gasket and oil seal, rocker cover gasket, oil filter gasket, sump gasket, sump plug washer	Identify source of leak and renew seal as appropriate.
	Worn piston rings or cylinder bores resulting in oil being burnt by engine	Fit new rings or rebore cylinders and fit new pistons, depending on degree of wear.
	Worn valve guides and/or defective valve stem seals	Remove cylinder heads and recondition valve stem bores and valves and seals as necessary.
Excessive mechanical noise from engine	Wrong valve to rocker clearances	Adjust valve clearances.
	Worn crankshaft bearings	Inspect and overhaul where necessary.
	Worn cylinders (piston slap)	
	Slack or worn timing chain and sprockets	Adjust chain and/or inspect all timing mechanism.

Note: When investigating starting and uneven running faults do not be tempted into snap diagnosis. Start from the beginning of the check procedure and follow it through. It will take less time in the long run. Poor performance from an engine in terms of power and economy is not normally diagnosed quickly. In any event the ignition and fuel systems must be checked first before assuming any further investigation needs to be made.

Chapter 2 Cooling system

Contents

Specifications

System type	Thermo syphon with water pump assistance - pressurised
Thermostat	Opens 180°F (82°C)
Radiator pressure cap rating	7 lb in^2 (500 g cm^2)
System capacity	11½ pints (6.5 litres)

1 General description

The cooling system comprises the radiator, top and bottom water hoses, water pump, cylinder head and block water jackets, radiator cap with pressure relief valve and flow and return heater hoses. The thermostat is located in a recess at the front of the cylinder head. The principle of the system is that cold water in the bottom of the radiator circulates upwards through the lower radiator hose to the water pump, where the pump impeller pushes the water round the cylinder block and head through the various cast-in passages to cool the cylinder bores, combustion surfaces and valve seats. When sufficient heat has been absorbed by the cooling water, and the engine has reached an efficient working temperature, the water moves from the cylinder head past the now open thermostat into the top radiator hose and into the radiator header tank.

The water then travels down the radiator tubes when it is rapidly cooled by the in-rush of air when the vehicle is in forward motion. A four bladed fan, mounted on the water pump pulley, assists this cooling action. On models built after 1969, a thermostatically operated electromagnetic fan is installed (see Section 9).

On models built after 1969, a thermostatically operated electromagnetic fan is installed (see Section 9).

The water, now cooled, reaches the bottom of the radiator and the cycle is repeated.

When the engine is cold the thermostat remains closed until the coolant reaches a pre-determined temperature (see Specifications). This assists rapid warming-up.

Water temperature is measured by an electro-sensitive capsule screwed into the thermostat housing. Connection between the transmitter capsule and the facia gauge is made by a single cable and connector. The cooling system also provides the heat for the heater.

The heater matrix is fed directly with water from the hottest part of the engine (thermostat housing or cylinder head according to date of manufacture) and returns through a connection on the water pump housing.

2 Cooling system - draining

1 Should the system have to be left empty for any reason both the cylinder block and radiator must be drained, otherwise with a partly drained system corrosion of the water pump impeller seal face may occur with subsequent early failure of the pump seal and bearing.

2 Place the car on a level surface and have ready a container having a capacity of two gallons which will slide beneath the radiator and sump.

3 Move the heater control on the facia to HOT and unscrew and remove the radiator cap. If hot, unscrew the cap very slowly, first covering it with a cloth to remove the danger of scalding when the pressure in the system is released.

4 Unscrew the radiator drain tap at the base of the radiator and then when coolant ceases to flow into the receptacle, repeat the operation by unscrewing the cylinder block plug located on the left-rear of the block or right-front according to model and date of manufacture.

5 Retain the coolant for further use if required.

3 Cooling system - flushing

1 The radiator and waterways in the engine after some time may become restricted or even blocked with scale or sediment which reduces the efficiency of the cooling system. When this condition occurs or the coolant appears rusty or dark in colour the system should be flushed. In severe cases reverse flushing may be required as described later.

2 Place the heater control to the HOT position and unscrew fully the radiator and cylinder block drain taps.

3 Remove the radiator filler cap and place a hose in the filler neck. Allow water to run through the system until it emerges from both drain taps quite clear in colour. Do not flush a hot engine with cold water.

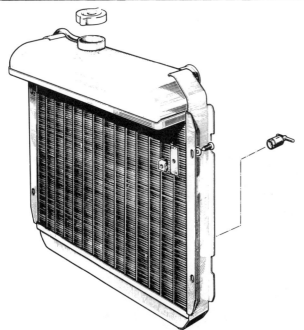

Fig 2.1 Radiator (early models)

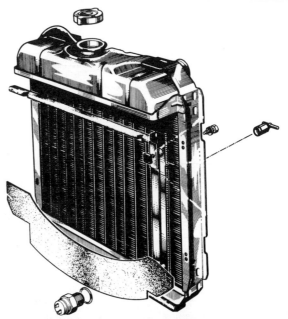

Fig 2.2 Radiator (after 1969) showing blanking plate and thermostatic switch for control of electromagnetic fan

4   In severe cases of contamination of the coolant or in the system, reverse flush by first removing the radiator cap and disconnecting the lower radiator hose at the radiator outlet pipe.
5   Remove the top hose at the radiator connection end and remove the radiator as described in Section 5.
6   Invert the radiator and place a hose in the bottom outlet pipe. Continue flushing until clear water comes from the radiator top tank.
7   To flush the engine water jackets, remove the thermostat as described later in this Chapter and place a hose in the thermostat location until clear water runs from the water pump inlet. Cleaning by the use of chemical compounds is not recommended.

4   Cooling system - filling

1   Place the heater control to the "HOT" position.
2   Screw in the radiator drain tap finger tight only and close the cylinder block drain plug.
3   Pour coolant slowly into the radiator so that air can be expelled through the thermostat pin hole without being trapped in a waterway.
4   Fill to the correct level which is 1 inch (25.4 mm) below the radiator filler neck and replace the filler cap.
5   Run the engine, check for leaks and recheck the coolant level.

5   Radiator - removal, inspection, cleaning, refitting

1   Drain the cooling system as described in Section 2.
2   Disconnect the top hose from the radiator header tank.
3   Disconnect the bottom hose from the radiator outlet pipe.
4   Unscrew and remove the 4 retaining bolts which secure the radiator to the front engine compartment mounting panel.
5   Lift out the radiator, taking care not to damage the cooling fins. Do not allow antifreeze solution to drop onto the bodywork during removal as damage may result.
6   Radiator repair is best left to a specialist but minor leaks may be tackled with Holts Radweld.
7   The radiator matrix may be cleared of flies by brushing with a soft brush or by hosing.

8   Flush the radiator as described in Section 3 according to the degree of contamination. Examine and renew any hoses or clips which have deteriorated.
9   Refitting is a reversal of removal.
10 Refill the system and check for leaks.

6   Thermostat - removal, testing, refitting

1   A faulty thermostat can cause overheating or slow engine warm up. It will also affect the performance of the heater.
2   Drain off enough coolant through the radiator drain tap so that the coolant level is below the thermostat housing joint face. A good indication that the correct level has been reached is when the cooling tubes are exposed when viewed through the radiator filler cap.
3   Unscrew and remove the two retaining bolts and withdraw the thermostat cover sufficiently to permit the thermostat to be removed from its seat in the cylinder head. (photo)

6.3 Thermostat removal

4 To test whether the unit is serviceable, suspend the thermostat by a piece of string in a pan of water being heated. Using a thermometer, with reference to the opening and closing temperature in Specifications, its operation may be checked. The thermostat should be renewed if it is stuck open or closed or it fails to operate at the specified temperature. The operation of a thermostat is not instantaneous and sufficient time must be allowed for movement during testing. Never replace a faulty unit; leave it out if no replacement is available immediately.

5 Replacement of the thermostat is a reversal of the removal procedure. Ensure the mating faces of the housing are clean. Use a new gasket with jointing compound.

Fig 2.3 Exploded view of the thermostat

7.6 Water pump body, gasket and plate

7.8 Refitting the water pump

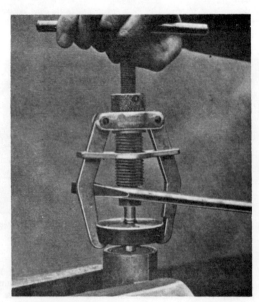

Fig 2.4 Removing flange from water pump shaft

Fig 2.5 Prising the sealing disc from the water pump body

Fig 2.6 Pressing water pump shaft from impeller

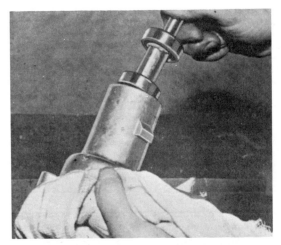

Fig 2.7 Extracting the water pump shaft and bearing assembly

7 Water pump - removal and installation

1 Drain the cooling system as previously described.

2 Disconnect the lower radiator hose.

3 Unbolt the adjusting strap from the dynamo and the water pump.

4 Slacken the dynamo mounting bolts and push the dynamo in towards the engine so that the driving belt can be removed from the dynamo pulley.

5 Unbolt the fan blades, remove the hub and driving belt, or belt only (electromagnetic fan).

6 Unscrew and remove the water pump securing bolts and then pull off the water pump, gasket, mounting plate and second gasket. (photo)

7 On late vehicles fitted with an elector-magnetic fan, disconnect the feed wire to the brush and then withdraw the fan unit from the water pump shaft using a suitable extractor.

8 Refitting is a reversal of removal but with electromagnetic type fan units, refer to Section 10 and 11 for precise assembly procedure. (photo)

8 Water pump - servicing

1 Provided regular lubrication has been carried out (see Routine Maintenance Section) the water pump will have a very long life. When a fault or wear develops it is recommended that a reconditioned unit is fitted but for those wishing to overhaul and repair the original pump, proceed as follows:

2 Press the water pump shaft from the fan hub mounting flange using a screwdriver as a lever to prevent the extractor rotating. (Fig 2.4)

3 Prise out the sealing disc. (Fig 2.5)

4 Extract the bearing circlip.

5 Immerse the pump assembly in very hot water (176°F - 80°C) for two or three minutes and then press the shaft from the impeller (Fig 2.6).

6 Withdraw the shaft, complete with two bearings, from the water pump housing; extract the seal, felt and cup washers. (Fig. 2.7)

7 Should either of the bearings require renewal, support the shaft assembly in a vice and using a soft faced mallet or a block of wood as an insulator, drive the shaft out of the bearing centre track. Retain the spacer (Fig 2.8)

8 Before commencing reassembly, renew the seal, impeller and felt ring, also the sealing disc.

9 Warm the pump in hot water as for dismantling and then place the felt washer in the pump housing followed by the cup washer (concave side towards shaft bearing).

10 Install the pump shaft complete with bearings and spacer so that the grooves on the shaft are nearest the impeller.

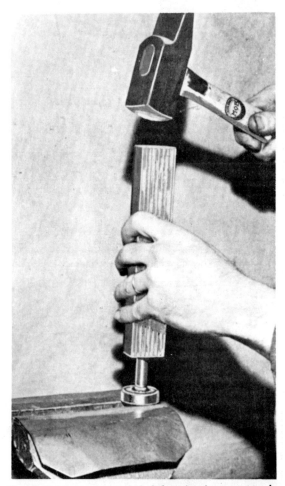

Fig 2.8 Driving water pump shaft from bearing centre track

11 Fit the bearing retaining circlips to the shaft.

12 Tap the new sealing disc into position in the water pump body using a piece of tubing (1.37 in/35.0 mm outside diameter) as an installation tool. Make sure that the crimped side faces outwards and when finally installed, the face of the disc should be fractionally below the surface of the adjacent water pump housing.

13 Locate the seal assembly to the impeller end of the shaft.

14 Position the impeller on the end of the shaft so that the driving lugs on the seal assembly engage with the matching recesses of the impeller (Fig 2.9).

15 Press the impeller onto the water pump shaft making sure that the opposite end of the shaft is securely supported. When correctly installed, the end of the shaft should be flush with the face of the impeller and there should be a maximum clearance between the impeller blades and the pump housing of 0.059 in (1.5 mm) without any sign of rubbing between the two components. (Figs 2.10/2.11)

16 Support the shaft at the impeller end and press on the fan hub mounting flange. When correctly installed the water pump shaft should project above the flange by 0.31 in (8.0 mm).

9 Electromagnetic fan - general description

1 On vehicles built after 1969, a thermostatically operated

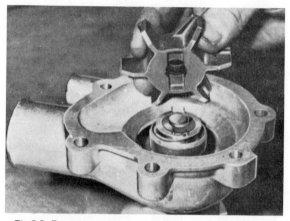

Fig 2.9 Engaging water pump impeller recesses with seal assembly projections

Fig 2.10 Pressing water pump impeller onto shaft

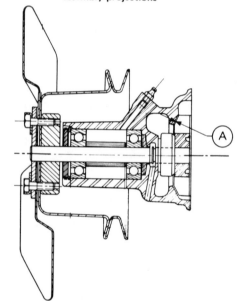

Fig 2.11 Cross-sectional view of water pump and fan (pre 1969)

A Impeller to body clearance (0.059 in/1.5 mm)

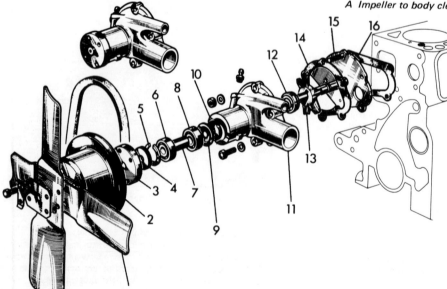

Fig 2.12 Exploded view of the water pump

1 Fan blades
2 Hub/pulley
3 Mounting flange
4 Sealing disc
5 Circlip
6 Front bearing
7 Spacer
8 Rear bearing
9 Cupped washer
10 Felt ring
11 Housing
12 Seal assembly
13 Impeller
14 Gasket
15 Plate
16 Gasket

electromagnetic fan is installed. It is actuated by a thermostat switch screwed into the radiator which cuts in when the coolant in the radiator reaches a temperature of 87.8 C (190°F) and switches off the fan when the coolant temperature drops to 80°C (176°F).

2 No maintenance is required except occasionally to check the security of the leads to the thermostat switch and to the fan brush holder. When the brush has worn down to a minimum length of 0.787 in (2.0 mm) the brush assembly must be renewed.

10 Electromagnetic fan - removal and installation

1 The fan blade assembly may be removed from the hub/pulley assembly after unscrewing and removing the three outer self locking nuts and detaching the support plate.

2 Slacken the dynamo mountings and adjusting strap and remove the driving belt.

3 Disconnect the lead from the brush holder.

4 Unbolt the water pump from the front face of the cylinder block.

5 Using a suitable two or three legged puller, extract the fan

mechanism from the water pump shaft.

6 Refitting is a reversal of removal but refer to the adjustment operation in the next Section.

11 Electromagnetic fan - servicing and adjustment

1 In the event of failure of the fan or after removal and refitting, the gap between the fan assembly and the hub mechanism must be checked.

2 The correct gap is 0.012 in (0.30 mm) and any adjustment can be carried out by releasing the locknuts on the three square-ended adjuster screws and then turning them equally. Check that the gap is constant by measuring it with a feeler gauge at several different points and then tighten the locknuts.

3 If the fan still fails to operate, check the condition of the brushes and renew if worn.

4 Remove the fan assembly and clean the brush contact ring.

5 Finally check all leads and connections and test the operation of the thermostatic switch (in the radiator) by removing it, connecting it to a battery and test bulb and then heating the switch in water.

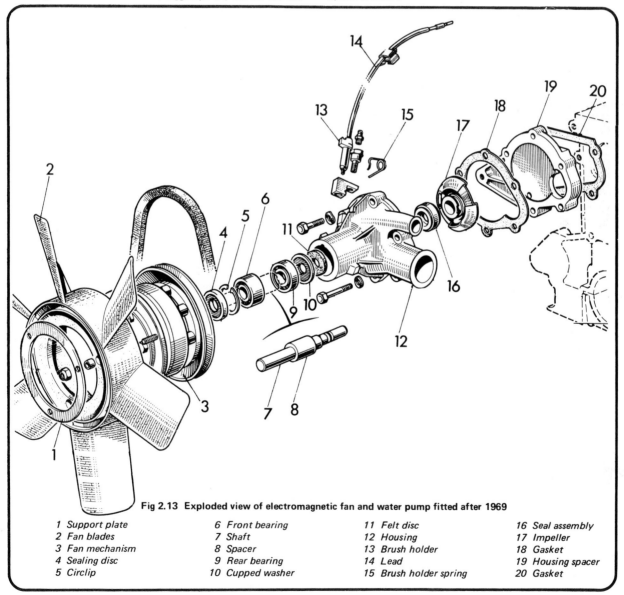

Fig 2.13 Exploded view of electromagnetic fan and water pump fitted after 1969

1 Support plate	6 Front bearing	11 Felt disc	16 Seal assembly
2 Fan blades	7 Shaft	12 Housing	17 Impeller
3 Fan mechanism	8 Spacer	13 Brush holder	18 Gasket
4 Sealing disc	9 Rear bearing	14 Lead	19 Housing spacer
5 Circlip	10 Cupped washer	15 Brush holder spring	20 Gasket

12 Drive belt - adjustment

1 The correct tension of the fan belt must be maintained at all times.
2 If it is overtightened, then the bearings in the water pump and the dynamo may wear prematurely. If the belt is slack, it will slip and cause overheating of the cooling system through lack of fan and pump rotation, also a discharged battery through low dynamo output.
3 The fan belt is correctly tensioned when there is a total deflection of ½ in (12.7 mm) at the mid-point of the top run of the belt.
4 Adjust the belt with the engine cold by slackening the dynamo mounting and adjustment strap bolts and moving the dynamo away from the engine. It will be easier to adjust the tension of the belt if the dynamo bolts are only released just sufficiently to permit the unit to move stiffly. Always recheck the fan belt tension after the dynamo mounting bolts have been retightened.

13 Drive belt - renewal

1 Examine the fan drive-belt regularly for fraying, cuts or burning (caused by slipping) and renew if necessary.
2 Release the dynamo mounting and adjusting strap bolts and push the dynamo in towards the engine as far as it will go.
3 The drive belt may now be pulled over the rim of the dynamo pulley and then off the pulley which comprises part of the centrifugal oil filter body, and finally manoeuvred off and over the fan blades. There is no need to remove the blades.
4 Fit the new belt and then adjust the tension as described in the preceding Section.

14 Water temperature gauge - fault finding

1 Correct operation of the water temperature gauge is very important as the engine can otherwise overheat without the condition being apparent.
2 The gauge is electrically operated and comprises a transmitter unit screwed into the thermostat housing (or rear of the cylinder head according to date of manufacture) and a facia mounted gauge and the interconnecting wiring. The gauge only operates when the ignition is switched on.
3 Should the water temperature gauge read high or low intermittently, or not at all, first check the security of the cable between the transmitter and the gauge.
4 Disconnect the head from the transmitter, switch on the ignition and there should be no reading on the gauge. Now earth the end of the lead to the engine block and the needle of the gauge should indicate "HOT". This test proves the gauge to be functioning correctly and that the fault must lie in the transmitter unit or the interconnecting cable. Renew as appropriate. A modified thermostat housing gasket providing a better earth contact for the transmitter is available.

15 Anitfreeze mixture

1 The cooling system should be filled with Castrol Antifreeze solution in early autumn. The heater matrix and radiator bottom tank are particularly prone to freeze if antifreeze is not used in air temperatures below freezing. Modern antifreeze solutions of good quality will also prevent corrosion and rusting and they may be left in the system to advantage all year round, draining and refilling with fresh solution each year.
2 Before adding antifreeze to the system, check all hose connections and check the tightness of the cylinder head bolts as such solutions are searching. The cooling system should be drained and refilled with clean water as previously explained, before adding antifreeze.
3 The quantity of antifreeze which should be used for various levels of protection is given in the table below, expressed as a percentage of the system capacity.

Antifreeze volume	Protection to	Safe pump circulation
25%	$-26^{\circ}C(-15^{\circ}F)$	$-12^{\circ}C(\ 10^{\circ}F)$
30%	$-33^{\circ}C(-28^{\circ}F)$	$-16^{\circ}C(\ \ 3^{\circ}F)$
35%	$-39^{\circ}C(-38^{\circ}F)$	$-20^{\circ}C(-\ 4^{\circ}F)$

4 Where the cooling system contains an antifreeze solution any topping-up should be done with a solution made up in similar proportions to the original in order to avoid dilution.

16 Fault diagnosis - cooling system

Symptom	Reason/s	Remedy
Overheating	Low coolant level	Top up.
	Slack fan belt	Adjust tension.
	Thermostat not operating	Renew.
	Radiator pressure cap faulty or of wrong type	Renew.
	Defective water pump	Renew.
	Cylinder head gasket blowing	Fit new gasket.
	Radiator core clogged	Clean.
	Radiator blocked	Reverse flush.
	Binding brakes	Rectify.
	Bottom hose or tank frozen	Drain and refill with antifreeze.
	Faulty electromagnetic fan	Renew.
	Faulty indicator fan switch (late models)	Renew.
	Radiator blanking panel left in position in hot weather (1301 models)	Remove.
Engine running too cool	Defective thermostat	Renew.
	Faulty water temperature gauge	Renew.
	Faulty radiator fan switch (late models)	Renew.
	Blanking plate not fitted to radiator (1301 models)	Install.
Loss of coolant	Leaking radiator or hoses	Renew or tighten.
	Cylinder head gasket leaking	Renew gasket.
	Leaking cylinder block core plugs	Renew.
	Faulty radiator filler cap or wrong type fitted	Renew with correct type.

Chapter 3 Carburation, fuel and exhaust systems

Contents

Specifications

Fuel pump

Type	Mechanical, camshaft operated
Make	SEV or AC

Fuel tank

Capacity	12.1 gals (55.0 litres)

Carburettor application

Simca 1300 (up to 1968)	Solex 32 PBIC
Simca 1300 (from 1968) and Simca 1301	Weber 32 ICB3
Simca 1500 and 1501 (up to body G.240814)	Weber 28/36 DCB
Simca 1500 and 1501 (from body G.240815)	Weber 28/36 DCB1
Simca 1500 (automatic transmission 1968 only)	Solex 35 TDIDA
Simca 1500 and 1501 (automatic transmission 1969 on) ...	Weber 28/36 DCB2

Solex 32 PBIC

	Engine 4100000 to 4102484	Engine 4102485 to 4161155	Engine 4161156 to 4188372	Engine 4188373 to 4315982
Year of manufacture	1963	1964	1965	1966–68
Choke lever ref no	14	17	23	24 or 26
Choke tube diameter	25 mm	25 mm	25 mm	25 mm
Main jet	120	122	122.5	122.5
Air correction jet	190	190	190	190
Idling jet	45	50	50	50
Air bleed under venturi	170	200	200	200
Idling air bleed	100	70	70	70
Emulsion tube	10	72	72	72
Power jet	Low 50	Low 50	Low 50	Low 50
Accelerator pump	54	54	54	54
Pump jet	40	40	40	40
Diffuser	3.2	3.2	3.2	3.2
Econostat vent	80	80	80	80
Econostat jet	110	110	95	95
Fuel inlet valve	1.5	1.5	1.5	1.5
Progression hole	100	100	60	60
By-pass	40	40	40	40
Starter air jet	3	3	5	5
Starter fuel jet	115	115	140	140

Weber ICB3

Choke tube diameter	25 mm
Main jet	130
Air correction jet	155
Idling jet	50
Idling air bleed	220
Emulsion tube	F 21
Accelerator pump	40
Accelerator pump jet	40
Econostat vent	190
Econostat	70
Fuel inlet valve	150

Weber 28/36 DCB

	Engine Nos 7000051 to 7002248 (1964)		Engine Nos 7002249 to 7016761 (1965)	
	Primary venturi	Secondary venturi	Primary venturi	Secondary venturi
Choke tube diameter	25 mm	26 mm	25 mm	26 mm
Main jet	135	140	135	140
Air correction jet	215	160	205	150
Idling jet	45	70	45	70
Idling air bleed	200	70	200	70
Emulsion tube	F 30	F 30	F 33	F 33
Fuel inlet valve	175	175	175	175
Centring tube (mixture adjustment)	F 4.5	F 4.5	F 4.5	F 4.5
Accelerator pump jet	60	—	50	—
Crankcase fume intake tube (diameter)	8	—	8	—
Starter air jet	150	—	150	—
Starter fuel jet	FL 180	—	FL 180	—

Weber 28/36 DCB1

	Engine Nos 7016762 to 7115475 (1965)		Engine Nos 7115476 to 7228167 (1966)	
	Primary venturi	Secondary venturi	Primary venturi	Secondary venturi
Choke tube diameter	25 mm	26 mm	25 mm	26 mm
Main jet	135	140	135	140
Air correction jet	205	150	205	150
Idling jet	45	70	45	70
Idling air bleed	200	70	190	70
Emulsion tube	F 33	F 33	F 33	F 33
Fuel inlet valve	175	175	175	175
Centring tube (mixture adjusting)	F 4.5	F 4.5	F 4.5	F 4.5
Accelerator pump jet	50	—	50	—
Crankcase fume intake tube (diameter)	8 mm	—	8	—
Starter air jet	150	—	100	—
Starter fuel jet *	FL 180	—	FL 160	—

From engine no 7073487 becomes FL 150

Later carburettors have similar specifications except that fuel inlet needle valve connecting spring to float is deleted and accelerator pump valves incorporate plastic balls.

Weber 28/36 DCB2

	Primary venturi	Secondary venturi
Choke tube diameter	25 mm	26 mm
Main jet	130	135
Air correction jet	205	155
Idling jet	45	70
Idling air bleed	190	70
Emulsion tube	F 33	F 33
Fuel inlet valve	175	175
Centring tube (mixture adjusting)	F 4.5	F 4.5
Accelerator pump jet	50	50
Crankcase fume intake tube (diameter)	8 mm	—
Choke air jet	100	—
Starter fuel jet	FL 205	—
Starter air vent	6.25	—

Solex 35 TDIDA (automatic choke)

	Primary venturi	Secondary venturi
Choke tube diameter	23 mm	27 mm
Main jet	117.5	130
Air correction jet	110	100
Idling jet	47.5	70
Fuel inlet valve	1.5	1.5
Accelerator pump injector	—	40
Air bleed (enrichment)	—	220
Fuel jet (enrichment)	—	120

Torque wrench settings

						lb ft	kg m
Exhaust pipe clamp nuts (to manifold)	...	...	...	...	...	13	1.7
Exhaust pipe bracket nuts	...	...	...	...	...	16	2.2
Exhaust pipe joint nuts	...	...	...	...	...	16	2.2
Fuel pump to crankcase nuts	...	...	...	...	...	25	2.8
Carburettor to inlet manifold flange nuts			...	...	...	20	3.5

1 General description

1 The fuel system comprises a rear mounted fuel tank, a mechanically operated fuel pump working from an eccentric on the camshaft, a carburettor and all necessary fuel lines.
   Various models of carburettor have been fitted and reference should be made to 'Specifications' and to Section 8.

2 Air cleaner - removal, servicing, refitting

1 Every 12000 miles (19000 km) the paper type air cleaner element should be renewed.
2 Remove the central wing nut from the air cleaner lid, lift off the lid and extract the element (photo).
3 Wipe the interior of the air cleaner body free from oil and dirt, install the new element and refit the lid and wing nut.
4 On all but the earliest models, an air intake preheater shield is fitted to the exhaust manifold and is connected to the spout of the air cleaner by means of a flexible rubber tube (photo).
5 A flap valve is fitted within the air intake spout so that the air can either be drawn from the preheater shield in Winter or directly through the open end of the spout in summer. Control of the flap valve position is by means of a spring type lever.
6 The air cleaner assembly may be completely removed by first detaching the lid and extracting the element and then removing the four securing bolts from within the air cleaner body or disconnecting the clamp and support bracket, according to type. Disconnect the rubber tube from the preheater shield and lift the assembly from the carburettor top flange.

3 Fuel pump - description

   The mechanically operated fuel pump may be of AC or SEV manufacture. Certain AC pumps have their upper and lower bodies swaged together and apart from cleaning the filter screen they cannot be serviced or repaired.
   Where the upper and lower bodies are detachable then the procedures described in the following Sections apply irrespective

of make although there are detail differences in the components used.

4 Fuel pump - removal and refitting

1 Disconnect the fuel supply line from the pump and plug the line to prevent loss of fuel.
2 Disconnect the fuel line between the pump and carburettor.
3 Unscrew and remove the two pump securing bolts and remove the pump, noting the insulating and sealing washers, fitted between the pump flange and the cylinder block.
4 Withdraw the pump in a downward direction so that the pump actuating arm can be extracted from between the crankcase wall and the camshaft.
5 Refitting is a reversal of removal but check the location and condition of the flange washers.

5 Fuel pump - servicing, repair and testing

1 Before deciding to overhaul a fuel pump, it will be wise to consider a factory exchange unit, particularly where the unit has been in service for a considerable mileage.
2 If you decide to overhaul the pump first obtain a repair kit which contains all necessary renewable items.
3 The method of overhaul applies to all makes of pump but components may vary in design detail.
4 Scribe a line on the two upper and lower body flange edges before dismantling so that they may be refitted in the same relative position. Withdraw the body flange securing screws.
5 Press down on the centre of the diaphragm and tilt it to disengage the lower end of the pull rod from the rocker arm. (AC pump eyelet and hook, SEV collar).
6 Remove the diaphragm assembly, spring, oil seal and washer. The diaphragm and pull rod cannot be separated and are renewed as an assembly. The rocker arm may be withdrawn after removal of its pivot circlips. If this component is sufficiently worn to warrant renewal then the pump should be renewed as a unit.
7 The valves in the AC pump are staked in position and should

2.2 Removing air cleaner element

2.4 Exhaust manifold air intake preheater plate

Fig 3.1 Exploded view of SEV fuel pump

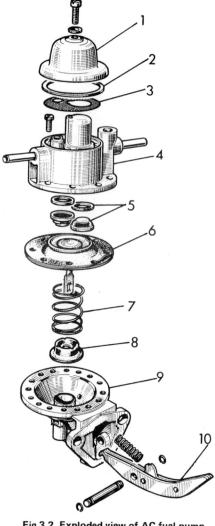

Fig 3.2 Exploded view of AC fuel pump

1 Cover	6 Diaphragm
2 Seal	7 Return spring
3 Filter gauze	8 Seal
4 Upper body	9 Lower body
5 Non-return valves	10 Pump operating lever

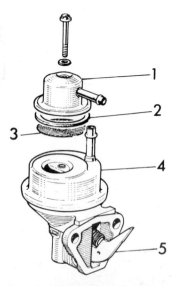

Fig 3.3 Sealed type of AC fuel pump

1 Cover	4 Sealed body
2 Seal	5 Pump operating lever
3 Filter gauze	

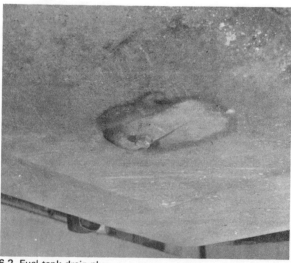

6.2 Fuel tank drain plug

only be removed for renewal with new components. Locate new gaskets in the valve seats, press the new valves fully home and secure them in position by staking at several points. The valves in the SEV pump are part of a plate assembly and the combined valve/plate unit is removed after withdrawal of the three securing screws. When refitting a new valve/plate assembly, use a new gasket.

8   When the fuel pump is dismantled, clean all parts in fuel and examine for wear and damage.

9   Reassembly is a reversal of dismantling. Use all the new components supplied in the repair kit. Tighten the body flange screws to finger tightness and then operate the rocker arm several times to centralise the diaphragm. Finally tighten the flange screws evenly and in diametrically opposite sequence.

10 When reassembly is complete, temporarily connect the fuel supply line from the tank. Operate the pump actuating rocker arm and after three or four movements of the arm, a well defined spurt of fuel should be ejected from the outlet nozzle of the pump.

11 Remove the fuel supply line and place a finger over the pump inlet nozzle. Operate the actuating arm when a distinct suction should be felt. Remove the finger when an inrush of air should be heard. These tests prove that the pump is in good operating condition and may be employed to test the pump at any time not only when the unit has been overhauled.

6   Fuel tank - removal and refitting

1   Disconnect the leads from the battery negative terminal.

2   Remove the drain screw from the fuel tank and collect the contents in a suitable container (photo).

3   On saloon models, remove the covering from the luggage boot floor.

4   On estate car versions, remove the luggage compartment floor.

5   Remove the spare wheel from its recess in the fuel tank.

6   Disconnect the fuel outlet pipe from the tank and plug the pipe and the tank to prevent the entry of dirt.

7   Disconnect the electrical leads from the fuel level transmitter unit.

8   Disconnect the vent pipe from the filler pipe of the tank.

9   Remove the two securing screws, the flange and the rubber seal which locate the filler pipe in position.

10 Unscrew and remove the four screws from the recessed filler cap pressing.

11 Remove the screws and clips which secure the fuel tank flange to the bodyshell floor.

12 Either cut round the tank to body sealing flange to release the tank or place a block of wood under the tank and jack it up until its seal with the bodyshell floor is broken.

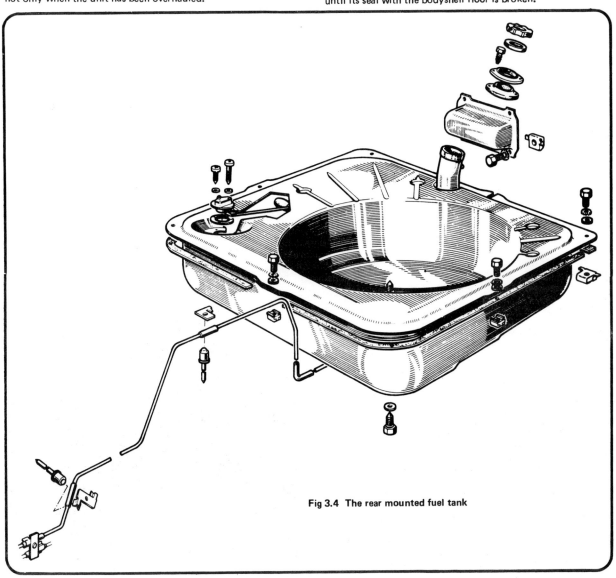

Fig 3.4 The rear mounted fuel tank

13 Lift the front edge of the tank out of the bodyfloor aperture and then remove the tank upwards.

14 Installation is a reversal of removal but clean the mating faces of the tank and bodyfloor and locate a new sealing strip or a bead of suitable mastic to provide a weatherproof seal.

15 Refit and tighten the drain plug using a new copper washer if necessary to make a good seal.

7 Fuel tank - cleaning and servicing

1 With time it is likely that sediment will collect in the bottom of the fuel tank. Condensation, resulting in rust and other impurities, will usually be found in the fuel tank of any car more than three or four years old.

2 Remove the tank as previously described and then remove the securing screws from the tank transmitter unit. Withdraw the transmitter taking great care not to damage the float or bend the float arm.

3 Shake the tank vigorously, using two or three changes of paraffin and finally rinsing out with clean fuel.

4 Never be tempted to repair a leak in a fuel tank by soldering. A temporary repair may be made using fibre glass or similar material but any other work should be given to a professional repairer or possibly just as economical is the purchase of a new tank.

8 Carburettors - general description

SIMCA 1300 models manufactured up until 1968 were fitted with Solex carburettors. SIMCA 1300 and 1301 models as from 1968 and all 1500 and 1501 models have Weber carburettors of differing types.

During one year only (1968) SIMCA 1500 models with automatic transmission were fitted with a Solex automatic choke carburettor, thereafter vehicles with this type of transmission also used a Weber carburettor.

Full specifications and applications are found in the 'Specifications' Section at the beginning of this Chapter.

9 Solex 32 PBIC Carburettor - slow running adjustment

1 Run the engine until normal operating temperature is reached.

2 Check that the ignition components are correctly set and adjusted.

3 Screw in the throttle stop screw until the engine is running at a fast idle (1000 rev/min).

4 Unscrew the volume control screw until the engine begins to run in a lumpy manner (hunts) and then turn the screw clockwise until the engine runs smoothly.

5 Unscrew the throttle stop screw until the desired idling speed is obtained (about 700 rev/min) and then readjust the volume control screw if necessary to smooth the idling performance.

6 It is recommended that a vacuum gauge is connected to the inlet manifold or a device such as a 'Colortune' is used to ensure precise adjustment and tuning of the carburettor slow running.

10 Solex 32 PBIC Carburettor - removal and refitting

1 Remove the air cleaner as described in Section 2.

2 Disconnect the choke cable from the clamp and swivel bolt on the carburettor.

3 Disconnect the throttle cable from the throttle valve lever on the carburettor.

4 Disconnect the fuel supply pipe from the carburettor (photo).

5 Disconnect the vaccum pipe from the carburettor.

6 Unscrew and remove the two nuts and washers which secure the carburettor flange to the inlet manifold.

7 Lift off the carburettor and remove the insulating and sealing

washers from the flange.

8 Refitting is a reversal of removal but always use new flange mounting gaskets.

9 Adjust the choke cable so that the choke valve plate lever is closed when the control knob is pushed fully home.

10 Ensure that the accelerator cable will open the throttle valve fully when the accelerator pedal is pushed to the floor and conversely, when the pedal is released, the throttle valve is closed with the throttle stop hard against the throttle stop screw.

11 Solex 32 PBIC Carburettor - dismantling, servicing, reassembly

1 Unscrew and remove the screws which secure the top cover to the carburettor body.

2 Lift off the cover and swivel it to disengage the fast idle interconnecting rod from the elongated cutout in the throttle valve lever.

3 Unscrew the fuel inlet pipe union and extract the seal and filter gauge.

4 Unscrew the fuel inlet needle valve from the top cover and check its action. If it is at all sticky, renew it. If the needle valve is serviceable, check its calibration against specifications and then refit the sealing washer and tighten the valve securely.
valve securely.

5 From the float chamber in the lower body, extract the float and pivot pin.

6 Unscrew all jets (including the accelerator pump nozzle) and check their calibration markings against those listed in specifications. Renew any which do not conform with those specified.

7 The cold starting device and the accelerator pump may be dismantled from the carburettor body if necessary.

8 Do not remove the throttle spindle or butterfly plate. If there is movement in the throttle spindle then the spindle holes in the body are worn and the carburettor should be renewed on an exchange basis.

9 Blow all jets and passages through with air from a tyre pump; **never probe them with wire** or their calibration will be ruined.

10 Obtain a repair kit from your dealer which will contain all the necessary gaskets and other components to be used during reassembly.

11 Reassembly is a reversal of dismantling but the following adjustments must be carried out.

12 Invert the carburettor and close the throttle butterfly valve. This will necessitate unscrewing the throttle stop screw to permit full closure of the plate.

13 Pull the accelerator pump operating lever fully back and test

10.4 Fuel pump to carburettor pipe support clip

the clearance between the edge of the throttle butterfly valve and the wall of the choke tube. This should be 2.5 mm for carburettors with a reference number 14 on the choke control lever and 3.0 mm for all others. The clearance is best tested with a twist drill.

14 Where adjustment is required, turn the control rod adjusting nut and locknut as appropriate.

15 Next check the fast idle setting. Again invert the carburettor and close the throttle butterfly plate fully after unscrewing the throttle stop screw.

16 Pull the cold starting device lever to the fully closed position and check the clearance between the edge of the throttle butterfly plate and the wall of the choke tube. This should be 1.0 mm using a twist drill as a gauge. If the clearance is incorrect, bend the interconnecting rod gently at its centre.

17 When the carburettor is reassembled and installed on the inlet manifold, carry out the slow running adjustment as described in Section 9.

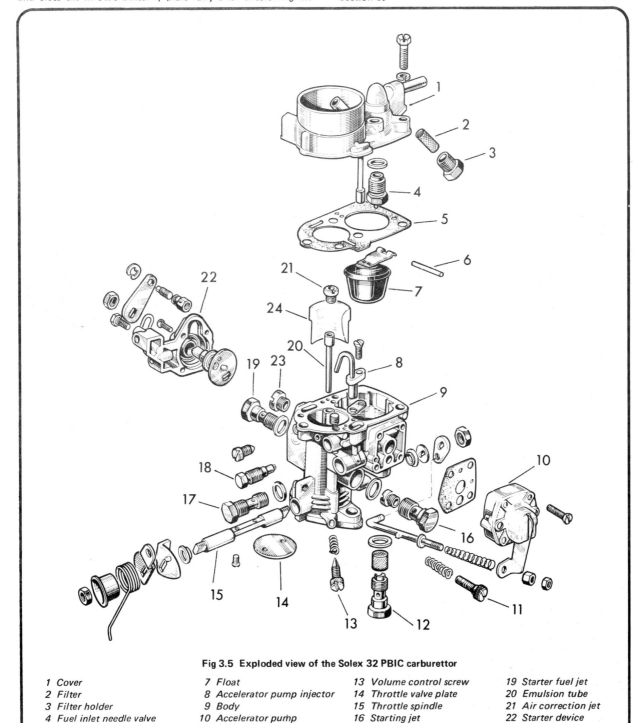

Fig 3.5 Exploded view of the Solex 32 PBIC carburettor

1 Cover	7 Float	13 Volume control screw	19 Starter fuel jet
2 Filter	8 Accelerator pump injector	14 Throttle valve plate	20 Emulsion tube
3 Filter holder	9 Body	15 Throttle spindle	21 Air correction jet
4 Fuel inlet needle valve	10 Accelerator pump	16 Starting jet	22 Starter device
5 Gasket	11 Throttle stop screw	17 Main jet carrier	23 Slow running air jet
6 Float pivot pin	12 Non-return valve	18 Pilot jet	24 Choke tube

12 Weber carburettors - slow running adjustment

1 Run the engine to normal operating temperature then switch if off.
2 Unscrew the throttle stop screw until the throttle butterfly plate is fully closed.
3 Screw in the throttle stop screw until it just touches the throttle arm stop and then screw it in a further 1½ to 2 turns.
4 Screw in the volume control screw until it seats (do not force it) and then unscrew it by between 1½ and 2 turns.
5 Start the engine and adjust the throttle stop screw if necessary, to give a slow running speed of between 700 and 800 rev/min.
6 Now adjust the volume control screw by screwing it in, or out, until the highest or smoothest idling speed is obtained.
7 If the tickover setting is not obtainable, or the engine is racing then you should recheck your carburettor controls for correctness of fitting and start again. If you still cannot obtain a reasonable tickover, and you are positive that the carburettor is not at fault, then proceed to check the ignition system. The static ignition timing of the engine affects idling speed, as well as the condition of the spark plugs, the compression in the cylinders, the inlet and exhaust valve tappet gaps, the condition of the inlet and exhaust valves themselves - all moving parts must be checked if the engine persists in ticking-over roughly and unevenly.
8 It is strongly recommended that a vacuum gauge or a 'Colortune' device is used for more precise setting.

13 Weber carburettors - removal and refitting

1 The procedure is essentially the same as described for Solex carburettors in Section 10.
2 The Weber 32 ICB 3 has two holes in the mounting flange but other types have four (photo).
3 On models other than the 32 ICB 3, the air cleaner is secured to the top face of the carburettor by four mounting studs.

14 Weber 32 ICB 3 Carburettor - dismantling, servicing, re-assembly

1 Disconnect the choke plate and throttle plate interconnecting rod by withdrawing the split pin from the upper end of the rod.
2 Unscrew and remove the securing screws from the top cover and lift the cover from the carburettor body.
3 If necessary unscrew the inlet needle valve and holder and the filter from the top cover. Check the needle vlave for freedom of action and also its calibration against that shown in Specifications.
4 When screwing the needle valve holder back into the top cover ensure that the spacing washer is located under it and tighten the holder securely.
5 Detach the float and pivot pin from the float chamber lid.
6 Unscrew and remove all jets using spanners and screwdriver blades of appropriate size in order not to burr the small components.
7 Thoroughly clean the carburettor in fuel and blow through the internal passages with air from a tyre pump.
8 Blow through the jets in a similar manner; never probe with wire to clear them.
9 Examine the choke and throttle valve plate spindles. If there is wear in the spindle holes in the body or top cover then the carburettor should be renewed on an exchange basis. Do not remove the valve plate or spindles unless absolutely necessary.
10 Dismantle the accelerator pump by disconnecting the link rod from its operating arm and then removing the four cover screws.
11 Reassembly is a reversal of dismantling but a repair kit should be obtained which will contain all the necessary gaskets and washers for replacement purposes.

12 During reassembly, carry out the following checks and adjustments.
13 Hold the top cover in a vertical attitude so that the tongue of the float arm is in light contact with the needle valve. The distance between the face of a gasket held in position on the top cover and the nearest point on the surface of the float should be 6.0 mm. If adjustment is required, bend the tongue on the float arm but then check that the float operating stroke is still 8.5 mm otherwise bend the tab at the end of the float arm (Fig. 3.6).
14 The accelerator pump operating rod should not normally require adjustment unless it has been bent or distorted. Should this be the case unscrew the throttle stop screw so that it is no longer in contact with the throttle lever stop. Pull the accelerator pump operating arm fully back and check the clearance between the edge of the throttle butterfly and the wall of the choke tube. This clearance should be 2.5 mm, otherwise bend the operating

13.2 Removing Weber type ICB3 carburettor

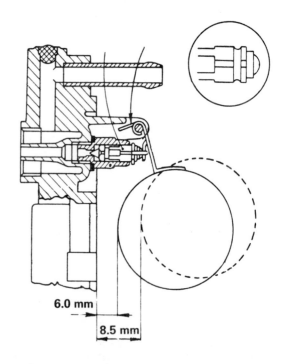

Fig 3.6 Weber carburettor float setting diagram

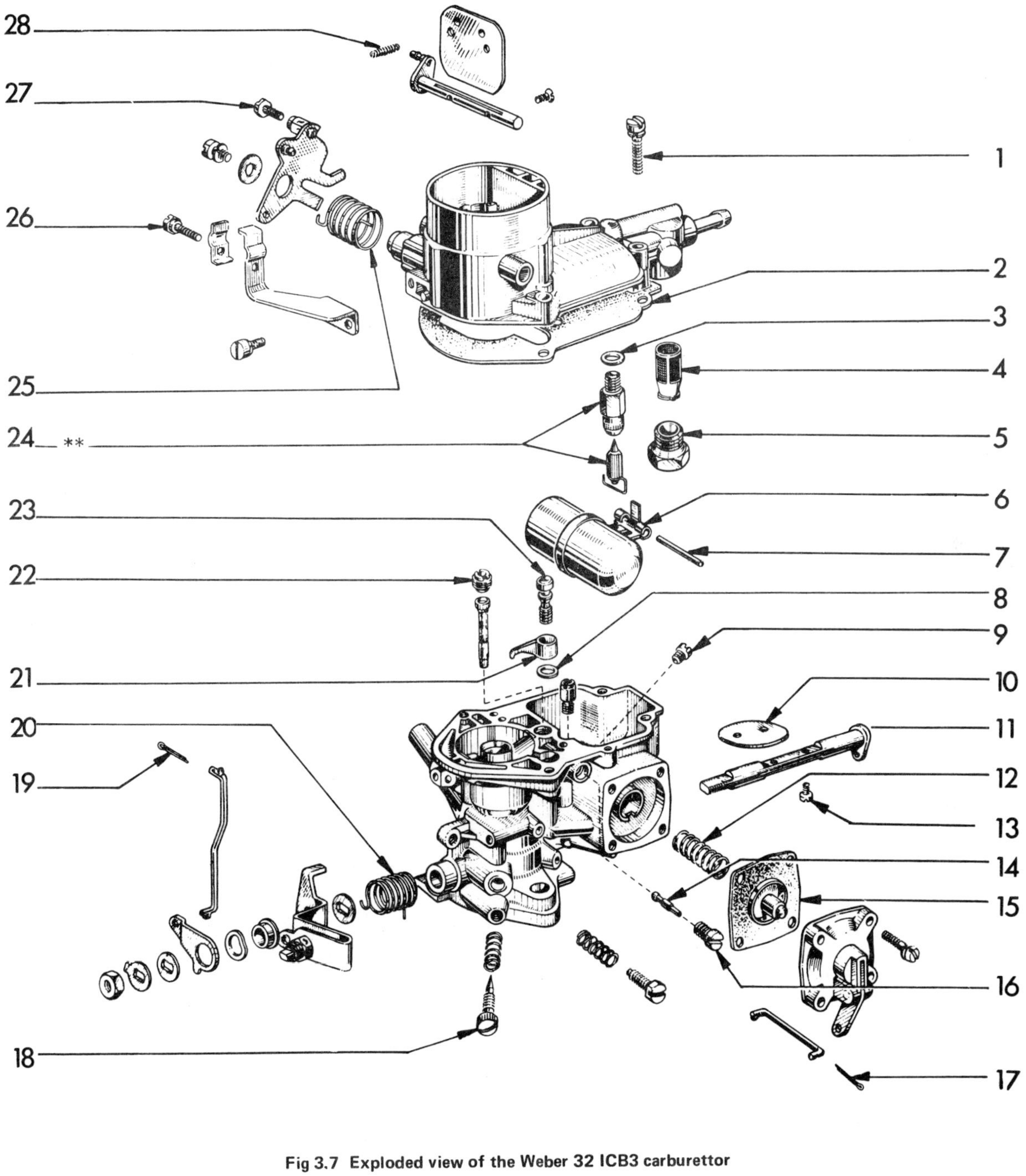

Fig 3.7 Exploded view of the Weber 32 ICB3 carburettor

1 Cover screw
2 Gasket
3 Inlet valve washer
4 Filter
5 Filter holder
6 Float
7 Float pivot pin
8 Washer
9 Main jet
10 Throttle butterfly plate
11 Throttle spindle
12 Return spring
13 Throttle plate screw
14 Idling jet
15 Accelerator pump diaphragm
16 Idling jet holder
17 Split pin
18 Volume control screw
19 Split pin
20 Throttle valve plate return spring
21 Accelerator pump ejector
22 Air correction jet
23 Pump jet
24 Fuel inlet needle valve
25 Choke valve plate return spring
26 Screw
27 Choke cable pinch bolt
28 Choke cable spring

rod.
15 Now check the fast idle setting. Close the choke valve plate fully and again check the clearance between the edge of the throttle valve plate and the wall of the choke tube. This should be 1.2 mm, otherwise bend the link rod. The clearances just described are best checked using a twist drill or rod of suitable diameter.
16 When the carburettor is reassembled and installed on the manifold, carry out the slow running adjustment as described in Section 12.

15 Weber Series 28/36 DCB Carburettors - dismantling, servicing, reassembly

1 These carburettors are of downdraft dual barrel type. The primary and secondary venturis are not detachable.
2 Dismantling, servicing and reassembly follow the pattern already described in Section 14 but of course no adjustment is required for the accelerator pump or the fast idle setting.
3 Checking and adjusting the float level should be carried out

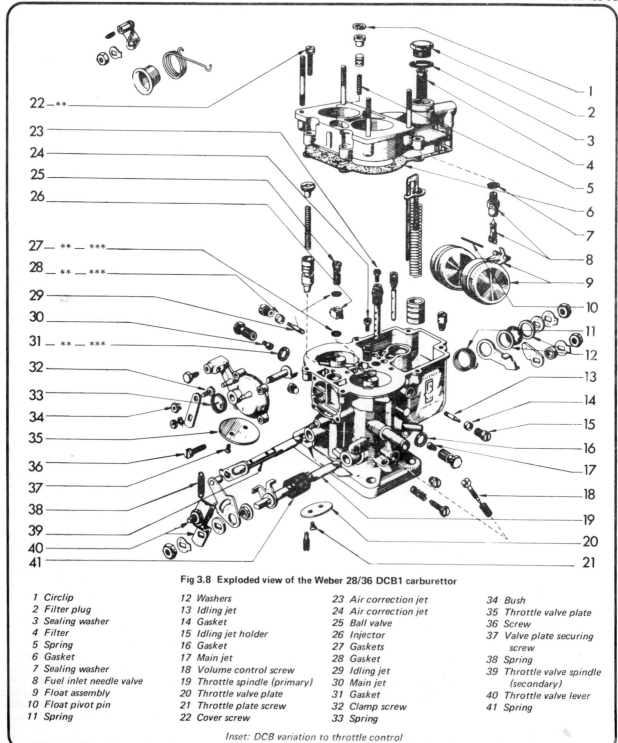

Fig 3.8 Exploded view of the Weber 28/36 DCB1 carburettor

1 Circlip
2 Filter plug
3 Sealing washer
4 Filter
5 Spring
6 Gasket
7 Sealing washer
8 Fuel inlet needle valve
9 Float assembly
10 Float pivot pin
11 Spring
12 Washers
13 Idling jet
14 Gasket
15 Idling jet holder
16 Gasket
17 Main jet
18 Volume control screw
19 Throttle spindle (primary)
20 Throttle valve plate
21 Throttle plate screw
22 Cover screw
23 Air correction jet
24 Air correction jet
25 Ball valve
26 Injector
27 Gaskets
28 Gasket
29 Idling jet
30 Main jet
31 Gasket
32 Clamp screw
33 Spring
34 Bush
35 Throttle valve plate
36 Screw
37 Valve plate securing screw
38 Spring
39 Throttle valve spindle (secondary)
40 Throttle valve lever
41 Spring

Inset: DCB variation to throttle control

in exactly the same way as described for the Weber 32 ICB 3 in the preceeding Section.
4   On the Weber type 28/36DCB1, the secondary butterfly valve travel is limited by a stop screw which is set and locked during production. Never attempt to alter the setting of this screw.

16 Solex 35 TDIDA carburettor - slow running adjustment

1   This type of carburettor was fitted to vehicles with automatic transmission built during 1968 only. The method of adjusting the slow running is as described for Weber carburettors in Section 12.
2   The engine idling speed on vehicles equipped with automatic transmission should be slightly higher (850 to 900 rev/min) than with manual gearbox vehicles. This will prevent stalling when 'Drive' is engaged and offset the drag caused by the fluid in the torque converter.
3   It is strongly recommended that a vacuum gauge or a device similar to a 'Colortune' be used for more precise setting of the slow running.

17 Solex 35 TDIDA carburettor - removal and refitting

1   Remove the air cleaner assembly from the four locating studs on the top flange of the carburettor.
2   Disconnect the accelerator control from the throttle lever of the carburettor.
3   Disconnect the 'kick-down' (downshift) cable from the carburettor.
4   Disconnect the fuel supply pipe from the carburettor.
5   Partially drain the cooling system and then disconnect the flexible hoses from the automatic choke housing and the coolant heated valve plate housing.
6   Unscrew and remove the flange securing nuts and lift off the carburettor and gaskets.
7   Installation is a reversal of removal but use new flange gaskets and remember to refill the cooling system.

18 Solex 35 TDIDA carburettor - dismantling, servicing, reassembly

1   Unscrew and remove the air cleaner mounting flange.
2   Unscrew and remove the securing screws from the top cover and then lift off the top cover and gasket.
3   Unscrew and remove the automatic choke housing.
4   Extract the float and pivot from the float chamber.
5   Unscrew all jets and blow them through with air from a tyre pump; never probe them with wire to clear them. Compare the jet calibration markings with those listed in 'Specifications' and renew any which deviate.
6   If necessary dismantle the accelerator pump and pre-atomiser assembly but do not dismantle the throttle butterfly valves or spindles unless essential. If wear is evident in the throttle spindles or their holes, then the carburettor must be renewed as an assembly on an exchange basis.
7   Blow all internal passages through with air from a tyre pump and then obtain a repair kit which will contain all the necessary gaskets and washers for use during reassembly.
8   Reassembly is a reversal of dismantling but the following adjustments must be carried out.
9   When refitting the automatic choke housing, engage the bi-metallic spring on its peg and make sure that the marks on both halves of the housing are in alignment. The alignment of these marks should not be varied in temperate climates but in extremes of heat or cold the position may be altered either side of the central index mark to provide longer or shorter duration of the choke action as required.
10 Pull the accelerator pump operating arm fully back and check the clearance between the edge of the secondary throttle valve plate and the wall of the choke tube. This should be 3.0 mm;

otherwise adjust the pump operating rod by means of its nut and locknut.
11 When the carburettor is reassembled and installed on the manifold, the slow running should be adjusted as described in Section 16.

19 Weber 28/36 DCB2 carburettor - description and servicing

1   This type of manually operated choke carburettor was fitted to vehicles equipped with automatic transmission after the end of 1968 and the unit was a successor to the Solex type 35TDIDA.
2   Slow running adjustment, removal, refitting, dismantling and reassembly all follow the operations described for dual venturi type Weber units earlier in this Chapter.
3   This carburettor is fitted with a dashpot to control the last section of throttle closure to idling speed when the accelerator pedal is released.
4   With the engine running at about 3000 rev/min. if the accelerator pedal is released the engine speed should fall to about 1000 rev/min in 5 seconds. The operating stroke of the dashpot plunger should be 4.5 mm ($\pm$ 0.5 mm) to achieve this. If adjustment is required, rotate the plunger nut and locknut.
5   Refer to 'Specifications' for full details of calibrations of jets and other components.

20 Accelerator and choke controls - maintenance and renewal

1   Both these controls are of cable operated type.
2   The accelerator cable is connected to the accelerator pedal by means of a clevis fork.
3   At the carburettor end, the method of attachment varies according to model and date of manufacture but is of pinch bolt or swivel type.
4   Occasionally apply a little oil to the accelerator pedal pivots and the cable connecting links.
5   If renewal is required, ensure that with the pedal fully depressed, the throttle valve plate is fully open but not under tension from an overtight cable. Conversely, ensure that with the pedal released, the throttle valve plate is fully closed.
6   The choke cable requires no maintenance. Should renewal be required, unscrew the choke control knob grub screw and pull off the knob. Release the pinch bolt from the cable at the choke plate lever on the carburettor.
7   Unscrew and remove the locknut at the choke control on the facia panel and withdraw the complete assembly through the bulkhead grommet into the vehicle interior.
8   Refit the new cable by reversing the removal operations. Before tightening the cable pinch bolt at the carburettor make sure that the control knob is pushed fully home and that the choke valve plate is closed (or starting device lever fully released).

21 Exhaust system

1   The system comprises two sections, a downpipe and primary expansion chamber and a rear mounted main silencer and tail pipe.
2   The downpipe is connected to the exhaust manifold by means of a bolted two piece clamp and further supported by a rigid bracket at the rear of the primary expansion chamber (photo).
3   The rear mountings are by flexible, circular straps (photo).
intervals is worthwhile as small defects may be repairable when, if left they will almost centainly require renewal of one of the sections of the system. Also, any leaks, apart from the noise factor, may cause poisonous exhaust gases to get inside the car which can be unpleasant, to say the least, even in mild concentrations. Prolonged inhalation could cause sickness and giddiness.
5   As the sleeve connections and clamps are usually very difficult to separate it is quicker and easier in the long run to

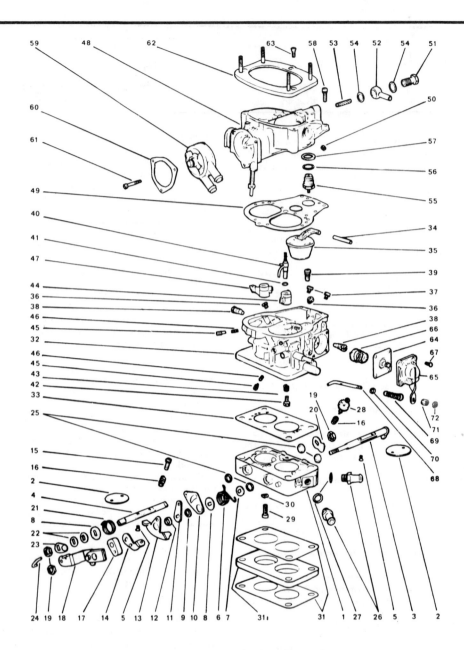

Fig 3.9 Exploded view of the Solex 35 TDIDA carburettor

1 Throttle valve plate housing	21 Return spring	39 Ball valve	57 Sealing washer
2 Valve plate	22 Spacers	40 Accelerator pump ejector	58 Retaining screw
3 Throttle spindle (primary)	23 Relay lever	41 Gasket	59 Automatic choke housing
4 Throttle spindle (secondary)	24 Link rod	42 Overriding pin	60 Housing retainer
5 Valve plate securing screw	25 Sealing washers	43 Spring	61 Retaining screw
6 Spring	26 Coolant hose connectors	44 Pre-atomizer (primary)	62 Air cleaner mounting
7, 8 & 9 Spacers	27 Sealing washer	45 Screw	flange
10 Lever	28 Volume control screw	46 Spring	63 Flange securing screw
11 Lever	29 Retaining screw	47 Pre-atomizer (secondary)	64 Accelerator pump
12 Spacer	30 Spring washer	48 Cover	diaphragm
13 Fast idle lever	31 Gasket	49 Gasket	65 Accelerator pump cover
14 Throttle valve lever	32 Body	50 Enrichment jet	assembly
15 Throttle stop screw	33 Gasket	51 Hollow bolt	66 Spring
16 Spring	34 Float pivot pin	52 Banjo inlet connection	67 Retaining screw
17 Spacer	35 Float	53 Filter	68 Link rod
18 Relay lever	36 Air correction jet	54 Sealing washer	69 Spring
19 Spindle nut	37 Main jet	55 Fuel inlet needle valve	70 Washer
20 Stop arm	38 Idling jet	56 Sealing washer	71 Adjusting nut for link
			rod
			72 Locknut

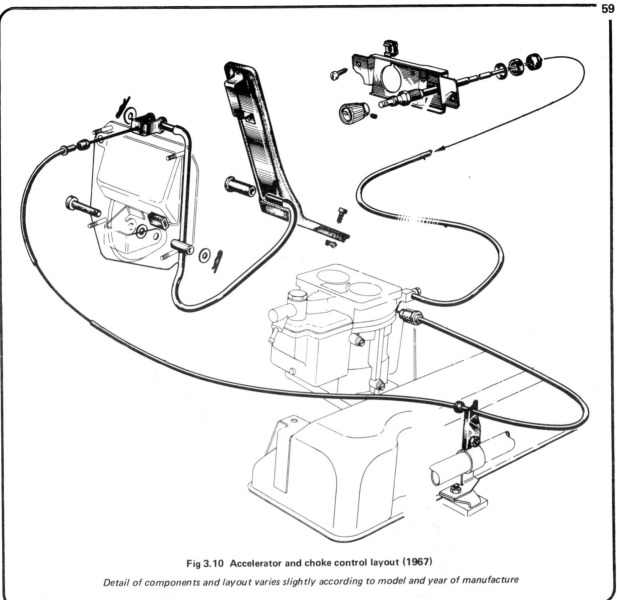

Fig 3.10 Accelerator and choke control layout (1967)

Detail of components and layout varies slightly according to model and year of manufacture

21.2 Exhaust pipe rigid mounting

21.3 Exhaust pipe rear flexible mounting

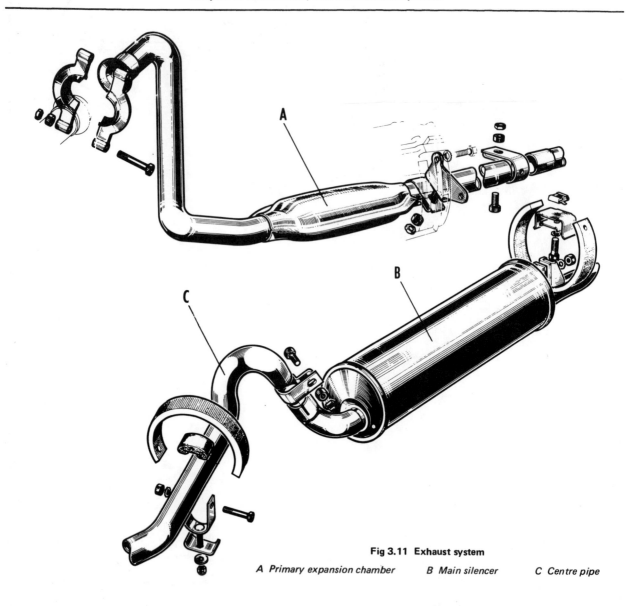

Fig 3.11 Exhaust system

A Primary expansion chamber   *B Main silencer*   *C Centre pipe*

remove the complete system from the car when renewing a section. It can be expensive if another section is damaged when trying to separate a bad section from it.

6   To remove the system, support the rear silencer on a jack and then disconnect the rear flexible mounting.

7   Disconnect the remaining mountings and finally uncouple the manifold to downpipe clamp.

8   Lower the jack and withdraw the complete assembly from below and to the rear of the vehicle. If necessary jack up the rear of the vehicle to provide more clearance and better access.

9   When separating the damaged section to be renewed cut away the damaged part from the adjoining good section rather than risk damaging the latter.

10 If small repairs are being carried out it is best, if possible, not to try and pull the sections apart.

11 Refitting should be carried out after connecting the two sections together. De-burr and grease the connecting socket and make sure that the clamp is in good condition and slipped over the front pipe but do not tighten it at this stage.

12 Connect the new or repaired system to the manifold and attach the rear support strap. Now adjust the attitude of the silencer so that it hangs evenly within its mountings and will not knock against adjacent components when deflected slightly in an upward or sideways direction.

13 Tighten all bolts fully.

22 Fault diagnosis - carburation and fuel systems

Symptom	Reason/s	Remedy
Excessive fuel consumption	Air filter choked	Renew element.
	Leakage from pump, carburettor or fuel lines or fuel tank	Renew or tighten as necessary.
	Float chamber flooding	Check and adjust level.
	Distributor capacitor faulty	Renew.
	Distributor weights or vacuum capsule faulty	Service or renew.
	Mixture too rich	Adjust.
	Contact breaker gap too wide	Check and reset.
	Incorrect valve clearances	Adjust.
	Incorrect spark plug gaps	Adjust.
	Tyres under inflated	Inflate.
	Dragging brakes	Check for air in system or faulty wheel or master cylinder.
Insufficient delivery or weak mixture	Petrol tank air vent restricted	Remove petrol cap and clean out air vent.
	Partially clogged filters in pump and carburettor	Remove and clean filters. Remove and clean out float chamber and needle valve assembly
	Incorrectly seating valves in fuel pump	Remove and fit new fuel pump.
	Fuel pump diaphragm leaking or damaged	Remove and fit new fuel pump.
	Gasket in fuel pump damaged	Remove and fit new fuel pump.
	Fuel pump valves sticking due to petrol gumming	Remove and thoroughly clean fuel pump.
	Too little fuel in fuel tank (prevalent when climbing steep hills)	Refill fuel tank.
	Union joints on pipe connections loose	Tighten joints and check for air leaks.
	Split in fuel pipe on suction side of fuel pump	Examine, locate and repair.
	Inlet manifold to block or inlet manifold to carburettor gasket leaking	Test by pouring oil along joints - bubbles indicate leak. Renew gasket as appropriate.

Chapter 4 Ignition system

Contents

Specifications

Distributor

Make	Ducellier or SEV
Drive	From camshaft
Rotational direction	Clockwise
Advance method	Centrifugal weights and vacuum from manifold
Firing order	1 3 4 2
Dwell angle (1300/1301 up to 1969)	$56^{o} \pm 1^{o}$
(all other models)	51 to 58°

Initial (static setting):
Advance marked by notch on oil filter pulley and line on timing cover

1301S saloon (Solex)	10°
1301S estate car (Weber)	12°
1501S estate car	14°
All other models	12°

	1300/1301 up to 1969	1301 1969 onwards	1500	1501
Centrifugal advance:				
Starts rev/min	1500	1000	1500	1000
degrees	1	0	1	0
Ends rev/min	4400	4400	4800	4800
degrees	26	26	30	30
Vacuum advance:				
Starts (mm Hg)	139.7	152.2	165.1	127.0
Ends (mm Hg)	298.7	304.8	393.7	406.4
Contact breaker gap	0.018 to 0.020 in (0.4572 to 0.5080 mm)			
Condenser rating	0.20 to 0.30 microfarad			

Spark plugs

Make	Marchal

	1300/1301 up to 1969	1301 after 1969	1500	1501
Type	35SN4	35 HN	34 HSN4	35 HS
Gap	0.024 in (0.6096 mm)	0.021 in (0.5334 mm)	0.025 in (0.6350 mm)	0.024 in (0.6096 mm)

1 General description

1 In order that the engine can run correctly it is necessary for an electrical spark to ignite the fuel/air mixture in the combustion chamber at exactly the right moment in relation to engine speed and load. The ignition system is based on feeding low tension (LT) voltage from the battery to the coil where it is converted to high tension (HT) voltage. The high tension voltage is powerful enough to jump the spark plug gap in the cylinders many times a second under high compression pressures, providing that the system is in good condition and that all adjustments are correct.

The ignition system is divided into two circuits. The low tension circuit and the high tension circuit.

The low tension (sometimes known as the primary) circuit consists of the battery lead to the control box, lead to the ignition switch, lead from the ignition switch to the low tension or primary coil windings, and the lead from the low tension coil windings to the contact breaker points and condenser in the distributor.

The high tension circuit consists of the high tension or secondary coil windings, the heavy ignition lead from the centre of the coil to the centre of the distributor cap, the rotor arm, and the spark plug leads and spark plugs.

The system functions in the following manner. Low tension voltage is changed in the coil into high tension voltage by the opening and closing of the contact breaker points in the low tension circuit. High tension voltage is then fed via the carbon brush in the centre of the distributor cap to the rotor arm of the distributor cap, and each time it comes in line with one of the four metal segments in the cap, which are connected to the spark plug leads, the opening and closing of the contact breaker points causes the high tension voltage to build up, jump the gap from the rotor arm to the appropriate metal segment and so via the spark plug lead to the spark plug, where it finally jumps the spark plug gap before going to earth.

The ignition is advanced and retarded automatically, to ensure the spark occurs at just the right instant for the particular load at the prevailing engine speed.

The ignition advance is controlled both mechanically and by a vacuum operated system. The mechanical governor mechanism comprises two weights, which move out from the distributor shaft as the engine speed rises due to centrifugal force. As they move outwards they rotate the cam relative to the distributor shaft, and so advance the spark. The weights are held in position by two light springs and it is the tension of the springs which is largely responsible for correct spark advancement.

The vacuum control consists of a diaphragm, one side of which is connected via a small bore tube to the carburettor, and the other side to the contact breaker plate. Depression in the inlet manifold and carburettor, which varies with engine speed and throttle opening, causes the diaphragm to move, so moving the contact breaker plate, and advancing or retarding the spark. A fine degree of control is achieved by a spring in the vacuum assembly.

2 Distributor - description and type

A Ducellier or SEV distributor may be fitted. The points of a Ducellier distributor are of so called self cleaning type, use being made of the vacuum movement of the baseplate to 'wipe' the spark. Pitting and burning of the contact breaker points is much reduced and when the faces are eroded, the points should not be dressed but renewed. Points of SEV distributors may be dressed on an oilstone in the usual way.

Apart from detail differences in components, the two makes of distributor are very similar and should be serviced in the same

manner. The distributor drive connection on 1300 models is the large and small segment dog type whereas on all other models the distributor shaft terminates in a gear which meshes directly with the camshaft.

3 Contact breaker points - adjustment

1 Turn the engine until (with the distributor cap removed), the contact points are opened to their fullest extent with the heel of the movable contact arm on one of the high points of the distributor cam. The easiest way to turn the engine is to engage top gear and release the handbrake and then push the vehicle forward. (On automatic vehicles, use the starter or turn the oil filter). Removal of the spark plugs will facilitate engine rotation.
2 Using feeler gauges check the points gap which should be between 0.018 and 0.020 in (0.4572 and 0.5080 mm). If necessary loosen the screw which secures the fixed contact breaker plate to the baseplate and move the contact breaker until the gap is correct (photos).
3 Retighten the contact breaker plate screw.

4 Contact breaker points - removal and refitting

(a) Ducellier

1 Pull off the distributor cap retaining springs and lift off the cap.
2 Pull off the rotor arm.
3 Extract the spring clip from the top of the contact arm pivot post. Remove the washer.
4 Loosen the LT terminal on the distributor body enough to permit removal of the contact breaker arm lead and spade terminal.
5 Lift off the movable contact breaker arm.
6 Unscrew and remove the screw from the fixed contact breaker arm and lift the arm from the baseplate.
7 Do not disturb or remove the toothed cam or pivot arm.
8 Refitting is a reversal of removal but adjust the points gap as described in the preceding Section.

(b) SEV

1 The procedures for removing and refitting the points are similar to those described for the Ducellier type except that after removal of the distributor cap and rotor arm, a dust cap and seal must be extracted before access to the contact breaker assembly can be obtained.

3.2A Checking points gap with a feeler gauge

3.2B Loosening the fixed contact breaker arm screw

5 Condenser (capacitor) - removal, testing, refitting

1 The condenser ensures that with the contact breaker points open, the sparking between them is not excessive to cause severe pitting. The condenser is fitted in parallel and its failure will automatically cause failure of the ignition system as the points will be prevented from interrupting the low tension circuit.

2 Testing for an unserviceable condenser may be effected by switching on the ignition and separating the contact points by hand. If this action is accompanied by a blue flash then condenser failure is indicated. Difficult starting, missing of the engine after several miles running or badly pitted points are other indications of a faulty condenser.

3 The surest test is by substitution of a new unit.

4 The condenser is mounted on the exterior of the distributor body and retained by a single screw.

6 Distributor (1300 and 1301 up to 1969 models) - removal and installation

1 Disconnect the leads from the spark plugs and the LT and HT leads from the coil.

2 Unscrew the flange bolts at the base of the distributor shaft housing and pull the distributor from its crankcase recess (photo).

3 If the engine has not been turned, then the distributor is simply installed by aligning the large and small segments of the drive dog and pushing it into its recess. Tighten the flange bolts securely.

4 If the engine has been turned then retiming must be carried out as follows: Rotate the crankshaft by pushing the vehicle with top gear engaged (on automatic vehicles remove the plugs and use the starter or turn the centrifugal oil filter on the front of the engine) until no.1 piston (rearmost) is at tdc on its compression stroke. The compression stroke may be ascertained by placing a finger over the rear plug hole and feeling the compression being generated.

5 Continue turning the crankshaft until the first notch on the oil filter pulley groove is opposite the mark on the timing cover.

6 Now insert the distributor driving sleeve into the crankcase recess so that when it is engaged with the driveshaft splines, its groove will be parallel to the centre line of the engine block with the smaller segment furthest from the engine (photos).

7 Push the distributor into its recess so that the large and small segments of its driving dog mate with those of the driving sleeve.

8 The rotor arm should now be pointing at No.1 contact in the distributor cap.

9 Check the ignition timing (Section 8) and refit the distributor cap and leads. Tighten the flange and pinch bolts.

7 Distributor (1301 after 1969, 1500 and 1501 models) - removal and installation

1 The driveshaft of this type of distributor meshes directly with the camshaft driving gear.

2 With No.1 piston (rearmost) at tdc on its compression stroke and the leading notch on the oil filter pulley groove opposite the long mark on the timing cover (ignore any shorter mark on the cover), the rotor arm of the distributor must point towards no.1 contact in the distributor cap.

3 As the distributor is pushed into its recess, the action of the meshing of the drive gears will automatically turn the rotor arm. It is therefore very important to turn the rotor arm back in an anti-clockwise direction about 30° before installing the distributor to compensate for this and to ensure that when the drive gears are fully meshed the rotor will point directly at No.1 contact in the distributor cap.

4 Check the ignition timing (Section 8) and tighten the distributor clamp plate bolt.

8 Timing the ignition

1 Rotate the crankshaft until No.1 (rearmost) piston is on its compression stroke. This may be ascertained by removing the rear spark plug and feeling the compression being generated. Alternatively, if the rocker cover is removed both No. 1 cylinder valves will be closed.

2 Continue turning the crankshaft until the leading notch on the oil filter driving pulley is opposite the mark on the timing cover. There is a slight difference in these marks according to engine type and both are illustrated in Chapter 1.

3 Connect a test lamp in parallel with the contact breaker points, one lead from the bulb holder being connected to the LT terminal on the side of the distributor body and the other lead to earth.

4 Slacken the distributor pinch bolt or clamp plate bolt (according to type) and switch on the ignition.

5 Turn the distributor body until the contact breaker points are closed and then turn the body in an anti-clockwise direction until the test lamp illuminates, this will indicate that the points have just opened.

6 This is the correct static ignition setting and the distributor pinch bolt or clamp plate bolt must now be tightened.

7 Switch off the ignition, remove the test lamp and refit the distributor cap.

8 If a stroboscope is used to set the timing, the manufacturer's instructions should be closely followed regarding connection.

9 Mark the line on the timing cover with white chalk or paint.

10 Determine at what speed the engine will run during the timing and read off the number of degrees of centrifugal advance from the curve. Note that the distributor speed shown is half engine speed (crankshaft speed). This number of degrees must be added to the number of degrees of static setting listed in Specifications. The total will then be marked on the oil filter pulley (in advance of tdc) again in white paint or chalk (Fig. 4.2).

11 Disconnect the vacuum pipe from the distributor and plug the pipe with a thin rod.

12 Start the engine and set the throttle stop so that the engine runs at the predetermined speed, checked against a tachometer.

13 With the stroboscope pointing at the timing marks, these marks should appear stationary and opposite each other.

14 If they are not in alignment, slacken the distributor clamp and rotate the distributor until the marks are opposite each other.

15 Tighten the distributor clamp, switch off the ignition, remove the stroboscope and reconnect the vacuum pipe.

9 Distributor - dismantling, servicing, reassembly

1 In the event of wear occurring in the main components of the distributor, it is strongly advised that a factory reconditioned unit is obtained. However, where the spares are available the unit may be stripped in the following manner.

2 Remove the cap by pulling off the two securing clips.

3 Pull off the rotor from the distributor shaft.

4 On SEV units extract the dust cover and seal.

5 Dismantle the LT terminal from the distributor body and then remove the contact breaker assembly.

6 On Ducellier type units mark carefully which notch of the toothed cam is engaged with the coil spring end.

7 Remove the spring clip from the top of the toothed cam and lift the cam from its pivot so that the vacuum unit connecting rod can be released.

8 Remove the baseplate retaining screws and extract the baseplate from the distributor body.

9 On SEV units disconnect the vacuum unit connecting rod from the movable baseplate but on no account alter the effective length of the rod by screwing the vacuum unit in or out, (see Section 11).

10 It is not recommended that the centrifugal weight mechanism is dismantled but, if essential, mark the springs so that they can

6.2 Withdrawing the distributor

6.6A Inserting distributor driving sleeve

6.6B Driving dog segments correctly aligned

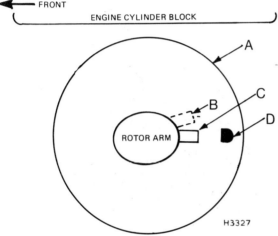

Fig 4.1 Distributor installation diagram (1301 after 1969, 1500 and 1501 models)

A distributor body B Position of rotor arm before installation of distributor C position of rotor arm after installation and drive gears have meshed D No 1 contact in distributor cap

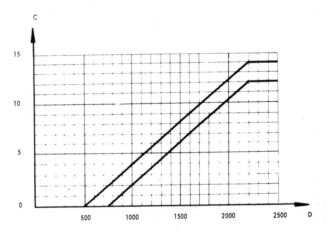

Fig 4.2 Centrifugal advance curve

C Distributor degrees   D Distributor rev/min (half engine speed)

be returned to their original locations on the securing posts and counterweight pivots. On Ducellier units, the counterweight springs differ and must not be interchanged. On SEV units, they are identical.

11 Great care must be observed in removing the counterweight springs and their retaining posts must not be bent, or the advance characteristics of the distributor will be changed (see next Section).

12 Drive out the shaft pin from the driving dog or gear according to type and extract the shaft from the distributor body, retaining the thrust washers and spacers in their original sequence.

13 Remove the vacuum unit (two screws) and the capacitor (one screw).

14 Clean all components and renew any that are worn or broken.

15 Reassembly is a reversal of dismantling but grease the shaft bushes and use a new pin to secure the driving dog or gear to the shaft.

10 Centrifugal advance mechanism - setting and adjustment

1 The mechanism is set during production and it is critical therefore that the tension or position of the counterweight springs is not altered.

2 Should changed characteristics of the distributor or engine require the mechanism to be reset or adjusted, it can only be carried out using the necessary meters and gauges.

3 Such setting and adjustment is made by bending the spring retaining post by levering them with a screwdriver inserted through the cutouts in the baseplate. The directional effect of such bending is that if they are bent towards each other, the point of static ignition setting is advanced and if they are bent away from each other, it is retarded (Fig. 4.4).

11 Vacuum advance mechanism - setting and adjustment

1 Here again, this is set during production and should not be altered during any dismantling or reassembly of the distributor.

2 On SEV units adjustment is carried out by unscrewing and removing the two vacuum capsule securing screws and then screwing the capsule in or out to effectively alter the length of the connecting rod.

3 On Ducellier units, the eccentric cam is rotated and locked in the desired position by the engagement of the toothed wheel with the end of the compression spring. The position of the cam in the baseplate cutout is reflected in the dwell angle curves (Fig. 4.6).

4 It is not recommended that the vacuum advance setting is altered unless the necessary dwell meter and other gauges are available.

12 Coil polarity and testing

1 High tension current should be negative at the spark plug

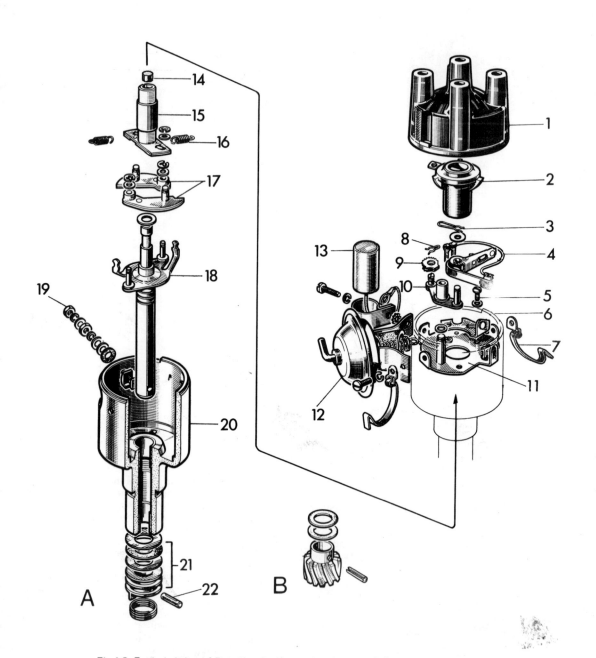

Fig 4.3 Exploded view of Ducellier distributor showing early (A) and later (B) drive gear

1 Cap
2 Rotor arm
3 Contact arm pivot clip
4 Movable contact arm and lead
5 Fixed contact arm securing
   screw
6 Fixed contact arm
7 Cap clip
8 Swivel arm clip
9 Toothed cam wheel
10 Swivel arm
11 Baseplate
12 Vacuum capsule
13 Condenser
14 Lubrication pad
15 Cam assembly
16 Counterweight spring
17 Counterweights
18 Shaft and centrifugal
   mechanism mounting
   plate
19 LT terminal components
20 Distributor body
21 Driving dog assembly
22 Shaft pin

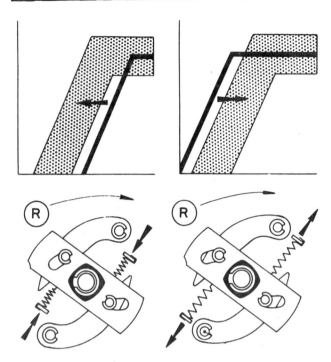

Fig 4.4 **Effect of bending counterweight spring retainer posts**

(left) Advancing the static setting (right) retarding the static setting. R Direction of distributor rotation. Solid line indicates specified static setting. SEV type distributor shown

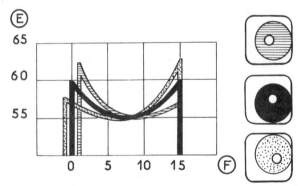

Fig 4.6 **Effect of rotating toothed cam eccentric within baseplate aperture (Ducellier type distributor)**

E Dwell angle *F Distributor degrees*

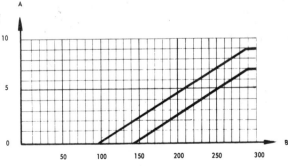

Fig 4.7 **Vacuum advance curve**

A Distributor degrees
B Vacuum (mm of mercury — mm Hg)

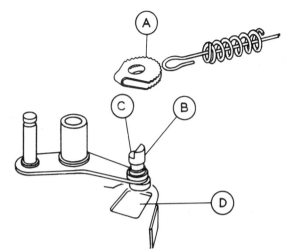

Fig 4.5 **Vacuum unit link rod and swivel arm components (Ducellier type distributor)**

A Toothed cam
B Eccentric post
C Cut-out for cam and eccentric post rotation
D Baseplate apperture

terminals. To ensure this, check that the LT connections to the coil are correctly made.
2 The LT wire from the distributor must connect with the negative (-) terminal on the coil.
3 The coil positive (+) terminal is connected to the ignition/ starter switch.
4 An incorrect connection can cause as much as a 60% loss of spark efficiency and can cause rough idling and misfiring at speed.

13 Spark plugs and leads

1 The correct functioning of the spark plugs is vital for the correct running and efficiency of the engine.
2 At intervals of 3,000 miles (5,000 km), the plugs should be removed, examined, cleaned, and if worn excessively replaced. The condition of the spark plugs will also tell much about the overall condition of the engine.
3 If the insulator nose of the spark plug is clean and white, with no deposits, this is indicative of a weak mixture, or too hot a plug (a hot plug transfers heat away from the electrode slowly - a cold plug transfers it away quickly).
4 The plugs fitted as standard are as listed in 'Specifications' at the head of this Chapter. If the tip and insulator nose are covered with hard black looking deposits, then this is indicative that the mixture is too rich. Should the plug be black and oily, then it is likely that the engine is fairly worn, as well as the mixture being too rich.
5 If the insulator nose is covered with light tan to greyish brown deposits, then the mixture is correct and it is likely that the engine is in good condition.
6 If there are any traces of long brown tapering stains on the outside of the white portion of the plug, then the plug will have to be renewed, as this shows that there is a faulty joint between the plug body and the insulator, and compression is being allowed to leak away.
7 Plugs should be cleaned by a sand blasting machine which will free them from carbon more thoroughly than cleaning by hand. The machine will also test the condition of the plug under compression. Any plug that fails to spark at the recommended pressure should be renewed.
8 The spark plug gap is of considerable importance, as, if it is too large or too small, the size of the spark and its efficiency will be seriously impaired. The spark plug gap should be set to the

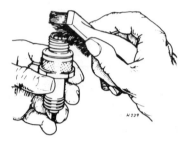

Cleaning deposits from electrodes and surrounding area using a fine wire brush.

Checking plug gap with feeler gauges

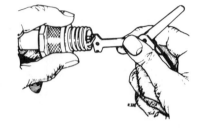

Altering the plug gap. Note use of correct tool.

Fig 4.8 Spark plug maintenance

White deposits and damaged porcelain insulation indicating overheating

Broken porcelain insulation due to bent central electrode

Electrodes burnt away due to wrong heat value or chronic pre-ignition (pinking)

Excessive black deposits caused by over-rich mixture or wrong heat value

Mild white deposits and electrode burnt indicating too weak a fuel mixture

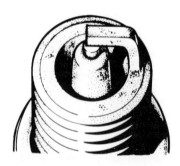

Plug in sound condition with light greyish brown deposits

Fig 4.9 Spark plug electrode conditions

figure given in 'Specifications' at the beginning of this Chapter.

9   To set it, measure the gap with a feeler gauge, and then bend open, or close, the outer plug electrode until the correct gap is achieved. The centre electrode should never be bent as this may crack the insulation and cause plug failure if nothing worse.

10 When replacing the plugs, remember to use new plug washers, and replace the leads from the distributor in the correct firing order, which is 1 3 4 2, No. 1 cylinder being the one furthest from the radiator.

11 The plug leads require no routine attention other than being kept clean and wiped over regularly.

12 After 10,000 miles (16000 km) the plugs should be renewed.

14 Ignition system - fault finding

By far the majority of breakdown and running troubles are caused by faults in the ignition system either in the low tension or high tension circuits.

There are two main symptoms indicating ignition faults. Either the engine will not start or fire, or the engine is difficult to start and misfires. If it is a regular misfire, ie. the engine is running on only two or three cylinders, the fault is almost sure to be in the secondary or high tension circuit. If the misfiring is intermittent, the fault could be in either the high or low tension circuit. If the car stops suddenly, or will not start at all, it is likely that the fault is in the low tension circuit. Loss of power and overheating, apart from faulty carburation settings, are normally due to faults in the distributor or to incorrect ignition timing.

15 Fault diagnosis - engine fails to start

1   If the engine fails to start and the car was running normally when it was last used, first check there is fuel in the petrol tank. If the engine turns over normally on the starter motor and the battery is evidently well charged, then the fault may be in either the high or low tension circuit. First check the HT circuit. **Note:** If the battery is known to be fully charged, the ignition light comes on, and the starter motor fails to turn the engine **check the tightness of the leads on the battery terminals** and also the secureness of the earth lead to its **connection to the body.** It is quite common for the leads to have worked loose, even if they look and feel secure. If one of the battery terminal posts gets very hot when trying to work the starter motor this is a sure indication of a faulty connection to that terminal.

2   One of the commonest reasons for bad starting is wet or damp spark plug leads and distributor. Remove the distributor cap. If condensation is visible internally dry the cap with a rag and also wipe over the leads. Replace the cap.

3   If the engine still fails to start, check that current is reaching the plugs, by disconnecting each plug lead in turn at the spark plug end, and holding the end of the cable about 3/16 inch (5 mm) away from the cylinder block. Spin the engine on the starter motor.

4   Sparking between the end of the cable and the block should be fairly strong with a strong regular blue spark. (Hold the lead with rubber to avoid electric shocks). If current is reaching the plugs, then remove them and clean and regap them. The engine should now start.

5   If there is no spark at the plug leads take off the HT lead from the centre of the distributor cap and hold it to the block as before. Spin the engine on the starter once more. A rapid succession of blue sparks between the end of the lead and the block indicate that the coil is in order and that the distributor cap is cracked, the rotor arm faulty, or the carbon brush in the top of the distributor cap is not making good contact with the rotor arm. Possibly the points are in bad condition. Clean and reset them as described in this Chapter, Section 3.   3

6   If there are no sparks from the end of the lead from the coil check the connections at the coil end of the lead. If it is in order start checking the low tension circuit.

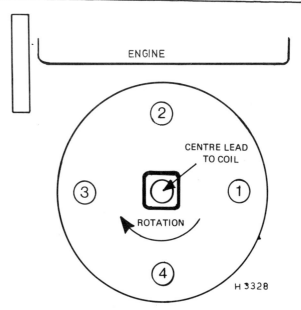

Fig 4.10 Distributor cap to spark plug HT lead connecting sequence diagram

Note: No 4 is nearest radiator

7   Use a 12v voltmeter or a 12v bulb and two lengths of wire. With the ignition switched on and the points open, test between the coil positive (+) terminal and earth. No reading indicates a break in the supply from the ignition switch. Check the connections at the switch to see if any are loose. Refit them and the engine should run. A reading shows a faulty coil or condenser, or broken lead between the coil and the distributor.

8   Take the condenser wire off the points assembly and with the points open test between the moving point and earth. If there now is a reading then the fault is in the condenser. Fit a new one and the fault is cleared.

9   With no reading from the moving point to earth, take a reading between earth and the coil negative (-) terminal. A reading here shows a broken wire which will need to be replaced between the coil and distributor. No reading confirms that the coil has failed and must be replaced, after which the engine will run once more. Remember to refit the condenser wire to the points assembly. For these tests it is sufficient to separate the points with a piece of dry paper while testing with the points open.

16 Fault diagnosis - engine misfires

1   If the engine misfires regularly run it at a fast idling speed. Pull off each of the plug caps in turn and listen to the note of the engine. Hold the plug cap in a dry cloth or with a rubber glove as additional protection against a shock from the HT supply.

2   No difference in engine running will be noticed when the lead from the defective circuit is removed. Removing the lead from one of the good cylinders will accentuate the misfire.

3   Remove the plug lead from the end of the defective plug and hold it about 3/16 inch (5.0 mm) away from the block. Restart the engine. If the sparking is fairly strong and regular the fault must lie in the spark plug.

4   The plug may be loose, the insulation may be cracked, or the points may have burnt away giving too wide a gap for the spark to jump. Worse still, one of the points may have broken off. Either renew the plug, or clean it, reset the gap, and then test it.

5   If there is no spark at the end of the plug lead, or, if it is weak and intermittent, check the ignition lead from the distributor to the plug. If the insulation is cracked or perished,

renew the lead. Check the connections at the distributor cap.

6 If there is still no spark, examine the distributor cap carefully for tracking. This can be recognised by a very thin black line running between two or more electrodes, or between an electrode and some other part of the distributor. These lines are paths which now conduct electricity across the cap thus letting it run to earth. The only answer is a new distributor cap.

7 Apart from the ignition timing being incorrect, other causes of misfiring have already been dealt with under the section dealing with the failure of the engine to start. To recap - these are that:-

a) The coil may be faulty giving an intermittent misfire.

b) There may be a damaged wire or loose connection in a low tension circuit.

c) The condenser may be short circuiting.

d) There may be a mechanical fault in the distributor (broken driving spindle or contact breaker spring).

8 If the ignition timing is too far retarded, it should be noted that the engine will tend to overheat, and there will be a quite noticeable drop in power. If the engine is overheating and the power is down, and the ignition timing is correct then the carburettor should be checked, as it is likely that this is where the fault lies.

Chapter 5 Clutch

Contents

Specifications

Type ... ... Single dry plate with coil spring pressure plate (up to 1969) and diaphragm spring pressure plate (after 1969)

Actuation ... ... Hydraulic

Free movement at release arm/operating rod ... ... 0.078 in (2.0 mm)

Free movement at pedal ... ... 5/8 in (15.9 mm)

Torque wrench settings

	lb ft	kg m
Clutch bellhousing to cylinder block with sealing washers ...	38	5.2
Clutch bellhousing to cylinder block without sealing washers ...	15	2.0
Flywheel cover plate bolts	7	1.0
Pressure plate to flywheel bolts	9	1.2
Slave cylinder mounting bolts	16	2.2

1 General description

The clutch mechanism comprises a single dry driven plate sandwiched between the coil spring type pressure plate and the rear face of the flywheel.

The driven plate is free to slide along the splined input shaft of the gearbox and is held in position between the flywheel and the pressure plate by the force of the pressure plate coil springs. Friction material is riveted to the driven plate which has a spring cushioned hub to abosrb transmission shocks and to ensure a smooth take off.

The clutch is actuated hydraulically through the medium of a master cylinder, a slave cylinder and interconnecting pipework.

The clutch release bearing is of carbon thrust type.

The principle of operation is that when the pendant foot pedal is depressed, the piston in the master cylinder moves forward and forces hydraulic fluid through the pipeline to the clutch slave cylinder. The piston in the slave cylinder moves forward and actuates the release arm by means of a short push-rod.

The release arm, in turn, pushes the release bearing forward to bear against the fingers of the pressure plate levers and so lifts the pressure plate from contact with the driven plate. With the flywheel and pressure plate assembly rotating at engine speed, the driven plate and input shaft are disconnected from the engine and change of gear may be carried out.

When the clutch pedal is released, the pressure plate coil springs force the pressure plate into contact with the friction linings of the driven plate and pushes the driven plate forward to engage it with the flywheel. The driven plate is now firmly, yet progressively, sandwiched between the pressure plate and the flywheel and the drive is taken up as the accelerator is depressed.

2 General description (vehicles built after 1969)

1 The description and operating principle of the clutch mechanism is similar to that described in the preceding Section except that a diaphragm spring pressure plate is incorporated and the release bearing is of sealed ball bearing type.

The diaphragm spring is sandwiched between two annular rings which act a fulcrum points. As the centre of the spring is pushed in, the outside of the spring is pushed out, so moving the pressure plate from its contact with the clutch driven plate.

When the clutch pedal is released, the diaphragm spring forces the pressure plate into contact with the friction linings of the driven plate and at the same time pushes the clutch driven plate fractionally forward on its splines so engaging it with the flywheel.

The clutch disc is now firmly sandwiched between the pressure plate and the flywheel (in a similar manner to coil spring type clutch mechanism) and the drive is taken up.

3 Clutch - adjustment

1 It is essential to maintain the clutch free movement. If no free movement exists then the clutch may 'slip' or the pressure plate springs may be over compressed when the clutch pedal is

Fig 5.1 Exploded view of clutch mechanism (coil spring pressure plate)

1 Driven plate (friction disc)
2 Pressure plate assembly
3 Clutch bellhousing

4 Carbon type thrust release bearing
5 Release arm
6 Release bearing retaining clip

7 Release arm pivot
8 Release arm pivot bush
9 Flywheel cover

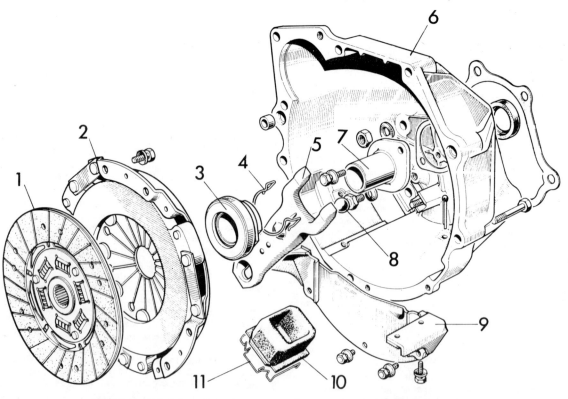

Fig 5.2 Exploded view of clutch mechanism (diaphragm spring pressure plate)

1 Driven plate (friction disc)
2 Pressure plate assembly
3 Ball bearing type thrust release
  bearing and hub

4 Release bearing retaining clip
5 Release arm
6 Clutch bellhousing
7 Input shaft bearing retainer

8 Release arm pivot ball
9 Flywheel cover
10 Release arm dust excluder
11 Dust excluder retaining clip

depressed.

2 If there is too much free movement at the pedal then it may be difficult to disengage the clutch fully and this will cause noisy or rough gear changing.

3 Carry out adjustment from underneath the vehicle by releasing the locknut from the slave cylinder pushrod.
4 Detach the return spring and loosen the locknut on the pushrod.
5 Screw the pushrod in or out until any movement in the release arm has been eliminated.
6 Unscrew the pushrod until a clearance of 0.078 in (2.0 mm) is obtained and then retighten the locknut and reconnect the return spring.
7 If the adjustment has been carried out correctly, a free movement of about 5/8 in (15.9 mm) will be observed at the clutch pedal itself.

4 Master cylinder - removal and installation

1 Disconnect the fluid inlet pipe from the master cylinder.
2 Disconnect the fluid outlet pipe from the master cylinder.
3 Plug both pipes to prevent loss of fluid and to prevent the entry of dirt.
4 Unscrew and remove the two master cylinder flange securing nuts and withdraw the unit from its mounting plate within the engine compartment, leaving the pushrod still attached to the clutch pedal.
5 Installation is a reversal of removal but bleed the hydraulic system as described in Section 8.

5 Master cylinder - dismantling, servicing, reassembly

1 Extract the circlip from the end of the master cylinder.
2 Extract the stop-washer.
3 The piston complete with secondary seal will now be ejected, followed by the primary seal and return spring.
4 Wash all components in hydraulic fluid or methylated spirit. Examine the surfaces of the piston and cylinder bore for scoring or 'bright' wear areas. If these are apparent, renew the master cylinder complete.
5 If the components are unworn, discard the seals and obtain a repair kit.
6 Manipulate the new seals into position using the fingers only and ensuring the lips and chamfers face the correct way.
7 Reassembly is a reversal of dismantling but dip the seals and piston in clean hydraulic fluid before inserting them into the master cylinder bore and make sure that the lips of the seals are not cut or trapped during the operation.
8 Later master cylinders are fitted with a double lipped secondary seal.

6 Slave cylinder - removal and installation

1 Disconnect the fluid inlet pipe and plug the pipe to prevent loss of fluid or entry of dirt.
2 Detach the return spring.
3 Unscrew and remove the two securing bolts and lift the slave cylinder from its location leaving the pushrod attached to the

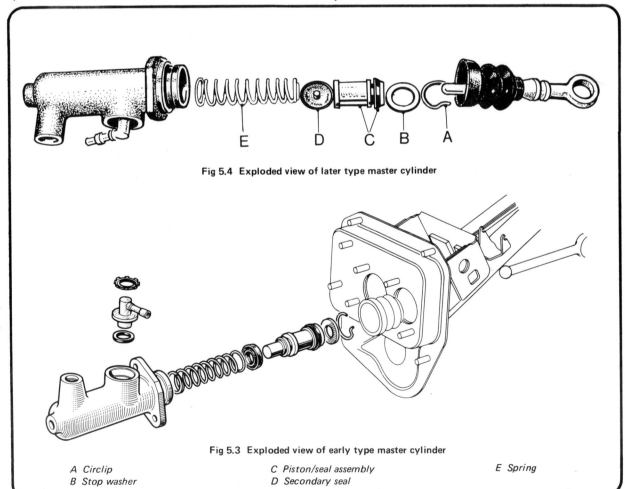

Fig 5.4 Exploded view of later type master cylinder

Fig 5.3 Exploded view of early type master cylinder

A Circlip
B Stop washer
C Piston/seal assembly
D Secondary seal
E Spring

release arm.

4   Retain the spring attachment bracket.

5   Installation is a reversal of removal but bleed the clutch hydraluic system (Section 8) and check and adjust the free-movement (Section 2).

7 Slave cylinder - dismantling, servicing, reassembly

1   Pull off the dust excluding boot. On later slave cylinders, the inner bore of the boot engages in a recess machined in the push-rod. It is recommended that this type of boot and the modified pushrod are installed at the time of overhaul to provide more positive dust sealing.

2   Extract the piston/seal assembly. This can normally be done by tapping the end of the cylinder on a piece of wood or by applying air pressure from a tyre pump at the fluid entry port. On later type slave cylinders, a spring and end stop are incorporated. To remove the end stop, pass a tube into the cylinder body to compress the stop fingers and then withdraw it.

3   If necessary, unscrew the bleed nipple.

4   Wash all components in clean hydraulic fluid or methylated spirit and examine the surface of the piston or cylinder bore for scoring or 'bright' wear areas. If these are evident, renew the slave cylinder complete.

5   If the components are unworn, discard the seal and obtain a repair kit.

6   Refit the seal using the fingers only to manipulate it into position.

7   Reassemble by dipping the piston/seal assembly in clean hydraulic fluid and inserting it into the cylinder taking care not to trap the lips of the seal.

8   Fit a new rubber boot and refit the bleed nipple.

8 Hydraulic system - bleeding

1   The need for bleeding the cylinders and fluid line arises when air gets into it. Air gets in whenever a joint or seal leaks or part has to be dismantled. Bleeding is simply the process of venting the air out again.

2   Make sure the reservoir is filled and obtain a piece of 3/16 inch (4.8 mm) bore diameter rubber tube about 2 feet (610 mm) long and a clean glass jar. A small quantity of fresh, clean hydraulic fluid is also necessary.

3   Detach the cap (if fitted) on the bleed nipple at the clutch slave cylinder and clean up the nipple and surrounding area. Unscrew the nipple ¾ turn and fit the tube over it. Put about ½ inch of fluid in the jar and put the other end of the pipe in it. The jar can be placed on the ground under the car.

4   The clutch pedal should then be depressed quickly and released slowly until no more air bubbles come from the pipe. Quick pedal action carries the air along rather than leaving it behind. Keep the reservoir topped up.

5   When the air bubbles stop tighten the nipple at the end of a down stroke.

6   Check that the operation of the clutch is satisfactory. Even though there may be no exterior leaks it is possible that the movement of the pushrod from the clutch cylinder is inadequate because fluid is leaking internally past the seals in the master cylinder. If this is the case, it is best to replace all seals in both cylinders.

7   Always use clean hydraulic fluid which has been stored in an airtight container and has remained unshaken for the preceding 24 hours.

9 Clutch pedal - removal and installation

1   The clutch and brake pedals operate on a common crossshaft.

2   To remove either pedal, disconnect the pushrod from the pedal arm by removing the spring clip and clevis pin.

3   Remove the spring clip and thrust washer from the end of the crossshaft and then withdraw either pedal off the end of the shaft.

4   Installation is a reversal of removal but apply grease to the pedal bushes before installing them on the crossshaft.

10 Clutch - removal

1   Remove the gearbox as described in Chapter 6, or if the engine is being removed for overhaul then the clutch will be accessible on the rear of the flywheel.

2   Mark the position of the clutch pressure plate assembly in relation to the flywheel.

3   Unscrew the pressure plate bolts from the flywheel in diametrically opposite sequence and only one turn at a time until the pressure of the coil springs or diaphragm spring has been relieved. Lift away the pressure plate assembly and catch the driven plate as it is released.

11 Clutch - inspection and renovation

1   Due to the slow wearing qualities of the clutch, it is not easy to decide when to go to the trouble of removing the gearbox in order to check the wear on the friction lining. The only positive indication that something needs doing is when it starts to slip or when squealing noises on engagement indicate that the friction lining has worn down to the rivets. In such instances it can only be hoped that the friction surfaces on the flywheel and pressure plate have not been badly worn or scored. A clutch will wear according to the way in which it is used. Much intentional slipping of the clutch while driving - rather than the correct selection of gears - will accelerate wear. It is best to assume, however, that the friction disc will need renewal every 35,000 miles (56000 km) at least and that it will be *worth* replacing it after 25,000 miles (40000 km). The maintenance history of the car is obviously very useful in such cases.

2   Examine the surfaces of the pressure plate and flywheel for signs of scoring. If this is only light it may be left, but if very deep the pressure plate unit will have to be renewed. If the flywheel is deeply scored it should be taken off and advice sought from an engineering firm. Providing it may be machined completely across the face the overall balance of engine and flywheel should not be too severely upset. If renewal of the flywheel is necessary the new one will have to be balanced to match the original.

3   The friction plate lining surfaces should be at least 1/32 in (0.8 mm) above the rivets, otherwise the disc is not worth putting back. If the lining material shows signs of breaking up or black areas where oil contamination has occurred it should also be renewed. If facilities are readily available for obtaining and fitting new friction pads to the existing disc this may be done but the saving is relatively small compared with obtaining a complete new disc assembly which ensures that the shock absorbing springs and the splined hub are renewed also. The same applies to the pressure plate assembly which cannot be readily dismantled and put back together without specialised riveting tools and balancing equipment. An allowance is usually given for exchange units.

12 Clutch release bearing (carbon type) - renewal

1   The release bearing should be renewed at the time of major clutch overhaul and in any event if the carbon thrust face has worn down to within 1/16 in (1.6 mm) of its metal holder.

2   The release bearing is retained in the grooves of the release arm fork by two spring clips and these must be removed before the release bearing can be withdrawn.

3   Refitting is a reversal of removal but ensure that the bearing retaining clips are secure and the ends of the clips are at the rear of the release arm fork. (photo)

4   The release arm/fork assembly is bushed and swivels on a

75

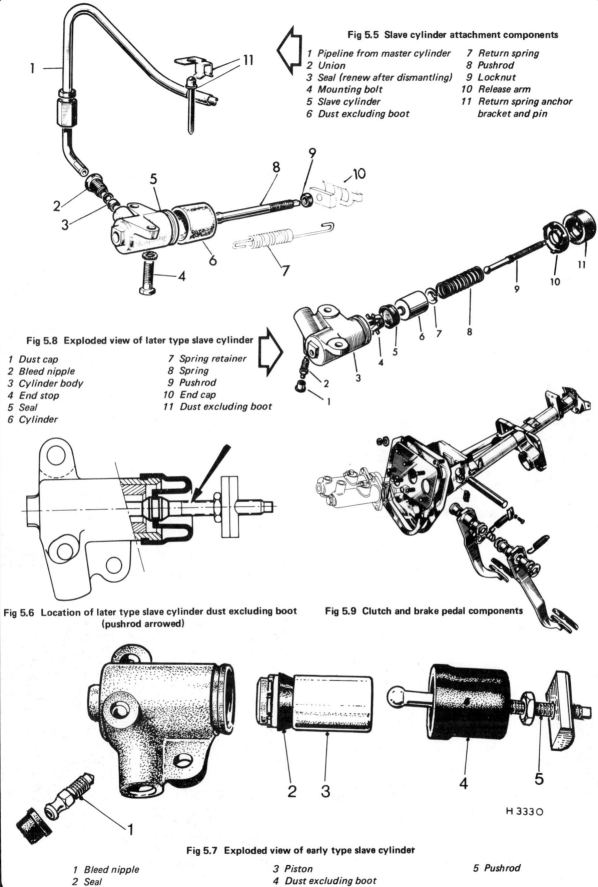

Fig 5.5 Slave cylinder attachment components

1 Pipeline from master cylinder
2 Union
3 Seal (renew after dismantling)
4 Mounting bolt
5 Slave cylinder
6 Dust excluding boot
7 Return spring
8 Pushrod
9 Locknut
10 Release arm
11 Return spring anchor bracket and pin

Fig 5.8 Exploded view of later type slave cylinder

1 Dust cap
2 Bleed nipple
3 Cylinder body
4 End stop
5 Seal
6 Cylinder
7 Spring retainer
8 Spring
9 Pushrod
10 End cap
11 Dust excluding boot

Fig 5.6 Location of later type slave cylinder dust excluding boot (pushrod arrowed)

Fig 5.9 Clutch and brake pedal components

H 3330

Fig 5.7 Exploded view of early type slave cylinder

1 Bleed nipple
2 Seal
3 Piston
4 Dust excluding boot
5 Pushrod

pivot which is secured to the rear of the clutch bellhousing by two studs. (photo)

13 Clutch release bearing (ball bearing type) - renewal

1   This type of bearing which is fitted in conjunction with the diaphragm spring type clutch should be renewed if there are signs of grease leakage from it or if it is noisy or rattles when spun with the fingers.
2   The bearing is press fitted to a hub which in turn is retained to the release fork by a spring.
3   Detach the spring and withdraw the hub/bearing assembly from the release fork.
4   Press the bearing from the hub and then press on the new one ensuring that all pressure is concentrated on the bearing centre track.
5   The release arm/fork assembly swivels on a ball pivot and a little grease should be applied to the pivot.

14 Clutch - refitting

1   Before the driven plate and clutch pressure plate assembly

can be refitted to the flywheel, a guide tool must be obtained. This may be either an old input shaft from a dismantled gearbox or a stepped mandrel.
2   Examine the spigot bush located in the centre of the flywheel. If it is worn or damaged, the bush must be renewed. If the bush is in good condition insert a quantity of high melting point grease into it.
3   Locate the driven plate against the face of the flywheel, ensuring that the projecting side of the centre splined hub faces towards the gearbox (away from the flywheel).
4   Offer up the pressure plate assembly to the flywheel aligning the marks made prior to dismantling and insert the retaining bolts finger tight. Where a new pressure plate assembly is being fitted, locate it to the flywheel in a similar relative position to the original by reference to the index marking and dowel positions. (photo)
5   Insert the guide tool through the splined hub of the driven plate so that the end of the tool locates in the flywheel spigot bush. This action of the guide tool will centralise the driven plate by causing it to move in a sideways direction. (photo)
6   Insert and remove the guide tool two or three times to ensure that the driven plate is fully centralised and then tighten the pressure plate securing bolts a turn at the time and in a diametrically opposite sequence, to a torque of 9 lb/ft (1.2

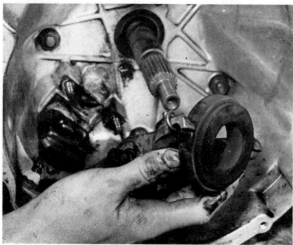
12.3 Carbon type thrust release bearing clips

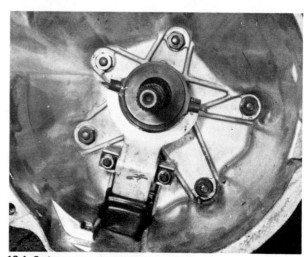
12.4 Carbon type release bearing and arm

14.4 Locating the clutch components to the face of the flywheel

14.5 Centralising the clutch driven plate

kg/m) to prevent distortion of the pressure plate cover.
7 Reconnect the gearbox to the engine. Do this by supporting the gearbox and engaging the input shaft with the driven plate hub splines and the flywheel spigot bush. Keep the input shaft and gearbox perfectly square during the refitting operation and do not allow the weight of the gearbox to hang, even

momentarily, upon the input shaft while it is only partially engaged with the driven plate otherwise damage to the clutch components may result.
8 Insert the clutch bellhousing to engine crankcase securing bolts and tighten them to a torque of 38 lb/ft (5.3 kg/m).
9 Adjust the clutch free movement (Section 3).

15 Fault diagnosis - clutch

Symptom	Reason/s	Remedy
Judder when taking up drive	Loose engine or gearbox mountings	Tighten and inspect rubber insulators for deterioration.
	Badly worn friction surfaces or contaminated with oil	Renew driven plate and rectify oil leakage, probably crankshaft rear oil seal or input shaft oil seal.
	Worn splines on gearbox input shaft or driven plate hub	Renew component.
	Worn input shaft spigot bush in flywheel	Extract old and fit new bush.
Clutch spin (failure to disengage) so that gears cannot be meshed	Incorrect release bearing to pressure plate clearance	Adjust.
	Driven plate sticking on input shaft splines due to rust. May occur after vehicle standing idle for long period	As temporary remedy, engage top gear, apply handbrake, depress clutch and start engine. If driven plate badly stuck, engine will not turn. When engine running, rev up and slip clutch until normal clutch disengagement is possible. Renew driven plate at earliest opportunity.
	Damaged or misaligned pressure plate assembly	Renew pressure plate assembly.
Clutch slip (increase in engine speed does not result in increase in vehicle road speed - particularly on gradients)	Incorrect release bearing to pressure plate clearance	Adjust clearance.
	Friction surfaces worn out or oil contaminated	Renew driven plate and rectify oil leakage.
Noise evident on depressing clutch pedal	Dry, worn or damaged release bearing	Renew bearing.
	Insufficient pedal free travel	Adjust.
	Weak or broken pedal return spring	Renew.
	Weak or broken clutch release lever return spring	Renew.
	Excessive play between driven plate hub splines and input shaft splines	Renew both components.
Noise evident as clutch pedal released	Distorted driven plate	Renew.
	Broken or weak driven plate cushion coil springs	Renew driven plate as an assembly.
	Insufficient pedal free travel	Adjust according to type, see Section 2 or 3.
	Weak or broken clutch pedal return spring	Renew.
	Weak or broken release lever return spring	Renew.
	Distorted or worn input shaft	Renew input shaft (see Chapter 6) and driven plate if necessary.
	Release bearing loose on retainer hub	Renew hub and bearing.

Chapter 6: Part 1/Manual gearbox

Contents

Specifications - manual gearbox

Type	Four forward gears and reverse. Synchromesh on all forward gears	

Ratios	Saloons	Estate
First	3.65 : 1	3.65 : 1
Second	2.06 : 1	2.14 : 1
Third	1.39 : 1	1.39 : 1
Fourth	1.00 : 1	1.00 : 1
Reverse	3.39 : 1	3.39 : 1

Speedometer driven gear	12 teeth	14 teeth

Speedometer worm drive	5 threads	6 threads

Oil capacity		
Up to number 1754406	2.53 pints (1.45 litres)	
After number 1754407	2.8 pints (1.6 litres)	

Torque wrench settings	lb ft	kg m
Rear mounting bolts	16	2.2
Half housing securing bolts	16	2.2
Rear drive flange bolt	58	8.0
Layshaft nut	108	14.9
Speedometer driven gear retainer bolt	7	1.0
Shift fork locking screws (1st/2nd, 3rd/4th)	7	1.0
Shift fork locking screw (reverse)	16	2.2
Input shaft bearing nut	108	14.9
Mainshaft synchro hub nut	108	14.9
Bearing retaining plate bolts	16	2.2
Rear cover bolts	16	2.2
Detent springs retaining plate bolts	15	2.1
Clutch bellhousing to cylinder block bolts (with special washers)	38	5.3
Clutch bellhousing to cylinder block bolts (without special washers)	15	2.1

1 General description of manual gearbox

Two light alloy half shells, split longitudinally form the gearbox housing which contains four forward gears and reverse. All forward gears are provided with synchromesh which is of the 'Porsche' type.

The rear of the gearbox is supported on a rubber mounted, cantilevered, leaf spring.

Gear selection may be by means of a steering column mounted lever on earlier models or by float mounted lever which has been fitted to all RHD models and vehicles for operation in markets where this type of gearchange is preferred.

The principle of operation is that power from the engine is transmitted by means of the clutch to the input shaft of the gearbox. The input shaft gear is in constant mesh with a gear on the layshaft which in turn is in constant mesh with second and third gears on the mainshaft.

First gear is engaged when the synchroniser sleeve (A) (Fig 6.1) moves towards the rear by the action of the shift fork.

The first speed gears on both the layshaft and the mainshaft are then in mesh.

Second gear is engaged in similar manner by moving the synchroniser sleeve towards the front.

To engage third gear move synchroniser sleeve (B) to the rear which meshes the layshaft and mainshaft third speed gearwheels.

Top (fourth) gear is engaged when the synchroniser sleeve (B) is moved in a forward direction to lock the input shaft to the mainshaft this providing direct drive at engine speed.

Reverse gear is engaged when reverse idler gear (C) is moved causing reverse gears (D) on the layshaft and (E) on the main-shaft to mesh.

A combined filler/lever plug is fitted, and also a drain plug.

---

2 Gearbox - removal and installation

1 Disconnect the lead from the battery negative terminal.
2 Drain the cooling system (Chapter 2) retaining the coolant for replenishment if it contains antifreeze.
3 Disconnect the radiator top hose from the radiator.
4 Disconnect the heater pipes from the rocker box cover.
5 Remove the starter motor.
6 Disconnect the clamp which secures the exhaust downpipe to the engine manifold. Mark the two halves of the clamp so that they can be refitted correctly, as the groove is offset.
7 Disconnect the gearchange linkage from beneath the vehicle.
On vehicles with float mounted gearlevers:
8 Prise up the spring clip from the ball type joint. (photo)

9 Remove the split pin, washer and bolt from the clevis fork type joint. (photo)
On vehicles with steering column gearlevers:
10 Disconnect the rod from the arm on the side of the gearbox and then disconnect the gearchange rod from the arm (A) (Fig 6.2)
On all vehicles
11 Unbolt and remove the flywheel cover plate. (photo)
12 Detach the clutch return spring at the clutch slave cylinder. (photo)
13 Unbolt the clutch slave cylinder and tie it up out of the way. There is no need ti disconnect the fluid pipes. (photo)
14 Disconnect the clip (C) from the exhaust pipe just to the rear of the front expansion box.
15 Disconnect the handbrake cable (D).
16 Remove the bolts from the three legged connecting flange at the rear of the gearbox ensuring that the flexible section remains bolted to the propeller shaft.
17 Unbolt the propeller shaft centre bearing support and move the propeller shaft to one side and tie it up or support it on a

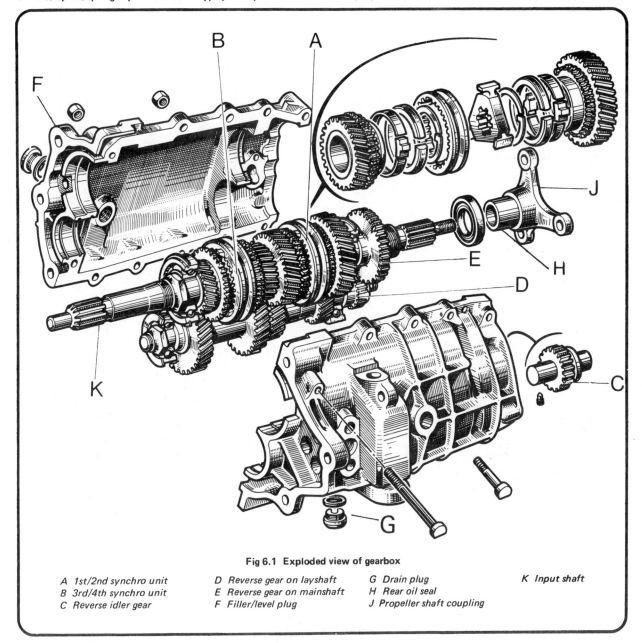

Fig 6.1 Exploded view of gearbox

A 1st/2nd synchro unit   D Reverse gear on layshaft   G Drain plug   K Input shaft
B 3rd/4th synchro unit   E Reverse gear on mainshaft   H Rear oil seal
C Reverse idler gear   F Filler/level plug   J Propeller shaft coupling

stand to prevent strain on the rear universal joint.

18 Place a piece of wood on a jack and support the gearbox under its bottom face. (photo)

19 Mark the position of the rear mounting (E) in its support clamps and unbolt it both from the gearbox and the bodyfloor. (photo)

20 Lower the support jack until the gearbox is inclined at a steep angle and the speedometer cable is accessible for disconnection by unscrewing the retaining collar. (photo)

21 Unscrew the bolts which secure the clutch bellhousing to the engine block and withdraw the gearbox from below and to the rear of the vehicle. (photo)

22 Installation is a reversal of removal but ensure that the clutch driven plate has been centralised (Chapter 5).

23 As the input shaft of the gearbox passes through the clutch mechanism, the gearbox may need rotating in either direction in order to engage the input shaft splines with those of the driven plate hub. Alternatively, the rear flange may be turned provided a gear has been engaged.

24 If the gearbox has been drained, remember to fill it with the correct grade and quantity of oil.

3 Gearbox - dismantling

1   Drain the oil from the gearbox.

2   Unscrew and remove the bolt which secures the retaining plate of the speedometer driven gear. Lift the speedometer gear from the transmission housing. Note that the sealing 'O' ring should be retained in the groove of the speedometer gear body. (photo)

3   From within the clutch bellhousing, remove the release arm

Fig 6.2 Components to disconnect before removing gearbox

A Gearchange arm (steering column   B Clutch slave cylinder   D Handbrake cable
   change)   C Exhaust clip and bracket   E Rear mounting

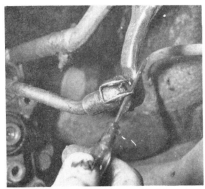
2.8 Disconnecting gearchange linkage

2.9 Disconnect gearchange clevis fork joint

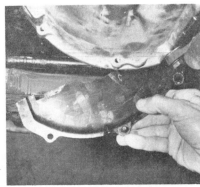
2.11 Removing flywheel cover plate

2.12 Detaching clutch release arm return spring

2.13 Disconnecting clutch slave cylinder from bellhousing

2.18 Supporting gearbox

2.19A Disconnecting gearbox mounting

2.19B Disconnecting gearbox mounting

2.20 Disconnecting speedometer drive cable

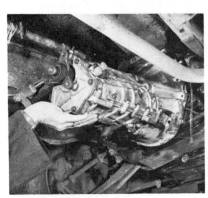
2.21 Withdrawing gearbox

3.2 Removing speedometer driven gear

3.4 Separating the gearbox from the clutch bellhousing

fork and release thrust bearing (see Chapter 5).

4 Remove the bolts which secure the bellhousing to the gearbox and withdraw the bellhousing and its sealing gasket. (photo)

5 Unscrew the centre bolt which secures the retaining plate for the selector rod detent balls and springs. (photo)

6 Withdraw the plate. (photo)

7 Withdraw the springs and turn the gearbox to eject the detent balls. (photo)

8 At the rear of the gearbox, remove the rubber spacer from the centre bolt of the driveshaft flange. (photo)

9 Bend back the tab of the locking plate and then holding the drive flange still with a bar, unscrew the centre bolt using a ring spanner. (photo)

10 Withdraw the driving flange from the shaft splines. (photo)

11 Remove the bolts from the rear cover, withdraw the cover and its gasket. (photo)

12 Extract the oil slinger from the rear end of the mainshaft (photo)

13 Withdraw the speedometer drive gear from the rear end of the mainshaft. (photo)

14 Withdraw reverse gear from the mainshaft. (photo)

15 Unbolt the front bearing lockplates. (photo)

16 Unbolt the rear bearing lockplates. (photo)

17 *On vehicles fitted with a floor mounted gearlever* disconnect the upper operating arm from the squared end of the splined selector shaft.

18 Disconnect the shorter speed selector rod from the selector finger. (photo)

19 Unscrew and remove the nuts from the bolts which secure the two halves of the gearbox casing together. Note that two of the rear bolts support the gear change rod guide tube. (photo)

20 Remove the upper half of the gearbox casing. (photo)

21 Lift the layshaft assembly from the gearbox. (photo)

22 Lift the mainshaft assembly from the gearbox. (photo)

23 Loosen the lockscrews on the 3rd/4th selector fork (1) and the 1st/2nd selector fork (2). (photo)

24 Withdraw the 3rd/4th selector rod and extract the fork. (photo)

25 Withdraw the 1st/2nd selector rod far enough to extract the interlocking ball and then remove the selector rod and fork from

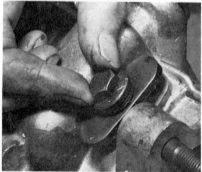

3.5 Removing the detent ball retaining plate bolt

3.6 Removing the detent plate

3.7 Removing a detent spring

3.8 Withdrawing the rubber spacer from the driving flange centre bolt

3.9 Unscrewing the driving flange centre bolt

3.10 Withdrawing the driving flange from the mainshaft splines

3.11 Removing the gearbox rear cover and gasket

3.12 Extracting the oil slinger from the rear end of the mainshaft

3.13 Withdrawing speedometer drive gear from the rear end of the mainshaft

3.14 Withdrawing reverse gear from the rear end of the mainshaft

3.15 Unbolting a lockplate from the input shaft bearing

3.16 Unbolting a lockplate from the mainshaft rear bearing

3.17 Disconnecting operating arm from splined selector shaft

3.18 Disconnecting selector rod from selector finger

3.19 Location of gearchange rod guide tube mountings

3.20 Removing upper half of gearbox casing

3.21 Lifting out the layshaft assembly

3.22 Lifting out the mainshaft assembly

3.23 3rd/4th selector fork (A) 1st/2nd selector fork (B)

3.24 Withdrawing 3rd/4th selector rod and fork

3.25 Removing 1st/2nd selector fork, rod and interlock ball

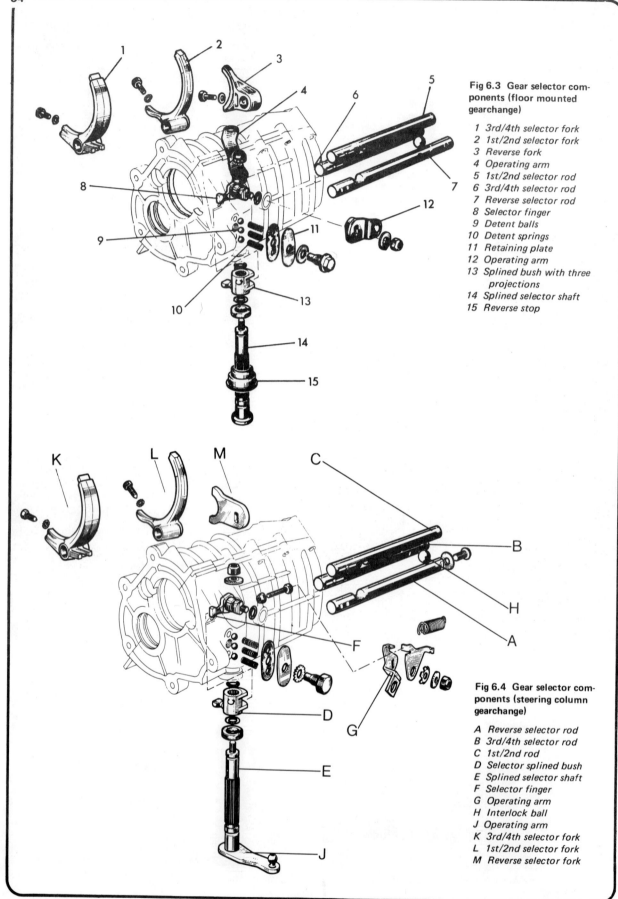

Fig 6.3 Gear selector components (floor mounted gearchange)

1 3rd/4th selector fork
2 1st/2nd selector fork
3 Reverse fork
4 Operating arm
5 1st/2nd selector rod
6 3rd/4th selector rod
7 Reverse selector rod
8 Selector finger
9 Detent balls
10 Detent springs
11 Retaining plate
12 Operating arm
13 Splined bush with three projections
14 Splined selector shaft
15 Reverse stop

Fig 6.4 Gear selector components (steering column gearchange)

A Reverse selector rod
B 3rd/4th selector rod
C 1st/2nd rod
D Selector splined bush
E Splined selector shaft
F Selector finger
G Operating arm
H Interlock ball
J Operating arm
K 3rd/4th selector fork
L 1st/2nd selector fork
M Reverse selector fork

the gearbox.

26 Unscrew the lockscrew from the reverse selector fork and withdraw the selector rod and fork. *On vehicles with steering column gearchange*, the reverse selector fork is retained by an end screw. (photo)

27 Mark the relative position of the splined bush to the splined selector shaft and remove the shaft from the gearbox. This is achieved by unscrewing and removing the nut at its threaded end but the operating arm is detachable and located at the top of the shaft on *vehicles with floor mounted gearchange levers* but is non-detachable and located at the bottom of the shaft on *vehicles having steering column change. (photo)*

28 As the gear selector shaft is withdrawn, extract the bush with the three projections, retaining any washers and 'O' ring seals and then unbolt and remove the gear selector finger. (photo)

29 Unscrew and remove the grub screw which secures the reverse idler shaft. (photo)

30 Withdraw the shaft and extract the idler gear. (photo)

4 Gearbox - inspection and renovation - general

1 Thoroughly clean out the gearbox half housings and inspect for cracks.

2 A magnetic drain plug is installed in the casing and this should be removed and wiped clean of fillings and swarf. (photo)

3 Examine the gearteeth of the components on both shaft gear trains for chipping and wear and renew as necessary. Unless the appropriate pullers are available take the shaft to your SIMCA dealer to have the necessary work carried out.

4 Inspect the bearings for visible wear or noisy operation by spinning them by hand. The bearings on each end of the layshaft incorporate oil seals and the complete bearing assembly will have to be renewed if the oil seals are faulty.

5 Check the condition of the synchromesh units. If the teeth on the sleeve are showing signs of wear, renew the unit. (photo)

6 If a long peripheral rubbing mark is visible on the

3.26 Removing reverse selector rod and fork

3.27 Withdrawing splined selector shaft

3.28 Location of splined bush (three projections), selector finger and reverse stop (floor mounted gearchange)

3.29 Unscrewing reverse idler shaft grub screw

3.30 Withdrawing reverse idler shaft and gear

4.2 Gearbox magnetic drain plug

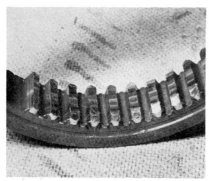

4.5 Wear on teeth of synchro unit sleeve

4.6 Position of wear mark on synchro spring band

synchroniser spring band, renew it and the circlip. (photo)

7   Inspect the condition of the shift rods, forks and other components. If the detent ball locking grooves are no longer well defined or are elongaged, renew the rods, balls and springs.

8   Renew the oil seals in the gearbox end cover and the clutch bellhousing using a piece of tubing as a drift.

5   Mainshaft - servicing

1   Grip the three legged driving flange (which was removed from the splined rear section of the mainshaft) in a vice or bolt it to a bench top.

2   Locate the splines of the mainshaft in the driving flange so that it can be utilised as a support.

3   Ensure top (fourth) gear is locked and unscrew the locknut from the front end of the input shaft. (Fig. 6.6)

4   Withdraw the input shaft complete with bearing and the 4th gearwheel and synchroniser sleeve. Extract the ball bearing from the front of the input shaft. (photo)

5   With the mainshaft still secured in the driving flange withdraw the needle roller bearing and then unscrew the locknut from the front of the mainshaft. (photo)

6   Mark the relative position of the 3rd/4th synchro. hub to the synchro. ring and withdraw the hub. (photo)

7   Withdraw the 3rd gear/synchro. ring assembly. (photo)

8   Withdraw the 2nd and 1st gears together with synchro. unit, again marking the hub in relation to the sleeve. (photo)

9   Remove the bearing from the rear end of the shaft. If an extractor is not available, the bearing may be removed by holding it in the hand and driving the mainshaft out using a soft faced hammer. This method should only be used if the bearing is to be renewed. (photo)

10 Reassembly of the input shaft/mainshaft assembly is a reversal of dismantling but observe the following:

(a) press on the bearings by applying pressure to their centre tracks only.

(b) check that the components of the synchro. units are correctly located (in their original position if no new parts have been used) and that the spring band and circlip are unmarked and a positive fit.

(c) tighten the mainshaft nut and input shaft nut to a torque of 108 lb/ft (15.0 kg/m).

6   Layshaft - servicing

1   To dismantle the layshaft, secure it in a vice fitted with jaw

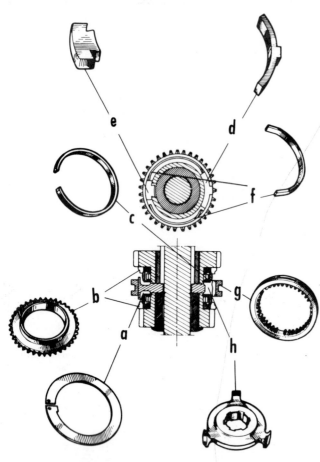

Fig 6.5 Exploded view of synchromesh unit

(a) Circlip
(b) Toothed ring
(c) Spring band
(d) Locking piece
(e) Retainer stop
(f) Spring
(g) Sliding sleeve
(h) Hub

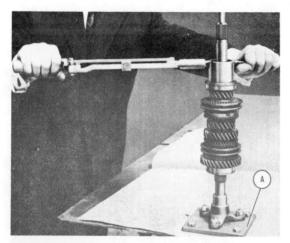

Fig 6.6 Unscrewing the nut from the front end of the input shaft

A Temporary retaining plate for driving flange

5.4 Input shaft separated from mainshaft

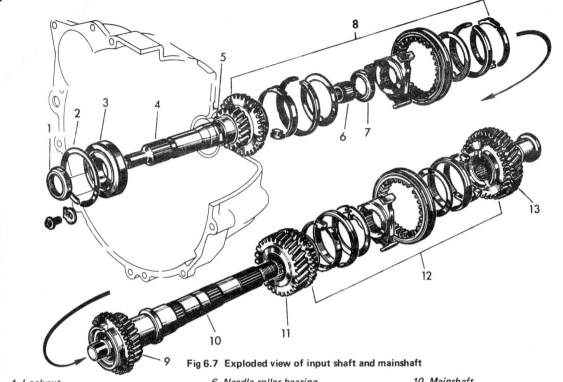

Fig 6.7 Exploded view of input shaft and mainshaft

1 Locknut	6 Needle roller bearing	10 Mainshaft
2 Bearing circlip	7 Locknut	11 2nd gear
3 Bearing	8 Components of 3rd/4th synchro	12 Components of 1st/2nd synchro unit
4 Input shaft	unit	13 1st gear
5 4th gear	9 3rd gear	

5.5A Withdrawing needle roller bearing from front of mainshaft

5.5B Unscrewing locknut from front of mainshaft

5.6 Withdrawing 3rd/4th synchro hub from mainshaft

5.7 Withdrawing the 3rd gear/synchro ring assembly from mainshaft

5.8 Withdrawing 2nd gear and 1st gear with synchro unit from mainshaft

5.9 Removing mainshaft rear bearing

protectors making sure that the shaft is gripped at a point midway between the gearwheels. On no account grip the gearwheels in the vice.

2 Unscrew the nut from one or both ends as required and draw off the bearings using a suitable puller.

3 Refit the new bearings using a press or a tubular drift but concentrate the pressure on the centre track of the bearing.

4 Use new locking plates under the nuts and tighten them to a torque of 108 lb/ft (15.0 kg/m).

7 Gearbox - reassembly

1 Reassembly is essentially a reversal of dismantling but follow the sequence given and the special operating and adjustment procedure described in the following paragraphs:

2 Install the reverse idler gear and shaft, locking the shaft in position with the grub screw.

3 Locate the gear selector finger in the gearbox, also the selector bush so that its single projection will face towards the shift rods when they are installed.

4 Install the reverse shift fork and rod.

5 Locate the interlocking ball and install the 3rd/4th shift fork and rod and then the 1st/2nd shift fork and rod. Ensure that the forks are correctly positioned on their rods so that the locking screws will engage in the dimples on the rods and then tighten the locking screws to a torque of 16 lb/ft (2.2 kg/m) for reverse and 7 lb/ft (1.0 kg/m) for the other two. *On vehicles equipped with steering column gearchange*, the reverse shift fork is retained on the flats at the end of the shift rod by a screw and washer screwed into a tapped hole in the end of the rod.

6 Fit the three detent balls and their springs into the holes of the neutral locking device; fit the retaining plate and retaining bolt.

7 Insert the splined gear selector shaft into the gearbox so that it will pass through the splined bush (previously placed in position to receive the shaft (see paragraph 3) with the mating marks made before dismantling in correct alignment.

8 If the splined shaft was dismantled from the bush without any alignment marks having been made then the larger projection of the bush must engage with the cutout in the 1st/2nd shift rod (positioned in neutral) and at the same time the flats on the upper end of the splined shaft must be parallel with the centre line of the gearbox. (photo)

9 *On vehicles equipped with steering column change,* the nut on the top of ths shaft should be tightened sufficiently to remove all endfloat. The lever which is permanently attached to the bottom of the splined shaft must point away from the gearbox.

10 Check for correct assembly of the splined shaft, bush and

selector finger by moving the 3rd/4th shift fork forward to engage top gear. Now move the operating arm of the splined shaft to the extremity of its travel when the longer projection of the splined bush should engage centrally in the notch of the 3rd/4th shift fork.

11 Lower the mainshaft/input shaft assembly into the gearcase.

12 Lower the layshaft assembly into the gearcase.

13 Smear the mating edges of both halves of the gearcase with gasket cement and fit the two halves together. Note that the securing bolts have milled heads to prevent them turning. They must be fitted to the appropriate half housing, the mating flange of which is designed to accept them. Tighten the nuts to 16 lb/ft (2.2 kg/m). (photo)

14 Fit the gearchange rod guide tube to the two rear casing bolts and connect the link rods to the gearchange levers on the gearbox *(floor mounted gearchange). (photo)*

15 Fit and bolt up the front and rear bearing lockplates to a torque of 16 lb/ft (2.2 kg/m).

16 Fit reverse gear to the mainshaft, the speedometer drive gear and the oil slinger.

17 Locate a new gasket on the rear face of the gearbox housing and position the end cover, complete with new oil seal. (photo)

18 Locate the exhaust expansion box support plate and screw in and tighten the end cover bolts to a torque of 16 lb/ft (2.2 kg/m). (photo)

19 Locate the drive flange on the splines at the rear end of the mainshaft, tighten the hollow bolt to a torque of 58 lb/ft (8.0 kg/m) using a new lockplate which must be bent up securely.

20 Locate a new gasket on the front face of the gearbox and bolt the clutch bellhousing into position, with special washers 38 lb/ft - 5.2 kg/m, without washers 15 lb/ft - 2.0 kg/m)

21 Reassemble the clutch release mechanism (see Chapter 5).

22 Install the speedometer driven gear, using a new 'O' ring seal and tightening the securing plate nut to a torque of 7 lb/ft (1.0 kg/m).

8 Floor mounted gearchange linkage - maintenance and adjustment

1 Earlier types of linkage benefit from an occasional application of oil to the joints and swivels.

2 Access to the moving points of the hand lever can be obtained from within the vehicle.

3 Lift up the covering from the transmission tunnel. (photo)

4 Prise out the rubber grommet which surrounds the gearchange lever. (photo)

5 A number of modifications have been carried out to this type of linkage and it is therefore essential when renewing worn components to ensure that if a modified part only is available

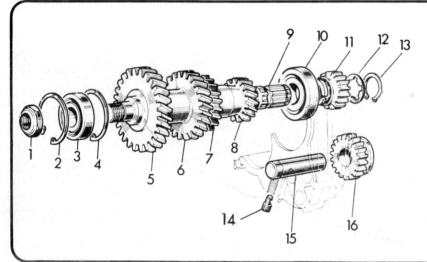

Fig 6.8 Exploded view of the layshaft

1 *Locknut*
2 *Bearing circlip*
3 *Bearing*
4 *Bearing circlip*
5 *4th gear*
6 *3rd gear*
7 *2nd gear*
8 *1st gear*
9 *Layshaft*
10 *Bearing*
11 *Reverse gear*
12 *Lockwasher*
13 *Circlip*
14 *Grub screw*
15 *Reverse idler shaft*
16 *Reverse idler gear*

then any other essential complementary items are also available and obtained at the time of purchase. (photo)

6 Apart from renewing worn components to correct faulty gear selection the only other adjustment is to check the length (between centres) of the selector rod (E) (Fig 6.9) If necessary, loosen the locknut and adjust the rod to conform with the diagram. (Fig 6.10)

7 On earlier types of floor mounted gear linkage, a persistent vibration of the hand lever may be encountered. To rectify this, the nylon bushes which are fitted between the gearchange guide tube (A) and the inner control rod (D) should be packed with a piece of aluminium foil to make them a force fit in the guide tube. If this does not completely cure the problem, the return spring should either be changed for a stiffer type which is available or packing washers fitted to the front of the existing spring to increase its tension.

8 On some models not fitted with a later, modified, reverse stop, the two gearchange control rods rub against each other in some selector positions and thick grease should be applied to the rubbing surfaces.

9 Steering column gearchange linkage - maintenance and adjustment

1 Very little maintenance is required except occasionally to apply a little oil to the joints and pivots and to check the security of the retaining bolts.

2 Examine the linkage for wear and renew any worn components. Should the linkage have been dismantled and re-assembled or new parts fitted or faulty gearchanging be experienced then the following adjustments must be carried out.

3 Move the hand control lever (H) (Fig 6.11) to 3rd or 4th gear position.

4 Disconnect the rod (O) from the selector arm (P) on the gearbox.

5 Disconnect the exhaust pipe from its support bracket on the

7.8 Splined bush projection in engagement with cut-out in 1st/2nd shift rod

7.13 Gearbox casing securing bolt

7.14 Gearchange linkage attached to gearbox (floor mounted gearchange)

7.17 Fitting gearbox end cover and gasket

7.18 Fitting exhaust support plate

8.3 Removing transmission tunnel covering

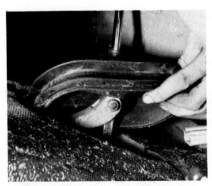
8.4 Prising out gearlever aperture grommet

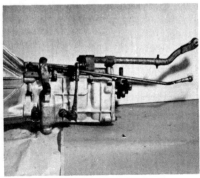
8.5 Gearchange linkage and control rods (floor mounted type)

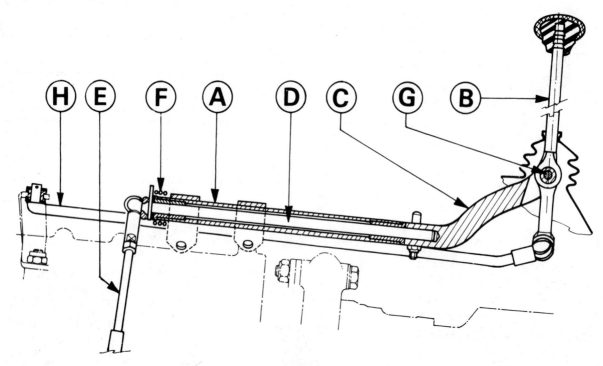

Fig 6.9 Components of floor mounted gearchange lever and linkage

A Guide tube   C Connecting crank   E Link to side operating arm   G Pivot bolt
B Hand lever   D Gearchange rod   F Return spring   H Link to upper operating arm

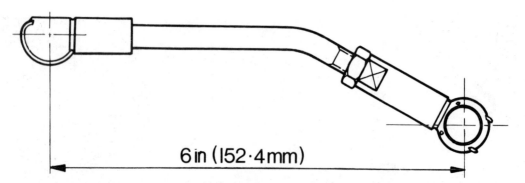

6 in (152·4mm)

Fig 6.10 Adjustable link rod to side operating arm (floor mounted gearchange)

gearbox rear cover.

6   Disconnect the front of the propeller shaft by uncoupling the flexible joint so as to leave the three legged drive flange only still attached to the gearbox splined shaft.

7   Disconnect the gearbox rear mounting from the body floor.

8   Lower the gearbox slowly and only enough to gain access to carry out the following operations. If the gearbox is pulled down too far, the engine connections and coolant hoses may be damaged or strained.

9   Release the locknut on the threaded rod (U) and screw the rod fully home.

10 Move the selector arm (P) towards the rear of the gearbox until the splined bush which is fitted to the splined selector shaft within the gearbox can be felt to impinge upon the reverse shift rod.

11 Hold the gearchange hand control quite still in its previously selected position and turn the threaded adjusting rod (U) until its head just makes contact with the reverse gear stop (V).

12 Now move the selector arm (P) fully towards the front of the gearbox until the internal splined bush can be felt to impinge upon the 1st/2nd shift rod.

13 Again hold the gearchange hand control quite still and rotate the adjusting rod, counting carefully the number of turns required to make the head of the rod just contact the reverse gear stop.

14 Screw the adjuster rod in by half the number of turns just counted and tighten the locknut.

15 Reconnect the gearbox rear mounting, the propeller shaft, the exhaust pipe and the selector rod (O).

16 Test the gear selection in all positions by means of the hand control and make any final precise adjustments by means of the rods (M) and (R) to provide positive engagement in each gear selector detent without any tendency to override the selector arms on the gearbox.

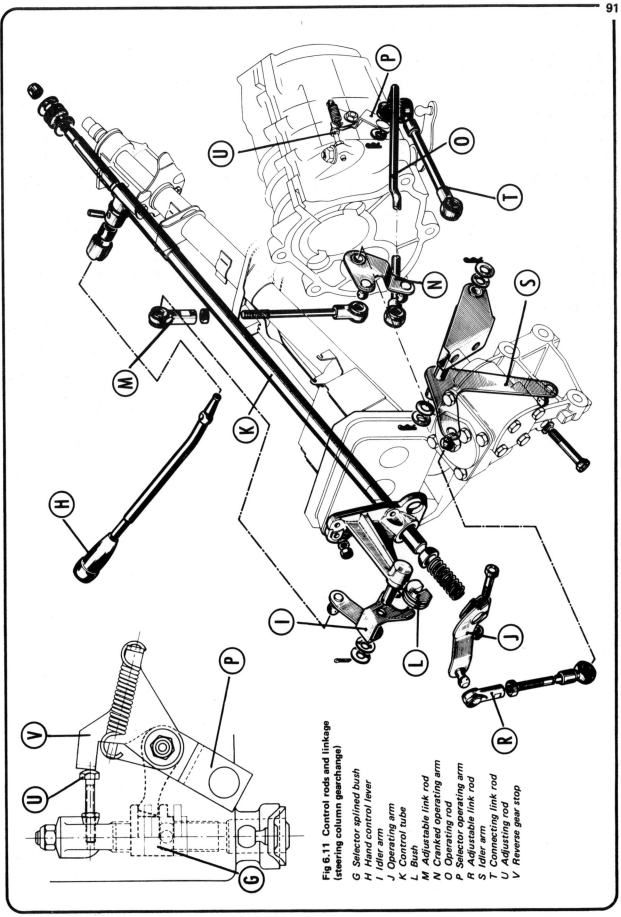

Fig 6.11 Control rods and linkage
(steering column gearchange)

G Selector splined bush
H Hand control lever
I Idler arm
J Operating arm
K Control tube
L Bush
M Adjustable link rod
N Cranked operating arm
O Operating rod
P Selector operating arm
R Adjustable link rod
S Idler arm
T Connecting link rod
U Adjusting rod
V Reverse gear stop

10 Fault diagnosis - manual gearbox

Symptom	Reason/s	Remedy
Ineffective synchromesh	Worn synchromesh units	Dismantle and renew.
Jumps out of one or more gears (on drive or over-run)	Weak detent springs or worn selector forks or worn gears	Dismantle and renew.
Noisy, rough, whining and vibration	Worn bearings (initially) resulting in extended wear generally due to play and backlash	Dismantle and renew.
Noisy and difficult engagement of gears	Clutch fault	Examine clutch operation.

Note: It is sometimes difficult to decide whether it is worthwhile removing and dismantling the gearbox for a fault which may be nothing more than a minor irritant. Gearboxes which howl, or where the synchromesh can be 'beaten' by a quick gear change, may continue to perform for a long time in this state. A worn gearbox usually needs a complete rebuild to eliminate noise because the various gears, if re-aligned on new bearings will continue to howl when different wearing surfaces are presented to each other.

The decision to overhaul therefore, must be considered with regard to time and money available, relative to the degree of noise or malfunction that the driver has to suffer.

Chapter 6: Part 2 /Automatic transmission

Contents

Specifications - automatic transmission

Type	Borg Warner 35
Torque converter range	Infinitely variable between 1 : 1 and 1.91 : 1
Fluid capacity	11.25 pints (6.4 litres)

Speed ratios

First	2.395 : 1
Second	1.450 : 1
Third	1 : 1
Reverse	2.094 : 1

Torque wrench settings

	lb ft	kg m
Drive plate to torque converter	25 - 35	3.5 - 4.1
Converter housing to transmission case	8 - 13	1.1 - 1.8
Starter inhibitor switch locknut	4 - 6	0.6 - 0.8
Oil pan bolts	13	1.8
Rear extension housing bolts	18	2.5

11 General description of automatic transmission

Automatic transmission (Borg Warner Type 35) has been optionally available on all models, both saloon and estate wagons. When fitted, the speed selection is made by a steering column mounted hand lever.

The system comprises two main assemblies:

(a) a three element hydrokinetic torque connecter coupling capable of torque multiplication at an infinitely variable ratio between 1.91 : 1 and 1 : 1.

(b) a torque/speed responsive and hydraulically operated epicyclic gearbox comprising a planetary gearset providing three forward ratios and one reverse ratio.

Due to the complexity of the automatic transmission unit, if performance is not up to standard, or overhaul is necessary, it is imperative that checking is carried out by your SIMCA main dealer to diagnose the fault. Any adjustments carried out yourself should be restricted to those described in this Chapter. In the event of a major fault being diagnosed or wear after an extended mileage, then consideration should be given to installation of a factory reconditioned unit which may prove to cost the same or even less than that of overhaul or repair.

Should this policy be adopted then the original torque converter, torque converter housing, securing bolts, starter inhibitor switch and filler/dipstick tube must be retained as these components are not supplied with the new transmission unit.

12 Automatic transmission - fluid level

It is important that transmission fluid manufactured only to the correct specification such as 'Castrol TQF' is used. The capacity of the complete unit is 11.25 pints (6.4 litres). Drain and refill capacity will be less as the torque converter cannot be completely drained, but this operation should not be necessary except for repairs.

13 Maintenance

1 Keep the exterior of the converter housing and the transmission casing clean and free from mud which might cause overheating. Brush the air inlet grilles clear of dirt.

2 Every 6,000 miles (10,000 km) or more frequently, check the automatic transmission fluid level. With the engine at its normal operating temperature move the selector to the 'P' position and allow the engine to idle for two mintues. With the engine still idling in the 'P' position withdraw the dipstick, wipe it clean and replace it. Quickly withdraw it again and if necessary top-up with 'Castrol TQF' automatic transmission fluid. The difference between the 'LOW' and 'FULL' marks on the dipstick is 1 pint (0.57 litre).

3 If the unit has been drained, it is recommended that only new fluid is used. Fill up to the correct 'HIGH' level by gradually

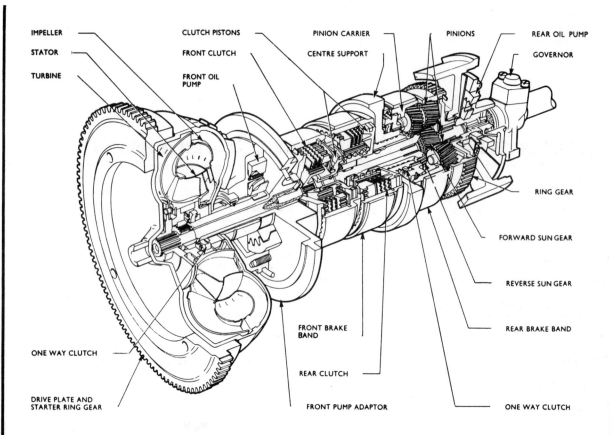

IMPELLER

STATOR

TURBINE

CLUTCH PISTONS

FRONT CLUTCH

FRONT OIL
PUMP

PINION CARRIER

CENTRE SUPPORT

PINIONS

REAR OIL PUMP

GOVERNOR

RING GEAR

FORWARD SUN GEAR

REVERSE SUN GEAR

REAR BRAKE BAND

ONE WAY CLUTCH

FRONT BRAKE
BAND

REAR CLUTCH

FRONT PUMP ADAPTOR

ONE WAY CLUTCH

DRIVE PLATE AND
STARTER RING GEAR

Fig 6.12 Cut-away view of the automatic transmission unit

Fig 6.13 Selector linkage at transmission unit

refilling the unit. The exact amount will depend on how much was left in the converter after draining.

14 Speed selector linkage - adjustment

1   Slackness in the selector linkage may be due to severe wear in the joints and swivels. Any worn parts should be renewed before carrying out the following procedure. The following description applies where the selector control or linkage has been dismantled and reassembled.
2   Disconnect the short rod from the operating arm on the left-hand side of the transmission. This is done by simply separating the balljoint connection.
3   Move the operating arm to the 'N' position. Do this by pushing the arm fully forward and then pulling it back two 'clicks'.
4   Set the steering column speed selector so that the pointer is opposite 'N'.
5   Under the vehicle check that the balljoint of the operating lever is in perfect alignment with the socket of the short link

rod. If this is not the case, slacken the locknut on the link rod and rotate the rod until correct alignment is obtained. Retighten the locknut.
6   Check the other selector positions and test that with the handlever in 'P' the car cannot be pushed or pulled when the handbrake is released.

Fig 6.15 Speed selector indicator (early types)

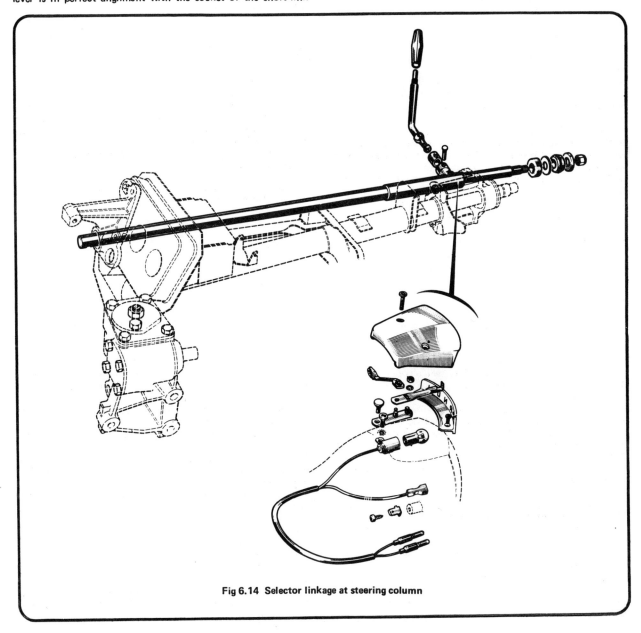

Fig 6.14 Selector linkage at steering column

On later type automatic transmission, two positions for low speed lock up are provided 'D1' and 'D2'.

15 Downshift cable - adjustment

1 The need for this adjustment will be due to cable stretch, the cable breaking and having to be renewed, or after removal and installation of a new unit.
2 Indications that the 'kick-down' cable requires adjustment are given when it is difficult to operate the 'kick-down' facility when the accelerator pedal is fully depressed.
3 During production, the downshift cable is set by means of a crimped stop on the inner cable at the carburettor end.
4 Adjustment is correct when, with the accelerator pedal released and the choke fully off, the crimped stop is just in sliding contact with the end of the threaded portion of the outer cable. To adjust, slacken the locknuts on the outer cable and rotate them as required.
5 If the crimped stop has become loose or a new cable is to be fitted then drain the transmission unit retaining the fluid in a suitably large container. Do not allow any grit or dirt to enter the container.
6 Unscrew and remove the oil pan bolts and remove the oil pan and gasket.
7 Engage the new cable in the cam of the downshift valve and connect it at its opposite end to the carburettor linkage.
8 With the accelerator fully released the valve position should be as (A) (Fig 6.17) and with the accelerator fully depressed in the 'Kick-down' position, the valve should appear as (B). Alter the position of the outer cable locknuts as required to provide the two specified settings.
9 Crimp the stop to the inner cable (new cables are supplied with the inner cable stops loose) so that it is in sliding contact with the end face of the outer cable.
10 Refit the oil pan using a new gasket and refill with clean fluid.

16 Starter inhibitor switch - adjustment

1 The starter inhibitor switch can include two terminals for reversing lights but as this type of lamp is not normally included in SIMCA 1301/1501 models it is unlikely that reversing lamp terminals are incorporated in the switch.
2 A substitute switch may be fitted which has the four terminals and the method of adjustment is described in the next Section.
3 Pull the two leads from the terminals of the switch and join the wires together with a clip.
4 Check that the starter can be operated.
5 Disconnect the switch leads from each other and then release the locknut on the threaded stem of the switch body.
6 Unscrew the switch several turns and place the speed selector lever in 'N' or 'P'.
7 Connect a torch battery and bulb across the two switch terminals and screw the switch in until the lamp just lights, plus one further quarter-turn. Tighten the switch locknut.
8 Remove the test bulb and battery and reconnect the switch leads.
9 Check that the starter motor operates only in selector positions 'N' and 'P'.

17 Starter inhibitor/reversing lamp switch - adjustment

1 Where this type of switch is installed or fitted as a substitute for a starter inhibitor switch, carry out adjustment in the following manner.
2 Disconnect the leads from the switch terminals, marking the leads so that they can be correctly replaced on the larger (angled) terminals for the reversing lamps and the smaller starter terminals.

3 Place the speed selector lever in 'D' or 'L' position (on later models 'D', '1' or '2').
4 Connect a test lamp and torch battery across the two larger reversing lamp terminals of the switch.
5 Unscrew the switch about two turns and then slowly screw it in again until the test lamp goes out. Mark the relative position of the switch body to the transmission casing by making a pencil mark.
6 Transfer the test lamp and battery to the two smaller starter inhibitor terminals and continue to screw in the switch until the test lamp illuminates. Mark the transmission casing at a point opposite to the mark previously made on the switch body.
7 Unscrew the switch until the mark on the switch body is half way between the two marks made on the transmission casing. Tighten the switch stem locknut.
8 Reconnect the leads to the switch terminals and check that the starter motor operates only when the selector lever is in 'N' or 'P' and that the reversing lamps illuminate only with the lever in 'R' and the ignition switched on.

18 Front brake band - adjustment

1 This is not normally required but can be checked where there is slip during downshift from third to second speed. Refer also to fault diagnosis chart (Section 24).
2 Access to the front brake servo is obtained after draining the fluid and removing the oil pan.
3 Loosen the locknut on the adjuster screw and then rotate the screw until a flat metal plate, ¼ in (6.35 mm) thick can be inserted between the end of the screw and the servo piston pin. Tighten the adjuster screw to a torque of 10 lb/in, then retighten the locknut and remove the metal plate.
4 Refit the oil pan, using a new gasket and refill the transmission with fluid.

19 Rear brake band - adjustment

1 The rear brake band may be out of adjustment if selection or operation of reverse gear is faulty; also refer to Fault diagnosis chart (Section 24).
2 The adjuster for the rear brake band is located on the right-hand side of the upper surface of the transmission casing. Access to it may be obtained by removing an inspection plug from underneath the carpet within the vehicle.
3 Slacken the locknut and then tighten the adjuster screw to a torque of 10 lb/ft (1.4 kg/m). Unscrew the adjuster one complete turn and retighten the locknut.

20 Extension housing oil seal - renewal

1 Persistent leakage of fluid from the rear end of the extension housing may be due to a faulty or worn oil seal. An out of balance propeller shaft can cause the leakage to continue even after renewal of the oil seal.
2 To renew the seal, disconnect the propeller shaft from the transmission rear driving flange.
3 Unscrew and remove the centre bolt from the driving flange in a similar manner to that described in Section 2 of Part 1 of this Chapter.
4 Pull the driving flange from the splines of the transmission rear shaft.
5 Prise out the oil seal taking great care not to damage the seating or housing which is of light alloy. If the seal is particularly tight, unscrew and remove the bolts which secure the rear extension housing to the main transmission casing. Remove the speedometer driven gear and then draw the extension housing off over the transmission rear splined shaft. The oil seal may then be drifted from its seat using a long rod or bar. Take care not to damage the bush which is located just in front of the oil seal.

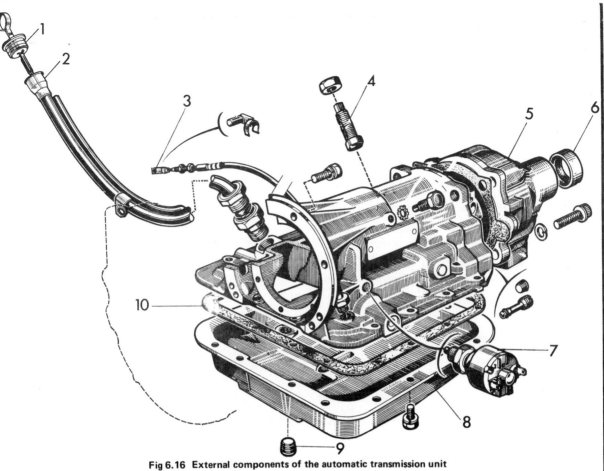

Fig 6.16 External components of the automatic transmission unit

1 Fluid dipstick
2 Combined fluid filler, dipstick and breather tube
3 Downshift cable (attachment to carburettor)
4 Rear brake band adjuster
5 Rear extension housing
6 Oil seal
7 Starter inhibitor switch
8 Oil pan
9 Drain plug
10 Gasket

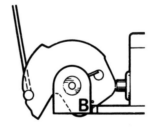

Fig 6.17 Downshift valve cable adjusting diagram

A Position of cam with accelerator pedal released

B Position of cam with accelerator pedal in 'kickdown' position

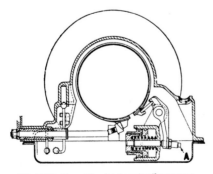

Fig 6.18 Front brake band adjustment

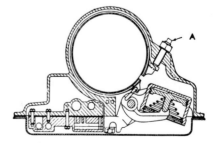

Fig 6.19 Rear brake band adjustment

6 Press in the new seal until it is flush with the end of the extension housing.

7 Refitting the propeller shaft and speedometer drive gear is a reversal of removal.

21 Automatic transmission - removal and installation

1 Disconnect the lead from the battery negative terminal and the leads from the starter inhibitor switch.

2 Drain the cooling system and disconnect the radiator top hose.

3 Release the heater hoses from their clips on the rocker box cover.

4 Disconnect the exhaust pipe from the manifold clamp ring.

5 Remove the starter motor.

6 Disconnect the downshift cable from the carburettor.

7 Disconnect the fluid filler tube/dipstick assembly from the cylinder block, unscrew the union nut at the base of the tube and remove the filler tube. Plug the hole with a piece of rag.

8 Disconnect the speed selector linkage from the operating lever balljoint on the transmission casing.

9 Disconnect the exhaust pipe from the support bracket on the transmission casing.

10 Disconnect the propeller shaft from the driving flange at the rear of the transmission unit.

11 Drain the fluid from the transmission unit.

12 Remove the four bolts which secure the driveplate to the torque converter. These are accessible, one at a time through the lower front section of the torque converter housing or the starter motor aperture. In order to bring each bolt into view rotate the engine by means of the driving flange at the rear of the transmission.

13 Raise the rear of the vehicle to provide adequate clearance

for the overall depth of the torque converter housing. Support the engine on a jack and an insulating block of wood placed to the rear and below the sump and then remove the transmission rear mounting and withdraw the bolts which secure the torque converter housing to the engine block.

14 Carefully lower the jack and withdraw the transmission unit to the rear from below the vehicle. There may be some loss of fluid from the torque converter if it becomes displaced from the oil pump drive as the transmission is being withdrawn. The transmission is quite heavy and the use of a trolley jack is recommended or carry out the operation over a pit with the help of an assistant.

15 Installation is a reversal of removal but ensure that the torque converter is pushed fully rearwards and is engaged with the tangs of the oil pump drive.

16 If the starter ring gear on the driveplate is worn or the teeth are chipped, now is the time to renew it.

17 When the transmission is installed, check the adjustment of the selector linkage and the downshift cable as described earlier in this Chapter.

18 Refill the unit with fluid.

22 Towing - precautions

1 Vehicles up to engine no 6611/2 (saloon) and 6611/2 (estate wagon) fitted with automatic transmission can be tow started by switching on the ignition and moving the speed selector lever to 'D' at a road speed of approximately 25 mph (40 kph). These vehicles may also be towed indefinitely in the event of a breakdown.

2 Vehicles built after these specified engine numbers cannot be tow started nor must they be towed, in the event of a breakdown over a distance of more than 28 miles (45 km) nor at a

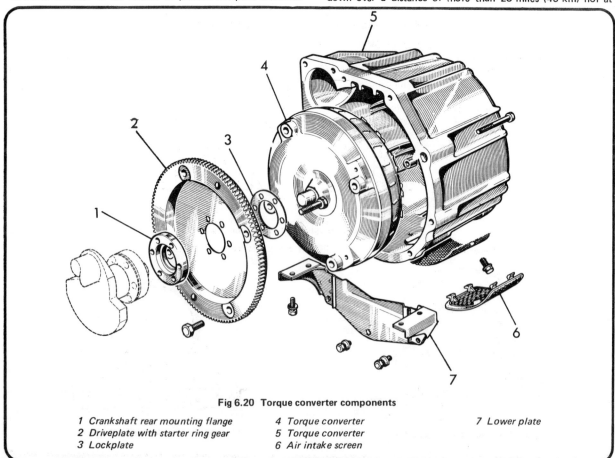

Fig 6.20 Torque converter components

1 Crankshaft rear mounting flange	4 Torque converter
2 Driveplate with starter ring gear	5 Torque converter
3 Lockplate	6 Air intake screen

7 Lower plate

road speed exceeding 30 mph (48 kph). It is also recommended that an additional 3½ pints (2 litres) of fluid is added to the transmission.

3 These restrictive conditions are due to the fact that the rear oil pump, fitted to earlier transmission units, is no longer incorporated and adequate lubrication is therefore not provided when the vehicle is being towed with the engine inoperative.

23 Testing for faults

Stall test procedure

The function of a stall test is to determine that the torque converter and gearbox are operating satisfactory.

1 Check the condition of the engine. An engine which is not developing full power will affect the stall test readings.

2 Allow the engine and transmission to reach correct working temperatures.

3 Connect a tachometer to the vehicle.

4 Chock the wheels and apply the handbrake and footbrake.

5 Select 'L' or 'R' and depress the throttle to the 'kick-down' position. Note the reading on the tachometer which should be 1,800 rev/min. If the reading is below 1,000 rev/min suspect the converter for stator slip. If the reading is down to 1,200 rev/min the engine is not developing full power. If the reading is in excess of 2,000 rev/min suspect the gearbox for brake bind or clutch slip. NOTE: Do not carry out a stall test for a longer period than 10 seconds, otherwise the transmission will become overheated.

Converter diagnosis

Inability to start on steep gradients, combined with poor acceleration from rest and low stall speed (1,000 rev/min) indicate that the converter stator unidirectional clutch is slipping. This condition permits the stator to rotate in an opposite direction to the impeller and turbine, and torque multiplication cannot occur.

Poor acceleration in third gear above 30 mph (48 kph) and reduced maximum speed indicate that the stator unidirectional clutch has seized. The stator will not rotate with the turbine and impeller and the 'fluid flywheel' phase cannot occur. This condition will also be indicated by excessive overheating of the transmission although the stall speed will be correct.

Road test procedure

1 Check that the engine will only start with the speed selector lever in 'P' or 'N' and that the reversing lamps (if fitted) operate only in 'R'.

2 Apply the handbrake and with the engine idling move the hand control lever from 'N' to 'D' then 'N' to 'R' and finally 'N' to 'L'. Engagement in each position should be positive.

3 With the transmission at normal running temperature, select 'D', release the handbrake and accelerate with minimum throttle opening. Check the 1 to 2 and 2 to 3 shift speeds and the smoothness of the changes.

4 On earlier type transmissions (see Section 22) at a minimum road speed of 30 mph (48 kph) select 'N' and switch off the ignition. Allow the road speed to drop to 25 mph (40 kph), switch on the ignition, select 'D' and the engine will start.

5 Stop the vehicle, select 'D' and then drive off using full throttle. Check 1 to 2 and 2 to 3 shift speeds and the smoothness of the changes.

6 At a roadspeed of 25 mph (40 kph) apply full throttle (not through to 'kick-down'). The vehicle should accelerate in third speed and not downshift to second.

7 At a maximum speed of 45 mph (72 kph) press the accelerator to the 'kick-down' position, the transmission should downshift to second.

8 At a maximum speed of 21 mph (34 kph) in 'L' the transmission should downshift to first speed when the accelerator is depressed to the 'kick-down' position.

9 Stop the vehicle, select 'D' and drive away using the 'kick-down' position of the accelerator pedal. Check the 1 to 2 and 2 to 3 shift speeds.

10 At a road speed of 40 mph (64 kph) in third speed, select 'L' and release the accelerator pedal. Check the 3 to 2 downshift and efficiency of engine braking.

11 With 'L' still engaged, stop the vehicle and accelerate to over 25 mph (40 kph) using the 'kick-down' position. Check for slip, squawk and absence of upshift.

12 Stop the vehicle and select 'R'. Reverse the vehicle using full throttle if possible, check for slip or squawk.

13 Stop the vehicle on a gradient. Apply the handbrake and then select 'P'. Release the handbrake and check the efficiency of the parking pawl. Turn the vehicle round and repeat the operation. If the parking pawl does not hold the vehicle or conversely, if it does not completely disengage when released (indicated by a clicking noise when the vehicle starts to roll) adjust the linkage of the speed selector mechanism (see Section 14).

The following shift speeds should be used as a guide when carrying out the foregoing tests:

	1 to 2	2 to 3	3 to 2	3 to 1	2 to 1
SELECTOR LEVER IN 'D'					
Minimum throttle	6 mph (9.6 kph)	13 mph (21 kph)	6 mph (9.6 kph)	-	2 mph (3.2 kph)
Full throttle	20 mph (32 kph)	40 mph (64.3 kph)	15 mph (24 kph)	2 mph (3.2 kph)	2 mph (3.2 kph)
'Kickdown' position	31 mph (50 kph)	55 mph (88.5 kph)	45 mph (72.4 kph)	25 mph (40 kph)	25 mph (40 kph)
SELECTOR LEVER IN 'L'					
Throttle released	-	-	10 mph (16 kph)	8 mph (12.8 kph)	8 mph (12.8 kph)

For 'Fault diagnosis' - see next page

24 Fault diagnosis - automatic transmission

The most likely causes of faulty operation are incorrect fluid level and linkage adjustment.

The faults and remedial action listed here are those which can be diagnosed and put right by the home mechanic. Where the transmission still does not operate correctly after the appropriate action has been taken then the fault can be assumed to be an internal one and the services of your Simca main dealer should be sought.

An indication of a major internal fault may be gained from the colour of the oil which under normal conditions should be transparent red. If it becomes discoloured or black then burned clutch or brake bands must be suspected.

Symptom	Reason/s	Remedy
Engine will not start in 'N' or 'P'	Faulty starter or ignition circuits	Check and repair.
	Incorrect linkage adjustment	Adjust.
	Incorrectly adjusted inhibitor switch	Adjust.
Engine starts in selector positions other than 'N' or 'P'	Incorrect linkage adjustment	Adjust.
Severe bump when selecting 'D', 'L', 'R' and excessive creep when handbrake released	Idling speed too high	Adjust.
	Downshift cable incorrectly adjusted	Adjust.
Poor acceleration and low maximum speed	Incorrect fluid level	Top up.
	Incorrect fluid level	Top up.
	Incorrect linkage adjustment	Adjust.
No drive in 'D'	Incorrect fluid level	Top up.
	Incorrect linkage adjustment	Adjust.
	Downshift cable incorrectly adjusted	Adjust.
Delayed or no 1 to 2 upshift	Downshift cable incorrectly adjusted	Adjust.
	Front brake band out of adjustment	Adjust.
Delayed or no 2 to 3 upshift	Downshift cable incorrectly adjusted	Adjust.
	Front brake band out of adjustment	Adjust.
Drag in 2nd or 3rd speeds	Rear brake band out of adjustment	Adjust.
Drag during 2 to 3 upshift	Front brake band out of adjustment	Adjust.
Slip or squawk in 'D' at full throttle	Incorrect fluid level	Top up.
	Incorrect linkage adjustment	Adjust.
	Downshift cable incorrectly adjusted	Adjust.
Transmission downshifts too easily	Downshift cable incorrectly adjusted	Adjust.
No downshift at all	Downshift valve inoperative	Clean or renew.
No 3 to 2 downshift or lack of engine braking	Incorrectly adjusted linkage	Adjust.
	Front brake band out of adjustment	Adjust.
Slip or squawk on take off in 'L'	Incorrect fluid level	Top up.
	Incorrect linkage adjustment	Adjust.
	Downshift cable incorrectly adjusted	Adjust.
Slip or squawk on take off in 'R' or slip	Incorrect fluid level	Top up.
	Incorrect linkage adjustment	Adjust.
	Downshift cable incorrectly adjusted	Adjust.
Drag in 'R'	Front brake band out of adjustment	Adjust.
No drive in 'R'	Incorrect fluid level	Top up.
	Incorrect linkage adjustment	Adjust.
	Downshift cable incorrectly adjusted	Adjust.
	Rear brake band incorrectly adjusted	Adjust.
Vehicle not held in 'P'	Incorrectly adjusted linkage	Adjust.

Chapter 7 Propeller shafts and universal joints

Contents

Specifications

Type ... ...   Two section with front flexible coupling, centre flexibly mounted bearing and two needle roller bearing type universal joints on rear section. Grease nipples provided on two splined sliding sections.

Torque wrench settings

	lb ft	kg m
Front flexible coupling bolts and nuts	38	5.2
Centre bearing mounting bolts	16	2.2
Rear drive flange bolts	16	2.2
Universal joint 'U' bolts	16	2.2

1 General description

The propeller shaft is of two section type and incorporates a splined sliding section on both the front and rear portions. These sliding sections are lubricated by a grease nipple and incorporate a felt lubricant seal.

The three legged driving flange which is attached to the splines of the output shaft of the gearbox or automatic transmission unit is bolted to a flexible coupling.

The centre of the propeller shaft is supported on a flexibly mounted bearing which is bolted to the bodyshell floor.

The universal joints at each end of the rear propeller shaft section are of spider and needle roller bearing type.

The centre bearing and the two rear universal joints are sealed and require no routine lubrication.

The complete propeller shaft assembly is balanced to fine limits during production and it is imperative that all components are marked in relation to those which are adjacent before any dismantling is undertaken.

2 Flexible coupling - renewal

1 Unscrew and remove the three bolts which secure the flexible coupling to the three legged drive flange at the rear of the transmission (photo).
2 Unscrew and remove the two bolts which secure the centre flexible mounted bearing to the bodyshell floor (photo).
3 Withdraw the front section of the propeller shaft complete

2.1 Disconnecting flexible coupling from transmission driving flange

2.2 Centre bearing retaining bolts

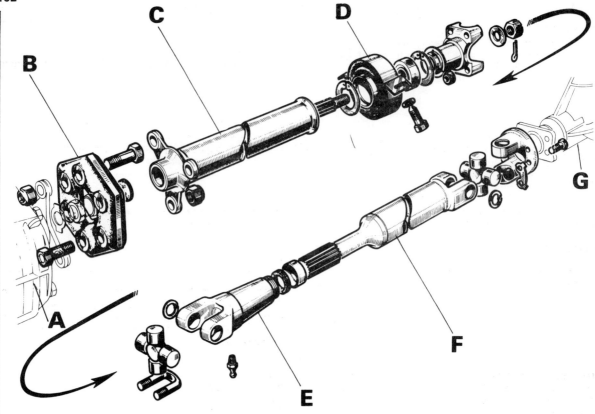

Fig 7.1 Exploded view of the propeller shaft assembly

A Transmission unit
B Flexible coupling
C Front propeller shaft

D Centre flexibly mounted bearing
E Internally splined sliding yoke
F Rear propeller shaft

G Rear axle

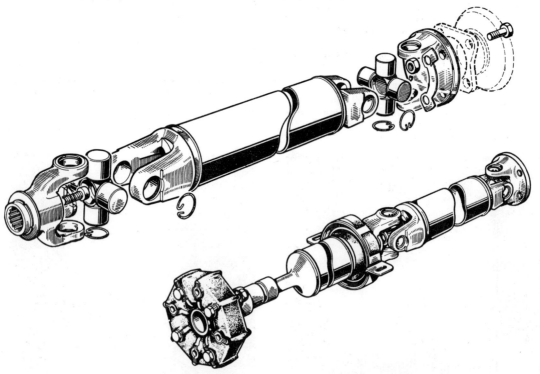

Fig 7.2 Modified propeller shaft and joints (automatic transmission)

with front flexible coupling and centre flexible bearing by pulling it forward to disengage it from the splines of the rear section of the propeller shaft.

4 Unbolt the flexible coupling from the propeller shaft.

5 Refitting and installation are reversals of dismantling and removal but the flexible coupling must be bolted to the spider of the propeller shaft so that the crosses moulded on the coupling are located one each side of the leg which has the punch mark. Note that the bolts which secure the coupling to the transmission driving flange have their heads nearest the propeller shaft and the bolts which secure the coupling to the spider of the propeller shaft have their heads nearest the gearbox.

3 Centre flexibly mounted bearing - renewal

1 Mark adjacent components to ensure that they will be refitted in their original positions (see Section 1).

2 Remove the nuts from the 'U' bolts of the centre universal joint and separate the joint.

3 Withdraw the split pin from the castellated nut which is now exposed at the rear end of the front propeller shaft.

4 Remove the washer and sliding sleeve from the rear face of the centre bearing.

5 Unscrew and remove the two securing bolts which hold the centre bearing to the bodyshell floor and then draw the bearing assembly off the end of the front propeller shaft.

6 The bearing is secured in its flexible mounting by two circlips which should be extracted if the bearing is being renewed.

7 Reassembly is a reversal of dismantling but check that the alignment marks made on components before dismantling mate, also that the elongated bolt slots of the centre bearing mounting are inclined *inwards* towards the gearbox. Do not fully tighten these bolts until the propeller shaft has been reconnected. Use a new split pin on the castellated nut and tighten all nuts and bolts to the specified torque.

4 Propeller shaft assembly - removal and installation

1 Disconnect the handbrake cable by unscrewing the nuts which secure the equaliser slide to the handbrake rod.

2 Unscrew and remove the two bolts which secure the centre flexibly mounted bearing to the bodyshell floor.

3 Disconnect the propeller shaft front flexible coupling from the three legged driving flange as described in Section 2.

4 Bend back the lock tabs of the nuts on the four bolts which secure the propeller shaft rear flange to the rear axle pinion drive flange.

5 Mark the edges of the two flanges so that they can be refitted in exactly the same relative position.

6 Remove the bolts, pull the propeller shaft slightly forward to separate the two driving flanges and then remove the complete propeller shaft assembly from below the vehicle.

7 Refitting is the reversal of removal but remember to align the rear flange mating marks and note that the rear flange securing bolts have their heads nearest the rear axle. Always use new locking tab washers (photo).

8 Note the location of the rubber insulator on the transmission driving flange bolt which should be renewed if worn (photo).

5 Universal joints - testing for wear

1 Wear in the needle roller bearings is characterized by

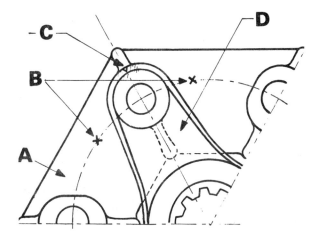

Fig 7.3 Fitting diagram — flexible coupling to front propeller shaft spider

A Flexible coupling
B Marks on flexible coupling
C Punch mark on propeller shaft spider

C Punch mark on propeller shaft spider
D Propeller shaft spider

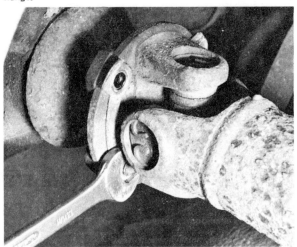

4.7 Refitting the propeller shaft to the rear axle pinion flange

4.8 Transmission driving flange and rubber insulator

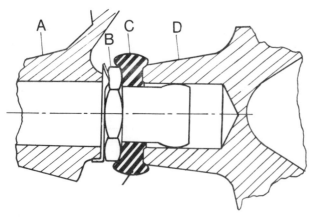

Fig 7.4 Sectional view of transmission driving flange bolt
and rubber insulator

A Transmission driving flange   C Rubber insulator
B Driving flange centre bolt   D Internally splined sliding
                                     yoke

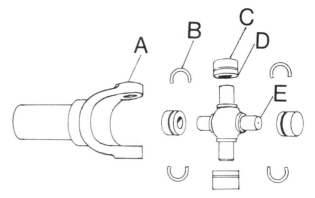

Fig 7.5 Components of universal joint

A Yoke   D Seal
B Circlip   E Spider
C Bearing cup

vibration in the transmission, 'clonks' on taking up the drive, and in extreme cases lack of lubrication, metallic squeaking and ultimately grating and shrieking sounds as the bearings break up.

2 It is easy to check if the needle roller bearings are worn with the propeller shaft in position, by trying to turn the shaft with one hand, the other hand holding the rear axle flange when the rear universal joint is being checked.

3 Now hold each propeller shaft section and try to turn them in opposite directions. Any movement here will indicate wear in the front universal joint.

4 If wear is evident in either of the needle bearing type universal joints, service them as described in the next Section.

5 A final test for wear is to attempt to lift the shaft and note any movement between the yokes of the joints.

6 Universal joints - servicing

1 Clean away all dirt from the ends of the bearings on the yokes so that the circlips may be removed using a pair of

contracting circlip pliers. If they are very tight, tap the end of the bearing cup (inside the circlip) with a drift and hammer to relieve the pressure.

2 Once the circlips are removed, tap the universal joints at the yoke with a soft hammer and the bearings and cup will come out of the housing and can be removed easily.

3 If they are obstinate they can be gripped in a self-locking wrench for final removal provided they are to be renewed.

4 Once the bearings are removed from each opposite journal the spider can easily be removed.

5 Refitting the new spiders, seals, needle rollers and cups (supplied as a repair kit) is a reversal of removal.

6 Place the needles round the inside of each cup, retaining them in position with some thick grease. Fill the bearing cup 1/3rd full with grease before placing it over the trunnion of the spider. Fit two cups and seals at a time and squeeze them into position in a vice making sure that the spider is held centrally and that the needles are not displaced.

7 Fit the new circlips supplied, ensuring that they locate securely in the grooves in the yokes.

7 Fault diagnosis - propeller shafts and universal joints

Symptom	Reason/s	Remedy
'Clonk' on taking up the drive	Worn universal joints	Service.
	Loose rear driving flange bolts	Tighten.
	Worn splines on sliding sections of shaft	Renew components.
Vibration during running on road	Out of balance propeller shaft	Rebalance or renew assembly.
	Worn centre bearing	Renew.
Noisy operation	Lack of lubrication	Lubricate.
	Wear in joints	Service.
	Wear in centre bearing	Renew.

Chapter 8 Rear axle

Contents

Specifications

Type	Semi-floating, hypoid bevel
Ratio	3.82 : 1
Number of pinion teeth	9
Number of crownwheel teeth	43
Oil capacity	2 pints (1.1 litres)

Torque wrench settings	lb ft	kg m
Pinion nut	94	13.1
Differential unit to axle casing	22	3.0
Differential unit to axle casing with 'Onduflex' washers ...	15	2.1

1 General description

The rear axle is of semi floating, hypoid bevel type. The differential assembly and crownwheel and pinion are mounted within a cast housing which is bolted to the front of the pressed steel axle casing. This housing may be removed for servicing after partially withdrawing the axle halfshafts without disturbing the rear axle casing or its attachments.

The axle halfshafts are forged with flanged ends and splined to the differential side gears. At the hub ends the axle shafts are supported on ball bearings, located by a retaining collar which is an interference fit on the shaft. An oil seal is installed in the end of the axle casing.

2 Halfshaft - removal and refitting

1 Remove the hub cap and slacken the wheel nuts.
2 Jack-up the rear of the vehicle and support it securely under the body frame and axle casing using axle stands or blocks.
3 Remove the roadwheel.
4 Mark the relative position of the brake drum to the axle end flange and then remove the dowel bolt which positions the road wheel, the brake drum securing screw, and withdraw the drum. If the drum is stuck, knock it off using a soft faced mallet applied at opposite points of the outer rim, do not strike the drum directly with a metal hammer or the drum may chip or crack.
5 Disconnect the fluid line from the wheel operating cylinder and plug the line to prevent loss of fluid.
6 Disconnect the handbrake cable from the lever on the brake backplate.
7 Unscrew and remove the nuts which secure the brake backplate to the flange on the end of the axle casing. These are accessible through holes in the halfshaft end-flange.
8 Bolt a slide hammer to the roadwheel bolt holes in the half-shaft flange and withdraw the shaft. It is quite useless to attempt to prise or lever the halfshaft from the axle casing as you will only succeed in pulling the vehicle off the jacks or stands. It is possible to bolt a spare wheel to the shaft flange and strike blows simultaneously at opposite points on its inner rim to remove the halfshaft but great care must be exercised to prevent damage to adjacent components. The halfshaft will be extracted complete with brake shoes and backplate (Fig. 8.2).
9 Refit the halfshaft by carefully entering its splined end into the axle casing taking great care not to damage the lips of the oil seal.
10 Hold the halfshaft horizontally and rotate it slightly until the splines of the shaft can be felt to engage with those of the differential side gear.
11 Push the shaft fully home so that the bearing is correctly seated in its recess.
12 Refitting of the other components is a reversal of removal but remember to align the marks on the brake drum and axle flange and finally bleed the brakes as described in the next Chapter.

3 Rear hub oil seal - renewal

1 Whenever the rear brake drums are removed check the internal surface of the backplate for oil contamination; also the linings of the brake shoes. Do not confuse leakage of hydraulic fluid from a faulty wheel operating cylinder (see Chapter 9) with oil seepage from the hub oil seal. Always keep the breather on top of the rear axle casing clean to prevent pressure building up within the axle casing which can cause oil to blow past the hub seals.

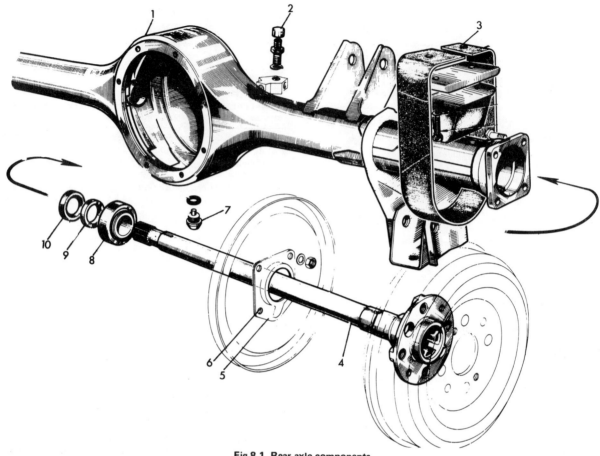

Fig 8.1 Rear axle components

1 Casing   overseas territories only)   6 Paper gasket   8 Bearing
2 Breather   4 Axle half shaft   7 Drain plug (magnetic type 9 Retaining collar
3 Rebound strap (certain   5 Oil baffle plate   for later models)   10 Oil seal

Fig 8.2 Removing a halfshaft using a slide hammer

2 Withdraw the halfshaft as described in the preceding Section.
3 Prise the oil seal from the recess in the end of the axle casing.
4 Wipe the recess clean and tap in the new seal so that its lips face the differential unit.
5 Check that the rubbing surface on the halfshaft is smooth and not grooved otherwise a new shaft will have to be installed. Any slight surface rust or corrosion may be removed by rubbing gently with very fine emery cloth.
6 Refit the halfshaft as described in the preceding Section.

4 Halfshaft bearing - renewal

1 Remove the halfshaft as described in Section 2.
2 Support the axle flange in the jaws of a vice and make a cut with a cold chisel in the bearing retaining collar to facilitate its later removal in conjunction with the bearing. Alternatively, the collar may be partially ground away or a hole drilled in it but great care must be taken to prevent damage to the shaft itself.
3 A press or puller will now have to be used to draw the bearing and its collar from the axle shaft. It will be easier to engage the bearing extractor if the bleed screw is first removed from the wheel operating cylinder (Fig. 8.4).
4 Discard the bearing and retaining collar.
5 Check that the following components are located in the correct sequence next to the halfshaft flange:
the oil baffle plate
the paper gasket
the brake backplate
the bearing
the bearing retaining collar.
      The retaining collar must be an interference fit on the shaft as it is the only component which retains the halfshaft in the axle casing. If for any reason it is a loose fit then the halfshaft must be renewed.

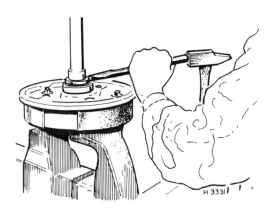

Fig 8.3 Expanding the halfshaft bearing retaining collar prior to removing it

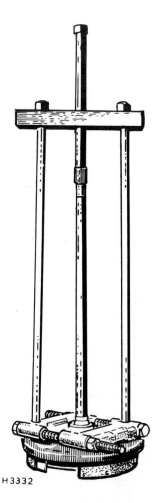

Fig 8.4 Withdrawing the bearing and collar from a halfshaft

6 Using a press with appropriate adaptors, press on the bearing and collar until they are fully seated on the shoulder of the shaft. Apply pressure only to the retaining collar which in turn will impinge on the bearing centre track. Never attempt to press on the bearing by applying pressure to its outer track.
7 Refit the halfshaft as previously described.

5 Pinion oil seal - renewal

1 Failure of the pinion oil seals may be assumed if oil leakage is observed from the nose of the differential carrier just behind the dust deflector.
2 Disconnect the propeller shaft from the pinion driving flange as described in Chapter 7.
3 Mark the position of the pinion nut in relation to the pinion drive flange.
4 Hold the pinion flange quite still using a long bar temporarily bolted to two of the flange holes and unscrew and remove the nut and washer. Mark the position of the flange in relation to the splined pinion shaft and remove the flange.
5 Pull off the dust deflector and prise out the two oil seals.
6 Tap the new seals into the pinion housing using a piece of tubing as a drift and making sure that the lips of the seals are towards the rear of the vehicle.
7 Fit the dust deflector, grease the rubbing surface of the pinion flange and push it onto the splines of the pinion, ensuring that the alignment marks coincide.
8 Fit the washer and screw on the nut until the alignment mark on it coincides with the one made on the pinion driving flange.
9 Reconnect the propeller shaft as described in Chapter 7.
10 Should the pinion nut, which is of self-locking type have been removed and refitted more than two or three times it should be renewed, in which case, tighten the new nut to a torque of 94 lb/ft (13.1 kg/m).

6 Differential - servicing

Due to the need for special tools and gauges, it is not recommended that the differential unit is dismantled. It is better to remove the original unit from the axle banjo casing as described in the next Section and have it serviced by your SIMCA dealer or to purchase a factory reconditioned unit or one in good condition from a car dismantler.

7 Differential unit - removal and installation

1 Jack-up the rear of the vehicle and partially extract both halfshafts as described in Section 2.
2 Disconnect the propeller shaft from the pinion driving flange.
3 Drain the oil from the rear axle.
4 Unscrew and remove the bolts which secure the differential housing to the rear axle banjo casing.
5 Pull the differential unit forward and remove it from the axle casing.
6 Installation is a reversal of removal but clean out the old oil from the axle casing and clean the mating surfaces and fit a new flange gasket.
7 Refit the drain plug and refill with the correct grade and quantity of oil.

8 Rear axle - removal and installation

1 Jack-up the rear of the vehicle and support it on stands placed under the body sideframe members.
2 Drain the oil from the rear axle and then support the axle casing on jacks or blocks.
3 Remove the rear road wheels.
4 Disconnect the propeller shaft from the rear axle pinion

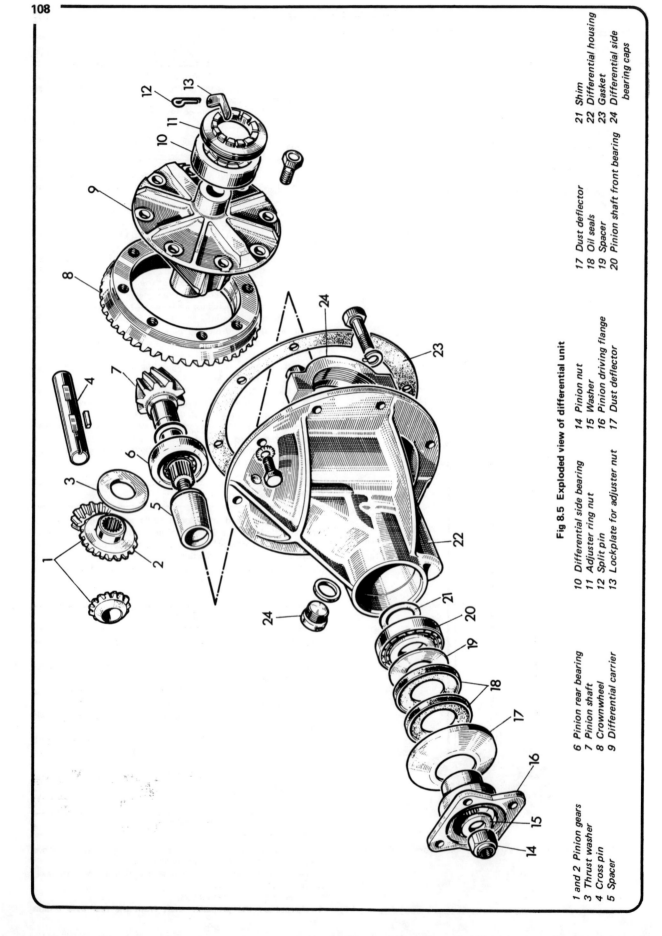

Fig 8.5 Exploded view of differential unit

1 and 2 Pinion gears	6 Pinion shaft	10 Differential side bearing	14 Pinion nut	17 Dust deflector	21 Shim
3 Thrust washer	7 Crownwheel	11 Adjuster ring nut	15 Washer	18 Oil seals	22 Differential housing
4 Cross pin	8 Differential carrier	12 Split pin	16 Pinion driving flange	19 Spacer	23 Gasket
5 Spacer	9 Differential carrier	13 Lockplate for adjuster nut	17 Dust deflector	20 Pinion shaft front bearing	24 Differential side bearing caps

driving flange as described in Chapter 7.

5 Disconnect the flexible brake pipe which runs between the three-way connector on the axle casing and the rigid brake pipe on the underside of the body floor (see Chapter 9). Plug the brake lines to prevent loss of fluid and to exclude dirt.

6 Disconnect the handbrake cables either by detaching them from the brake backplates and the operating levers or by disconnecting the equaliser slide from the pull rod and unbolting the cable cleats from the bodyframe.

7 Remove the rear shock absorbers and the coil springs as described in Chapter 11.

8 Disconnect the upper and lower suspension links from their attachment to the bodyframe by withdrawing their pivot bolts as described in Chapter 11.

9 Disconnect the transverse rod from its attachment to the axle casing.

10 Lower the jack or remove the blocks and withdraw the rear axle assembly from beneath the vehicle.

11 Installation is a reversal of removal but refer to Chapters 9 and 11 for precise details of brake bleeding and handbrake cable adjustment and the correct torque tightening figures for the suspension pivot bolts.

9 Modifications

1 In order to overcome oil leakage which sometimes occurs around the bolts which secure the differential unit to the rear axle banjo housing, special 'ONDUFLEX' sealing washers are fitted from rear axle serial no. "1797963". Where these washers are installed as original equipment or as substitutes for the original shakeproof type, they should be tightened to a torque of 15 lb/ft (2.1 kg/m).

2 Commencing with rear axle number "2170798" a magnetic type drain plug is fitted, similar in design to the one used in the gearbox. This type of drain plug cannot be fitted to earlier axle casings.

10 Fault diagnosis - rear axle

Symptom	Reason/s	Remedy
Oil leakage	Hub oil seals faulty	Renew.
	Pinion oil seals faulty	Renew.
	Defective differential unit to axle casing gasket	Renew.
	Old type lockwashers fitted	Install newer 'Onduflex' type.
Noise	Lack of oil	Top up.
	Worn bearings	Renew.
	General wear	Exchange differential unit or have serviced.
'Clonk' on taking up drive and excessive backlash	Incorrectly tightened pinion nut	Tighten to specified torque to provide correct bearing pre-load.
	Worn components	Renew.
	Incorrect pinion to crownwheel adjustment	Arrange for resetting by Simca agent.
	Worn axle halfshaft splines	Renew halfshaft.
	Elongated road wheel bolt holes (see also Section 7 of Chapter 7)	Renew road wheel.

Chapter 9 Braking system

Contents

Specifications

System types and applications

1300 models

Type ... ... Hydraulic four wheel drum with mechanical handbrake on rear wheels only

Front brakes ... ... Twinplex

Rear brakes ... ... Simplex

Drum diameter ... ... 10 in (254.0 mm)

Width of friction linings
Front ... ... 1.98 in (50.0 mm)
Rear ... ... 1.77 in (45.0 mm)

Length of friction linings ... ... 10.52 in (267.0 mm)

Thickness of friction linings ... ... 0.196 in (5.0 mm)

Total lining area (each front wheel) ... ... 37.5 in^2 (242.0 cm^2)

Total lining area (each rear wheel) ... ... 30.27 in^2 (196.0 cm^2)

Master cylinder diameter * ... ... 7/8 in (22.2 mm)

Front wheel cylinder diameter ... ... 1^1/8 in (28.6 mm)

Rear wheel cylinder diameter ... ... 15/16 in (23.8 mm)

* From body No J210669 master cylinder incorporates dual lip secondary cup seal

1301, 1500 and 1501 models

Type ... ... Hydraulic front disc and rear drum with servo option (1968 onwards). From 1970, Rhd vehicles are fitted with servo as standard. All vehicles have a mechanically operated handbrake on the rear wheels.

Girling front disc and rear drum brakes were originally installed but Teves/Ate front discs are substituted as from body Nos "U240556" (saloon) and "U230947" (estate wagon)

Disc diameter ... ...   9.7 in (246.0 mm)

Disc thickness ... ...   0.37 in (9.5 mm)

Friction pad thickness
    Friction material ... ...   0.413 in (10.5 mm)
    Backing plate ... ...   0.196 in (5.0 mm)

Friction area (one wheel)
    Pad ... ...   10.07 in^2 (65.0 cm^2)
    Disc ... ...   91.5 in^2 (590.0 cm^2)

Rear brakes ... ...   As for 1300 models except wheel cylinder diameter is 0.750 in (19.05 mm)

Hydraulic components ... ...   As for 1300 models

From body No A190802, master cylinder incorporates dual lip secondary cup seal

Torque wrench settings

	lb ft	kg m
Front brake backplate to stub axle carrier	34	4.7
Rear brake backplate to axle housing	18	2.4
Wheel operating cylinders to backplate	7	1.0
Disc to hub bolts	9	1.2
Disc shield to stub axle carrier	16	2.2
Caliper to stub axle carrier	51	7.0
Brake pressure distributor bolts	16	2.2
Caliper half shell securing bolts	25	3.6

1 General description

The braking system is of hydraulic type, acting on all four wheels with a mechanically operated handbrake on the rear wheels only and controlled by a facia mounted pull-out type lever.

1300 models are fitted with front and rear drum type brakes.

1301, 1500 and 1501 models are fitted with front disc brakes of either Girling or Teves/Ate manufacture according to the date of prodcution and rear drum type brakes. A pressure regulator valve is incorporated to prevent the rear wheels locking during heavy braking.

The master cylinder may be of Lockheed or Teves/Ate make and they differ only in component detail. The cylinders for the 1300 and 1500 range are not interchangeable. Commencing with 1968 models, servo assistance was optionally available on all models and when installed, the pressure regulator valve was changed for an interlocked adjuster valve which regulates the hydraulic braking pressure according to vehicle load.

1970 rhd models (onwards) are fitted with servo assistance as standard. Reference should be made to Specifications for full details of braking system types, makes and vehicle application.

2 Drum brakes - adjustment

1 To adjust the front brakes on 1300 models, jack-up the front roadwheels and turn one of the squared adjusters on the brake backplate until the wheel locks. Turn the wheel and the adjuster in the direction of normal rotation which would apply if the vehicle were moving forward (Fig. 9.3).

2 Now turn the adjuster in the reverse direction until the roadwheel is free to rotate without any drag or scraping of the shoe linings.

3 Repeat the operation on the second adjuster of the same brake.

4 Repeat the foregoing operations on the opposite front brake.

5 On all 1300, 1301, 1500 or 1501 models adjust the rear drum brakes in the following manner (Fig. 9.4).

6 Release the handbrake fully and chock the front wheels.

7 Raise the rear road wheels by jacking-up the vehicle under the axle casing.

8 Carry out the adjustment previously described for the front brakes by again turning each of the two squared backplate adjusters in the direction of normal road wheel travel.

3 Front disc pads - inspection, removal and refitting

1 The front disc brakes require no adjustment as due to the design of the caliper unit and its seals, the disc pads are kept in light contact with the brake disc at all times and any wear in the friction material is automatically compensated for.

2 Periodically, jack-up the front of the vehicle and remove the roadwheels.

3 On some later Teves type calipers a shield is fitted over the disc pad aperture and this should first be removed (Fig. 9.5).

4 On late Teves type calipers (without an external hydraulic bridge pipe) the pins which retain the cross shaped spring plate should be withdrawn. These pins have expanding ends and need to be pulled out of engagement sharply to release them from the holes in the caliper (Fig. 9.6).

5 On earlier type Teves calipers withdraw the spring clips from the ends of the retaining pins and pull out the pins (photo).

6 On all Teves calipers, now extract the cross shaped spring plate and inspect the thickness of the friction material of the disc pads. If it has worn down to 0.078 in (2.0 mm) the pads must be renewed as sets on both front wheels.

7 To extract the disc pads, grip their projections with a pair of pliers and pull them straight out from the caliper body (photo).

8 With 'Girling' type units, inspection of the disc pad friction linings can be made without any dismantling, once the road wheel is removed (Fig. 9.7).

9 To withdraw the 'Girling' type disc pads, first detach the spring clip from the retaining pins, pull out the pins and then extract the pads. On some models, anti-squeak shims are fitted behind the pads and must be retained for replacement with the new pads (Fig. 9.8).

10 Installation of new pads is a reversal of removal, according to

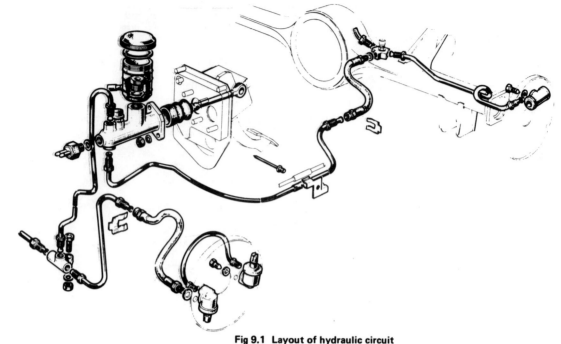

**Fig 9.1 Layout of hydraulic circuit
on 1300 models**

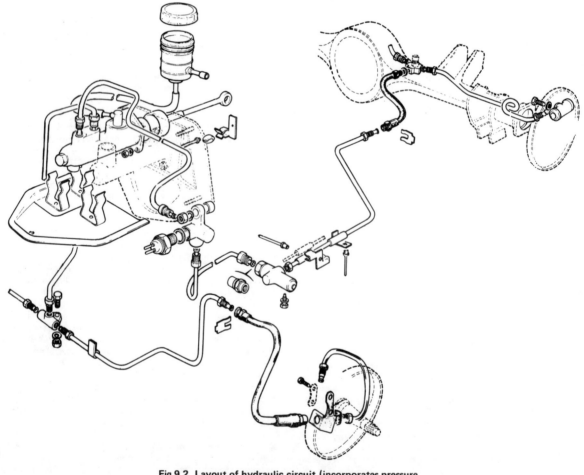

**Fig 9.2 Layout of hydraulic circuit (incorporates pressure
regulator) on 1301, 1500 and 1501 models**

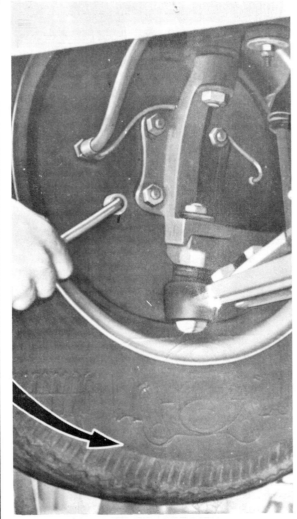

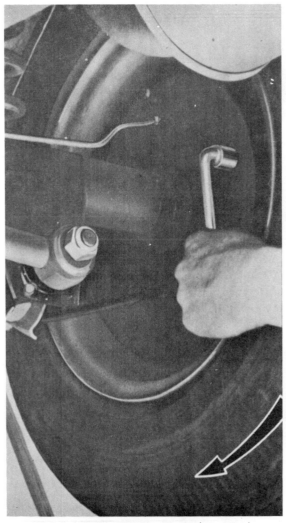

Fig 9.3 Adjusting a right hand front drum brake (1300 models)

Fig 9.4 Adjusting a rear drum brake (all models)

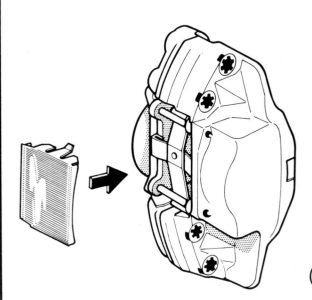

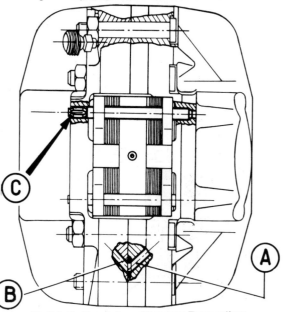

Fig 9.5 Shield fitted over disc pad aperture on some late type
Teves calipers

Fig 9.6 Sectional view of late type **Teves** caliper

A Internal fluid passage
B Sealing ring
C Expanded end of retaining
    pins

3.5 Removing pad retaining pins from Teves type caliper

3.7 Withdrawing disc brake pads (note anti-squeak slots)

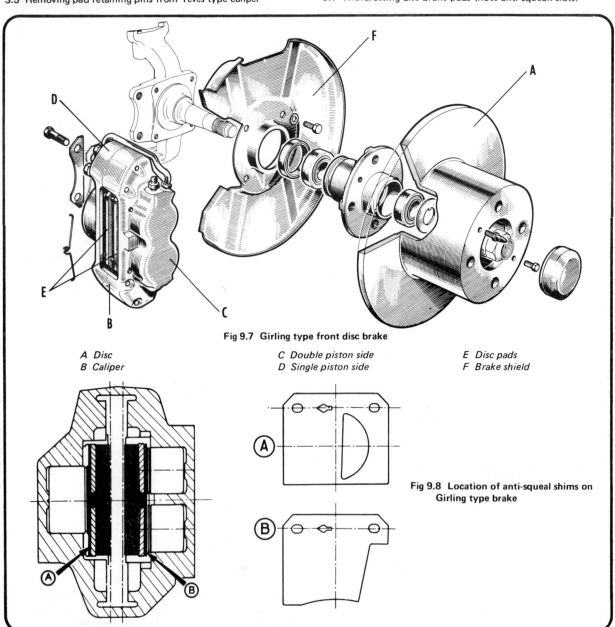

Fig 9.7 Girling type front disc brake

A Disc
B Caliper

C Double piston side
D Single piston side

E Disc pads
F Brake shield

Fig 9.8 Location of anti-squeal shims on Girling type brake

type but before doing so clean out the pad aperture in the caliper body using methylated spirit and then using a flat bar or piece of wood, press both caliper pistons squarely into the caliper until they are fully depressed. This operation will cause the level of fluid in the reservoir to rise and it will be wise to syphon some out beforehand. Alternatively as the pistons are being depressed, unscrew the caliper bleed nipple a turn, in order to allow excess fluid to be ejected.

11 Ensure that any anti-squeak shims are refitted and use the new pins and retaining clips supplied with the new pads.

12 When the pads have been fitted, apply the foot brake pedal several times in order to bring the pads into rubbing contact with the brake disc. Finally, check and top-up if necessary, the fluid reservoir with specified fluid.

4 Front drum brake shoes - inspection and renewal

1 Jack-up the front of the vehicle and remove the roadwheels.

2 Unscrew and remove the drum retaining screw and the roadwheel positioning dowel.

3 Withdraw the brake drum. Should it be stuck, **release** the shoe adjuster fully and then tap off the drum using a soft faced mallet.

4 If the friction linings have worn down almost to the level of the rivet heads then they must be renewed. If they are in good condition, brush all dust from the surface of the linings and from the interior of the drum. Refit the drum and adjust the brakes.

5 If the shoes are to be renewed, note carefully the holes in the shoe webs in which the return springs engage and also the way round that the shoes are fitted with regard to leading and trailing edges.

6 Release fully the two brake adjusters and then remove the two shoe steady springs.

7 Prise the ends of the shoes out of engagement with one operating cylinder, pull the shoes forward slightly and let the action of the return spring pull the shoes together.

8 Repeat the operation at the opposite wheel cylinder and then withdraw the shoes and return springs from the backplate.

9 If the pistons have a tendency to drop out of their cylinders use a piece of wire or rubber band to retain them. Do not touch the foot brake pedal while the shoes are removed.

10 Clean the slots in the wheel cylinders in which the brake shoes engage and apply a little high melting point or brake grease; also to the raised sliding surfaces of the brake backplate.

11 Lay the new shoes flat on a bench, the correct way round and engage the return shoes in their respective holes. Do not touch the linings with greasy hands.

12 Pull the shoes slightly apart to keep the return springs in engagement and then install the shoes by reversing the removal procedure.

Fig 9.9 Front brake assembly (1300 model)

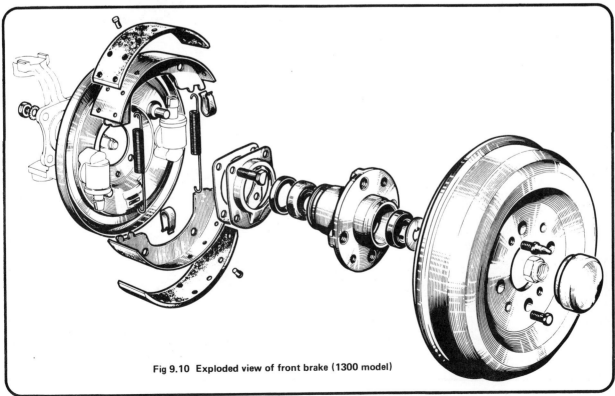

Fig 9.10 Exploded view of front brake (1300 model)

13 Fit the shoe steady springs, the brake drum with retaining screw and wheel dowel bolt and finally adjust the shoes as described in Section 2.

5 Rear drum brake shoes - inspection and renewal

1   The procedure is similar to that described for front shoes in the preceding Section but note the following points.
2   The handbrake must be fully released in addition to the two shoe adjusters before removing the shoes.
3   Disconnect the handbrake cable from the clip on the shoe actuating arm within the drum (photo).
4   Extract the connecting bar from between the two shoe webs as the shoes are prised apart.

6 Front drum wheel cylinders - removal and refitting

1   Raise the front of the vehicle and remove the roadwheel.
2   Remove the brake shoes as described in Section 4.
3   In order to prevent loss of fluid when the hydraulic line is disconnected, unscrew the lid of the fluid reservoir and place a piece of polythene sheet over the top of the reservoir and then screw on the lid. This will create a vacuum in the unit and prevent any fluid leaving the reservoir.
4   Disconnect the flexible hose from its connection with the rigid section of the pipeline by unscrewing the union nut and holding the flexible hose quite still by applying a spanner to the flats on its end fitting.
5   Remove the flexible hose from its retaining spring clip and

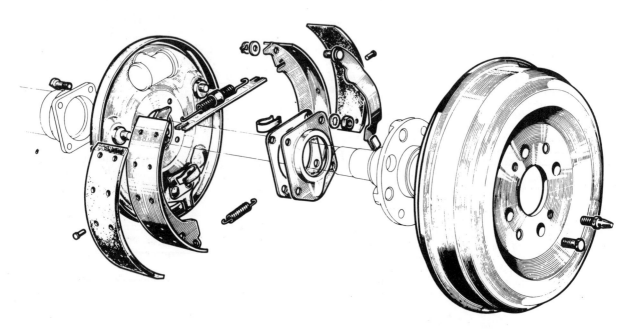

Fig 9.11 Exploded view of rear brake (all models)

5.3 Handbrake cable connection to shoe actuating arm

7.2 Removing a rear brake drum

then unscrew it from the wheel cylinder. Retain the sealing washer.

6 Disconnect the hydraulic bridge pipe which runs between the two wheel cylinders and unbolt the cylinders from the backplate.

7 Refitting is a reversal of removal but bleed the hydraulic system as described in Section 20 and adjust the brakes. Take great care not to twist or kink the flexible hose (Section 18). Remember to remove the polythene sheet from the reservoir.

---

7 Rear drum wheel cylinder - removal and refitting.

1 Raise the rear of the vehicle and remove the road wheel.

2 Remove the brake drum securing bolt and dowel bolt and withdraw the drum (photo).

3 Remove the brake shoes as described in Section 5.

4 Temporarily seal the fluid reservoir as described in the preceding Section.

5 Disconnect the rigid fluid line from the wheel cylinder by first unscrewing the union and then bending the pipe carefully away.

6 Unbolt the wheel cylinder from the backplate and remove it.

7 Refitting is a reversal of removal but remove the sealing sheet from the fluid reservoir, bleed the system (Section 20) and adjust the rear brakes (Section 2).

---

8 Front brake backplate (drum brakes) - removal and refitting

1 Remove the brake drum as previously described.

2 Tap the grease cap from the hub and unscrew the nut from the stub axle.

3 Remove the thrust washer and pull off the hub complete with bearings.

4 Disconnect the flexible brake hose as described in Section 6 and then unscrew and remove the bolts which secure the backplate to the stub axle carrier. Withdraw the backplate complete with brake shoes, wheel cylinders and the oil baffle plate and oil seal.

5 Refitting is a reversal of removal but tighten the backplate bolts to a torque of 34 lb/ft (4.7 kg/m), bleed the hydraulic system and adjust the hub bearings as described in Chapter 11 which includes staking the nut on the stub axle.

---

9 Rear brake backplate - removal and refitting

1 The removal of the rear brake backplate will necessitate the disconnection of the fluid pipeline to the wheel cylinder, also the handbrake cable to the operating lever.

2 Access to the bolts which secure the backplate to the rear axle end flange can be obtained through holes in the halfshaft flange.

3 The halfshaft will now have to be withdrawn using a slide hammer as described in Chapter 8. Removal of the backplate which is captive on the halfshaft will require removal of the bearing and retaining collar from the shaft also as described in Chapter 8.

4 The fitting of the backplate to the halfshaft is as described in Chapter 8 and installation is the reversal of removal but the brakes must be bled and adjusted when the work is completed.

---

10 Wheel operating cylinders - servicing

1 Clean the external surfaces of the cylinder and then pull off the dust excluders (Figs. 9.13/9.14).

2 Eject the pistons and seals from the cylinder by applying air from a tyre pump at the fluid inlet orifice.

3 Examine the surfaces of the pistons and cylinder bores. If there is evidence of scoring or 'bright' wear areas, renew the operating cylinder complete.

Fig 9.12 Tightening front brake backplate (1300 model)

4 If these components are in good condition, wash all parts in clean hydraulic fluid or methylated spirit and discard all rubber seals.

5 Obtain the appropriate repair kit which will contain the necessary replacement seals and other components.

6 Manipulate the seals into position using the fingers only and taking great care to see that the lips face the correct way.

7 Dip each part in clean hydraulic fluid before fitting.

---

11 Front caliper - removal and refitting

1 The removal of the Girling triple cylinder caliper and the Teves/ATE dual cylinder caliper is carried out in a similar manner (Figs. 9.15/9.16).

2 Jack-up the front of the vehicle and remove the road wheel.

3 Remove the disc pads as described in Section 3 (photo).

4 Remove the bolts which secure the caliper to the stub axle carrier and slide the caliper sideways from the brake disc. The hydraulic hose need not be disconnected from the caliper if work is to be carried out on the hub, disc or suspension components, the caliper simply being tied up out of the way.

5 Where complete removal of the caliper is required, seal the

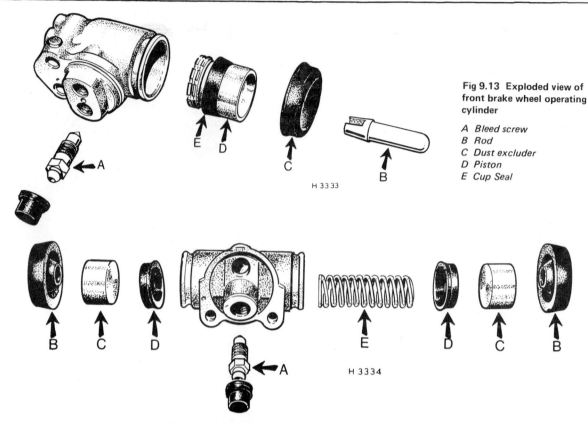

Fig 9.13 Exploded view of front brake wheel operating cylinder

A Bleed screw
B Rod
C Dust excluder
D Piston
E Cup Seal

H 3333

H 3334

Fig 9.14 Exploded view of rear brake wheel operating cylinder

A Bleed nipple   C Pistons   E Return spring
B Dust excluders   D Cup seals

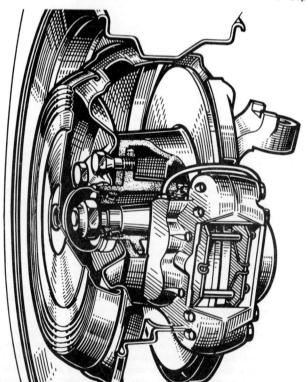

Fig 9.15 Girling type three piston caliper

Fig 9.16 Removing a Girling type caliper

fluid reservoir with polythene sheeting under the lid to prevent loss of fluid, unscrew the caliper from the flexible hose by holding the end fitting of the hose in a spanner and not allowing the hose to rotate by more than one half turn or it may be damaged.

6   Installation is a reversal of removal but tighten the securing bolts to a torque of 51 lb/ft (7 kg/m) and bleed the hydraulic system after having removed the sealing sheet from the reservoir and refitted the pads.

11.3 Brake caliper and disc showing one piston (pads removed)

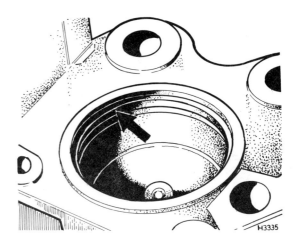

Fig 9.17 Girling type caliper piston seal

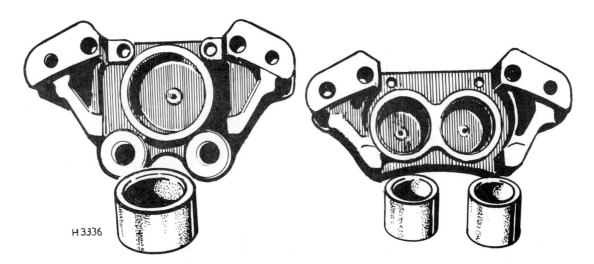

Fig 9.18 The two halves of a Girling type caliper with their pistons

12 Girling type caliper - servicing

1 Remove the hydraulic bridge pipe from the caliper unit by unscrewing the two unions.
2 Unscrew and remove the bolts which secure the two halves of the caliper unit together.
3 Extract the dust excluding sealing rings from between the rims of the three pistons and the cylinders.
4 Eject the pistons by applying air pressure from a tyre pump at the fluid inlet orifices. Mark each piston and its respective cylinder with a piece of masking tape so that the piston can be returned to its original location.
5 Carefully examine the surface of the pistons and cylinder bores for scoring or 'bright' wear areas. If these are evident, renew the caliper complete.
6 If these components are in good condition, obtain a repair kit which will contain all the necessary seals for replacement.
7 Wash all components in methylated spirit or clean hydraulic fluid, pick out the seals from their cylinder grooves and discard them.
8 Fit the new seals into the cylinder bore grooves using the fingers only to manipulate them into position.
9 Engage the new dust excluding rings with the outer grooves

of the cylinders and then dip each piston in clean hydraulic fluid and insert it (flat end first) into its respective cylinder. Use the fingers only for this operation so that the seals are not damaged.
10 Push the pistons to the limit of their travel and then engage the lips of the dust excluding rings in the piston outer grooves.
11 Fit the two half sections of the caliper together, tightening the securing bolts to a torque of 25 lb/ft (3.6 kg/m). Reconnect the bridge pipe.

13 Teves/Ate type caliper - servicing early models

1 Early type caliper units of this make incorporated a bridge pipe and their dismantling and servicing should be carried out in a manner similar to that described in the preceding Section for Girling units except that the following points must be observed.
2 The caliper has only two pistons.
3 When installing the pistons in their cylinders, the recessed portions of their rims must be at an angle of 45⁰ to the centre line of the caliper body in order to provide satisfactory anti-squeak properties. If it is necessary to rotate the piston in order to attain the required setting, insert a pair of pliers into the piston and turn the piston slowly (Figs. 9.20/9.21).

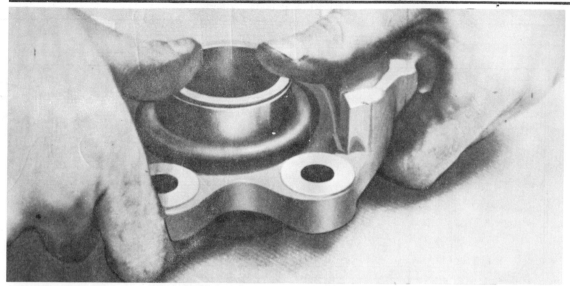

Fig 9.19 Fitting a piston to a Girling type caliper

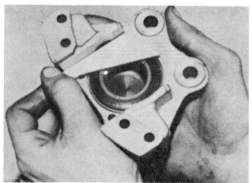

Fig 9.20 Checking the correct angle of the anti-squeak steps on a Teves type caliper piston

Fig 9.21 Rotating the piston in a Teves type caliper to align the steps

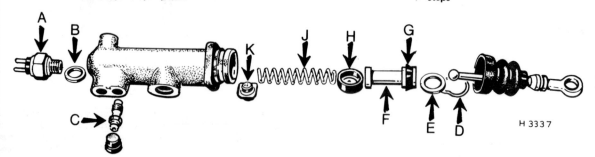

Fig 9.22 Exploded view of master cylinder (1300 model)

A Brake warning lamp switch	D Circlip	G Secondary cup seal	K Valve
B Sealing washer	E Stop washer	H Primary seal
C Bleed nipple	F Piston	J Spring

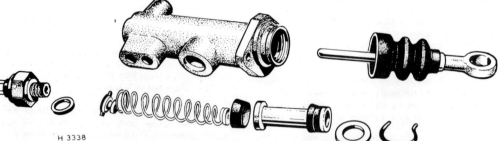

Fig 9.23 Exploded view of 1500/1501 type master cylinder (similar to 1300 models but does not incorporate bleed nipple

14 Teves/Ate type caliper - servicing later models

1 A modified form of caliper unit having no hydraulic bridge pipe but an internal connecting channel was fitted to 1301 vehicles from body no. "260510" and to 1501 models from body no "260525".
2 It is impertive that the two halves of this type of caliper are not separated by removal of the connecting bolts.
3 For servicing, the pistons must therefore be ejected in the following manner: Apply air pressure at the fluid inlet orifice, at the same time retaining the piston which is located on the same side as the orifice, in its cylinder. The opposing piston will be ejected. Now push out the remaining piston by passing a thin rod through the fluid inlet orifice.

15 Front brake disc and shield - removal, inspection, refitting

1 Periodically examine the faces of the brake disc. If it is deeply scored (light scoring or grooving is normal) it must either be renewed or reground. Disc run-out must not exceed 0.003 in (0.10 mm) otherwise the disc must be renewed.
2 Regrinding must not cause the disc to be reduced below 0.378 in (9.7 mm).
3 To remove a disc raise the car and remove the roadwheel.
4 Unbolt the caliper unit from the stub axle carrier and tie it up to the suspension without disconnecting the hydraulic flexible hose.
5 Mark the relative position of the disc to the inner hub and then unbolt the disc from the inner hub (one bolt and one roadwheel retaining dowel bolt).
6 Access to the bolts which secure the shield to the stub axle carrier may be obtained after removing the hub assembly from the stub axle by removing the grease cap and unscrewing the hub nut.
7 Refitting is a reversal of dismantling and removal but note the following points:
8 Tighten the shield bolts to a torque of 16 lb/ft (2.2 kg/m).
9 Tighten the disc to hub bolt and dowel bolt to a torque of 9 lb/ft (1.2 kg/m).
10 Tighten the caliper to stub axle carrier bolts to a torque of 51 lb/ft (7.0 kg/m).
11 Adjust the hub bearing preload as described in Chapter 11.

16 Master cylinder - removal and refitting

1 The master cylinders fitted to the 1300 and 1500 series vehicles are not interchangeable although similar in general design and construction.
2 Dependent upon the date of manufacture, the fluid reservoir may be screwed directly into the master cylinder body or remotely sited with a connecting tube. With the latter type of master cylinder, before removing it from the bulkhead, disconnect the tube from the reservoir and allow the fluid to drain into a container.
3 Disconnect the leads from the brake stop lamp switch which is screwed into the front end of the master cylinder body.
4 Unscrew the two unions and remove the two rigid pipelines from the master cylinder body.
5 Unscrew and remove the two nuts which secure the flange of the master cylinder to the mounting plate on the engine compartment rear bulkhead.
6 Draw the master cylinder forward leaving the operating pushrod still attached to the foot brake pedal.
7 Refitting is a reversal of removal but the hydraulic system must be bled as described in Section 20.

17 Master cylinder - servicing

1 Clean all dirt and grease from the external surface of the

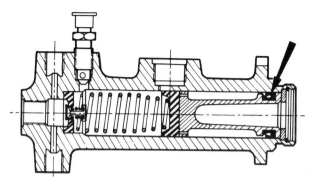

Fig 9.24 Sectional view of master cylinder with dual lipped cup seal

master cylinder.
2 Grip the master cylinder body securely in the jaws of a vice and unscrew the brake stop lamp switch.
3 *On 1300 models* remove the bleed nipple.
4 Extract the circlip from its recess in the end of the master cylinder.
5 Extract the piston stop washer and the piston/seal assembly.
6 Remove the cup seal, the spring and the valve. If these components are difficult to remove from the cylinder, pass a thin rod through the brake stop lamp switch hole and push them out.
7 Examine the surfaces of the piston and cylinder bore. If there is evidence of scoring or any bright wear areas are visible, renew the master cylinder complete.
8 If these components are in good order, discard the seals and obtain a repair kit.
9 Wash all the parts in clean hydraulic fluid or methylated spirit and then manipulate the new secondary seal into position using the fingers only. Check that the lips face the correct way.
10 Insert the valve, the spring and the cup seal followed by the piston/secondary seal assembly having first dipped it in clean hydraulic fluid.
11 Locate the stop washer and holding the piston depressed, fit the retaining circlip.
   On later master cylinders (1300 models) the secondary cup seal is of dual lipped type.
   Lockheed type master cylinder and Teves/Ate (1971 onwards) have the brake stop lamp switch located in a 3-way distribution union, sited remotely from the master cylinder. Internal construction details of these units is similar to those described in this Section for earlier Teves types.

18 Flexible hoses - inspection, removal and refitting

1 Regularly inspect the condition of the flexible hydraulic hoses which are located one to each front brake and a single one at the rear leading to a three-way union on the rear axle housing.
2 If they are swollen, chafed or perished, they must be renewed.
3 To remove a flexible brake hose, always unscrew the rigid pipe union at the rigid-to-flexible pipe connection. Prise the flexible hose from its supporting clip and then unscrew it from the wheel cylinder, caliper or three-way union as the case may be. As the hose is unscrewed, do not kink or twist it.
4 Commence refitting a flexible hose by screwing it into the wheel cylinder, caliper or three-way union. Then engage the groove in its end fitting with the support clip. At this stage check that the hose is not going to rub against adjacent suspension or other components. If necessary, remove the hose from the clip and turn it in either direction not more than a ¼ turn to provide the required 'set' to keep it from chafing. Finally engage it fully in the support clip.
5 Connect the flexible hose to the rigid line by tightening the union.

6 Always bleed the hydraulic system after disconnecting a flexible hose.

19 Rigid brake lines - inspection and renewal

1 At regular intervals wipe the steel brake pipes clean and examine them for signs or rust or denting caused by flying stones.
2 Examine the securing clips. Bend the tongues of the clips if necessary to ensure that they hold the brake pipes securely without letting them rattle or vibrate.
3 Check that the pipes are not touching any adjacent components or rubbing against any part of the vehicle. Where this is observed, bend the pipe gently away to clear.
4 Any section of pipe which is rusty or chafed should be renewed. Brake pipes are available to the correct length and fitted with end unions from most SIMCA dealers and can be made to pattern by many accessory suppliers. When installing the new pipes use the old pipes as a guide to bending and do not make any bends sharper than is necessary.
5 The system will of course have to be bled when the circuit has been reconnected.

20.12 Topping up the brake fluid reservoir

20 Bleeding the hydraulic system

1 Removal of all the air from the hydraulic system is essential to the correct working of the braking system, and before undertaking this examine the fluid reservoir cap to ensure that both vent holes, one on top and the second underneath but not in line, are clear; check the level of fluid and top up if required.
2 Check all brake line unions and connections for possible seepage, and at the same time check the condition of the rubber hoses, which may be perished.
3 If the condition of the wheel cylinders is in doubt, check for possible signs of fluid leakage.
4 If there is any possibility of incorrect fluid having been put into the system, drain all the fluid out and flush through with methylated spirit. Renew all piston seals and cups since these will be affected and could possibly fail under pressure.
5 Gather together a clean jam jar, a 9 in (229 mm) - length of tubing which fits tightly over the bleed nipples, and a tin of 'Castrol Girling' brake fluid which has been stored in an airtight tin.
6 To bleed the system clean the areas around the bleed valves, and start on the right-hand rear brake by removing the rubber cap over the bleed valve, and fitting a rubber tube in position.
7 Place the end of the tube in a glass jar containing sufficient fluid to keep the end of the tube submerged during the operation.
8 On vehicles with a vacuum servo unit, depress the brake pedal several times until the vacuum is destroyed.
9 Open the bleed valve with a spanner and quickly press down the brake pedal. After releasing the pedal, pause for a moment to allow the fluid to recoup in the master cylinder and then depress again. This will force air from the system. Continue until no more air bubbles can be seen coming from the tube. At intervals make certain that the reservoir is kept topped up, otherwise air will enter at this point again.
10 The bleeding sequence should be carried out in the following order: right rear; left rear; right front; left front and finally on 1300 models only, the bleed nipple on the master cylinder.
11 Always tighten (but not overtighten) the bleed screws when the pedal is in the fully depressed position.
12 Finally top up the level in the fluid reservoir to the 'maximum' mark (photo).

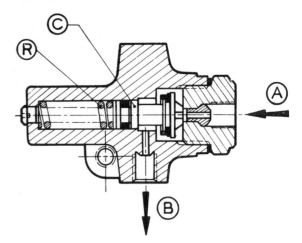

Fig 9.25 Pressure regulator valve

A Fluid inlet   C Valve
B Fluid outlet   R Spring

24.4 Handbrake primary cable and idler pulley

21 Brake pedal - removal and refitting

1 The brake and clutch pedals operate on a common crossshaft

and removal of the brake pedal is carried out in exactly the same way as described for the clutch pedal in Chapter 5.

22 Pressure regulator valve - description and testing

1 The design of this valve effectively limits the hydraulic pressure to the rear wheel cylinders whilst permitting the pressure to the front disc brake calipers to continue to increase during progressive application of the foot brake pedal.

2 With the brake pedal released, the valve (C) (Fig. 9.25) is held open by the action of the return spring.

3 During medium applications of the brake pedal when inlet pressure from the master cylinder is below that of the spring pressure, the valve is not restrictive and equal hydraulic pressure applied to both the front and rear brakes.

4 During heavy or sudden brake applications, the inlet pressure will exceed the return spring strength and the valve will close, thus restricting the pressure applied to the rear wheel cylinders.

5 To test the pressure regulator valve for serviceability, jack-up the vehicle and secure on stands.

6 Depress the brake pedal fully until the front wheels are locked and cannot be turned by hand. With the help of an assistant, keep the pedal depressed and open a rear wheel cylinder bleed nipple. The rear wheels should now rotate by hand and the foot pedal should not move any nearer the floor. If these two conditions are not met, renew the regulator valve complete. The valve is located on a bracket attached to the gearbox rear cantilever type mounting clamp bolts.

23 Handbrake - adjustment

1 Adjustment of the handbrake is normally automatic whenever the rear brake shoes are adjusted. However, in the event of cable stretch or after dismantling and reassembly, adjust the position of the equaliser slide.

2 Loosen the locknuts on the threaded rod at the equaliser and then turn them to move the equaliser slide until with the handbrake fully released, the slack is just removed from the cables.

3 Jack-up the rear road wheels and check that with the handbrake control fully released the rear wheels do not bind and that the brakes begin to be applied as the control is pulled to the 6th notch and fully applied at the 8th notch.

4 When adjustment is correct, retighten the locknuts and lower the vehicle.

24 Handbrake cables - renewal

1 To renew the primary cable, unscrew and remove the two securing screws from the handbrake control guide collar plate.

2 Rotate the handbrake control until the cable can be released by unhooking the nipple on the end of the cable from its notch.

3 Unscrew the cable pinch bolt at the relay lever and pull out the cable from the drilled bolt.

4 Release the cable from the idler pulley and then extract the inner cable from its outer conduit (photo).

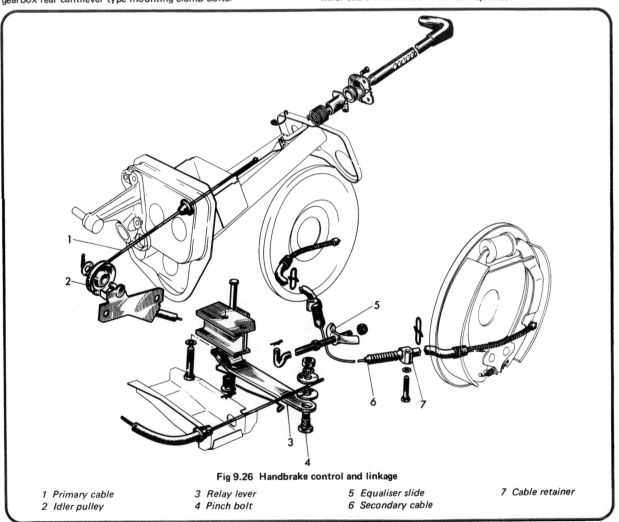

Fig 9.26 Handbrake control and linkage

1 Primary cable
2 Idler pulley
3 Relay lever
4 Pinch bolt
5 Equaliser slide
6 Secondary cable
7 Cable retainer

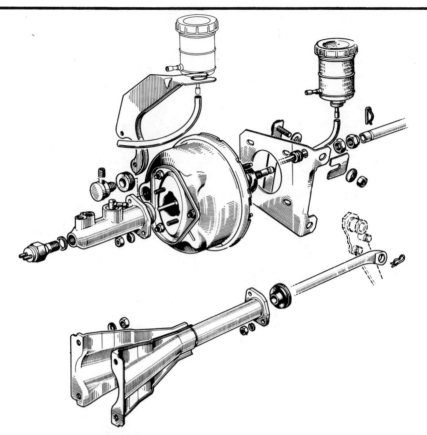

Fig 9.27 Vacuum servo unit with direct mounted type master cylinder

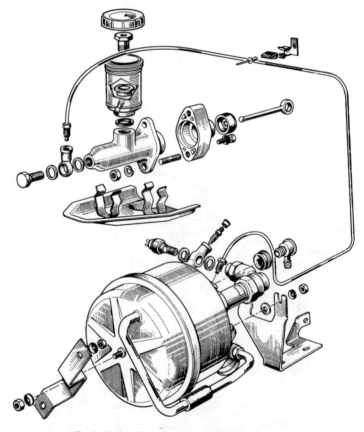

Fig 9.28 Remotely located vacuum servo unit

5 Installation of the new cable is a reversal of removal but only tighten the pinch bolt on the relay lever when the slack has just been removed from the primary and secondary cables.

6 The secondary cable may be removed by detaching the ends of the cables from the rear shoe operating levers and from the brake backplates.

7 Unbolt the cable retainers from the body side members and then prise open the lips of the equaliser slide, until the cable can be slid out.

8 Slide the cable from the body retaining clips and withdraw the complete secondary cable assembly. Refitting is a reversal of removal but move the equaliser slide to the end of the threaded pull rod before engaging the cable in it and finally adjust the handbrake as described in Section 23.

25 Vacuum servo unit - description and operation

1 The vacuum servo unit fitted to 1301 or 1501 models differs according to date of vehicle manufacture and the operating territory for which the car was destined.

2 The 'Master-Vac' unit is located between the brake pedal and the master cylinder and is operated by a very long pushrod.

3 The alternative unit is located remotely and is connected by means of a fluid line to a conventionally mounted master cylinder on the engine compartment bulkhead bracket.

4 The vacuum servo unit only assists in reducing the braking effort required and in the event of failure, it in no way affects the efficiency of the basic hydraulic system although of course higher foot pressures would be required.

5 The unit operates by vacuum obtained from the induction manifold and comprises basically a booster diaphragm and non-return valve.

6 In the 'Master-Vac' type unit, the servo unit and hydraulic master cylinder are connected together so that the servo unit piston rod acts as the master cylinder pushrod. The driver's braking effort is transmitted through another pushrod to the servo unit piston and its built in control system. The servo unit piston does not fit tightly into the cylinder, but has a strong diaphragm to keep its edges in constant contact with the cylinder wall, so assuring an air tight seal between the two parts. The forward chamber is held under vacuum conditions created in the inlet manifold of the engine and, during periods when the brake pedal is not in use, the controls open a passage to the rear chamber so placing it under vacuum conditions as well. When the brake pedal is depressed, the vacuum passage to the rear chamber is cut off and the chamber opened to atmospheric pressure. The consequent rush of air pushes the servo piston forward in the vacuum chamber and operates the main pushrod to the master cylinder.

7 With the alternative type remotely sited servo unit, the pressure from the primary master cylinder is relayed to a secondary cylinder located at the rear of the unit but the operating principle is similar.

8 The controls are designed so that assistance is given under all conditions and, when the brakes are not required vacuum in the rear chamber is established when the brake pedal is released. All air from the atmosphere entering the rear chamber is passed through a small air filter.

9 Under normal operating conditions the vacuum servo unit is very reliable and does not require overhaul except at very high mileages. In this case it is far better to obtain a service exchange unit, rather than repair the original unit.

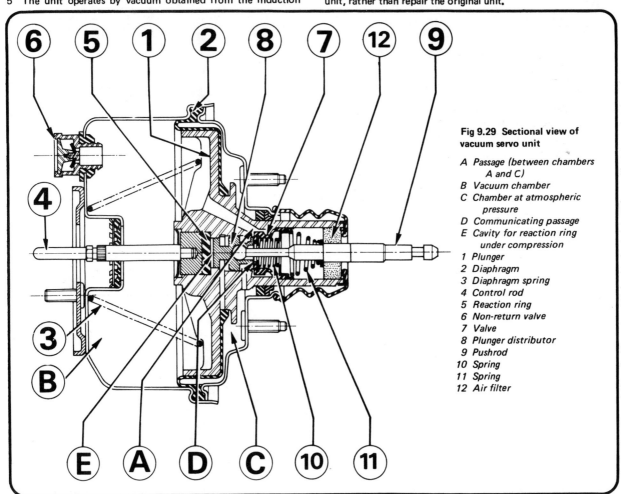

Fig 9.29 Sectional view of vacuum servo unit

A Passage (between chambers A and C)
B Vacuum chamber
C Chamber at atmospheric pressure
D Communicating passage
E Cavity for reaction ring under compression
1 Plunger
2 Diaphragm
3 Diaphragm spring
4 Control rod
5 Reaction ring
6 Non-return valve
7 Valve
8 Plunger distributor
9 Pushrod
10 Spring
11 Spring
12 Air filter

Fig 9.30 Removing direct mounted type master cylinder from servo unit

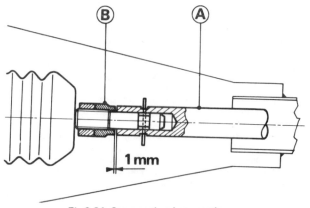

Fig 9.31 Servo pushrod connection

A Pushrod   B Adjuster and locknut

1mm

Fig 9.33 Adjusting servo pushrod nuts

Fig 9.32 Removing a vacuum servo unit

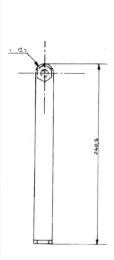
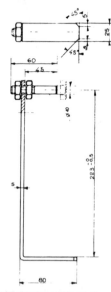

Fig 9.34 Pressure regulator/load sensitive valve guide tool diagram (dimensions in millimetres)

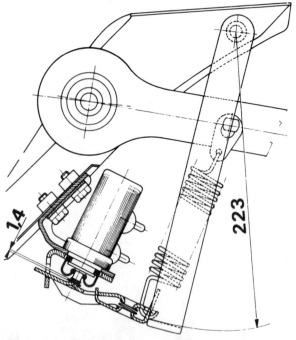

Fig 9.35 Pressure regulator/load sensitive valve adjustment diagram

26 Vacuum servo unit - removal and installation

1 On 'Master-Vac' direct acting types of unit, unscrew the nuts which secure the hydraulic master cylinder to the front face of the servo unit.

2 Pull the master cylinder forward to clear its holding studs without disconnecting the fluid lines.

3 Pull out the spring clip which secures the pedal push rod to the servo unit pushrod.

4 Pull the vacuum pipe from the nozzle on the servo unit.

5 Unscrew and remove the four nuts which hold the servo unit to its support bracket and withdraw the unit forward.

6 Installation is a reversal of removal but check and adjust if necessary the clearance between the pedal pushrod and the adjuster nuts on the servo unit pushrod. Using feeler blades, this clearance should be 0.039 in (1.0 mm) obtained by altering the position of the nut and locknut on the servo unit pushrod.

7 On alternative, remotely sited servo units, disconnect the fluid inlet and outlet pipes from the relay cylinder located at the rear of the servo unit, disconnect the leads from the brake stop lamp switch and pull off the vacuum pipe from the nozzle on the non-return valve at the rear of the unit.

8 Unbolt the complete servo/hydraulic relay unit from its supporting brackets.

27 Pressure regulator/load sensitive valve - adjustment

1 This device is installed on vehicles equipped with servo assisted brakes and is located on a body sidemember adjacent to the rear left-hand road spring (Fig. 9.38).

2 If adjustment is required, first make up a guide tool as illustrated made from a bolt and a flat metal strip (Fig. 9.34).

3 Loosen the two securing screws which retain the device in position and engage the bolt of the guide tool in the hole in the upper suspension arm support plate on the body sidemember. Move the guide tool so that its lower right-angular section is just contacting the lower loops of the two springs.

4 Move the regulator valve so that feeler blades of 0.054 in (1.4 mm) thickness can be inserted between the end face of the valve piston and the lever (Fig. 9.39).

5 Tighten the two securing screws and remove the feeler blades and the guide tool.

28 Modifications

1 Certain modifications and improvements have been carried out to brake components, the most important ones being the following:

2 Late type Teves caliper units are fitted with a small spring plate which increases the braking effort at the foot pedal as a warning that the friction pads have worn down beyond their safe limit.

3 The locknut on the pushrod of the direct acting type vacuum servo unit has been reduced in thickness to 0.023 in (6.0 mm) as the thicker one previously fitted tended to restrict the passage of air through the air filter of the servo unit (Fig. 9.40).

4 Anti-rattle springs are fitted to the disc pad retaining pins on later types of Girling calipers. The springs have washers at each end.

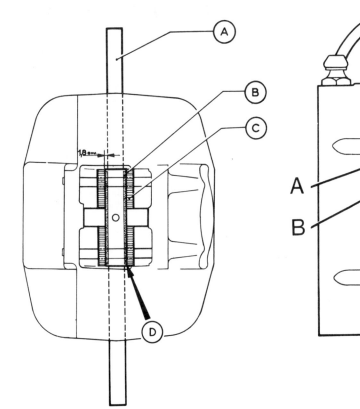

Fig 9.36 Disc pad wear warning plate (Teves type caliper)

A *Disc*
B *Friction pad*
C *Pad backing plate*
D *Sprung type warning plate*

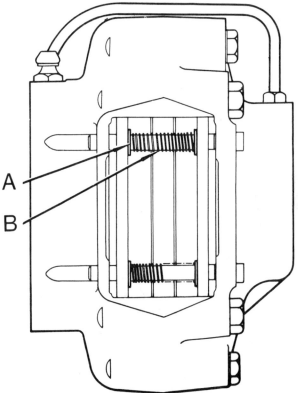

Fig 9.37 Disc pad anti-rattle springs fitted to late type Girling brakes

A *Washer*   B *Anti-rattle spring*

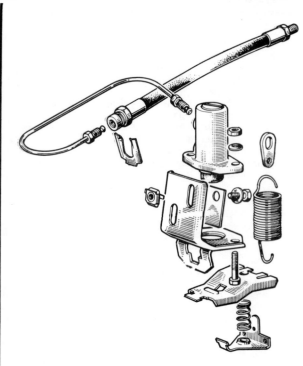

Fig 9.38 Exploded view of the pressure regulator/load sensitive valve

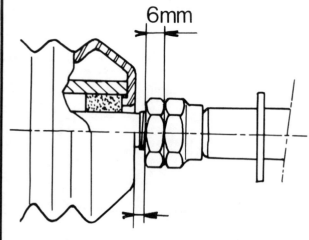

Fig 9.39 Checking the pressure regulator/load sensitive valve adjustment using feeler blades

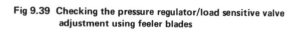

6mm

Fig 9.40 Thinner type pushrod nut on servo pushrod to prevent restriction of air filter

29 Fault diagnosis - braking system

Fault	Reason/s	Remedy
Pedal travels almost to floorboards before brakes operate	Brake fluid level too low	Top up master cylinder reservoir. Check for leaks.
	Caliper leaking	Dismantle caliper, clean, fit new rubbers and bleed brakes.
	Master cylinder leaking (bubbles in master cylinder fluid)	Dismantle master cylinder, clean and fit new rubbers. Bleed brakes.
	Brake flexible hose leaking	Examine and fit new hose if old hose leaking. Bleed brakes.
	Brake line fractured	Replace with new brake pipe. Bleed brakes.
	Brake system unions loose	Check all unions in brake system and tighten as necessary. Bleed brakes.
	Pad or shoe linings over 75% worn	Fit replacement pads or shoes.
	Brakes badly out of adjustment	Jack up car and adjust brakes.
Brake pedal feels springy	New linings not yet bedded-in	Use brakes gently until springy pedal feeling leaves.
	Brake discs or drums badly worn or cracked	Fit new brake discs or drums.
	Master cylinder securing nuts loose	Tighten master cylinder securing nuts. Ensure spring washers are fitted.
Brake pedal feels spongy and soggy	Caliper or wheel cylinder leaking	Dismantle caliper or wheel cylinder, clean, fit new rubbers and bleed brakes.
	Master cylinder leaking (bubbles in master cylinder reservoir)	Dismantle master cylinder, clean and fit new rubbers and bleed brakes. Replace cylinder if internal walls scored.
	Brake pipe line or flexible hose leaking	Fit new pipe line or hose.
	Unions in brake system loose	Examine for leaks, tighten as necessary.
Excessive effort required to brake car	Pad or shoe linings badly worn	Fit replacement brake shoes and linings.
	New pads or shoes recently fitted - not yet bedded-in	Use brakes gently until braking effort normal.
	Harder linings fitted than standard causing increase in pedal pressure	Remove pads or shoes and replace with normal units.
	Linings and brake drums contaminated with with oil, grease or hydraulic fluid	Rectify source of leak, clean brake drums, fit new linings.
	Servo unit faulty	Renew.
Brakes uneven and pulling to one side	Linings and discs or drums contaminated with oil, grease or hydraulic fluid	Ascertain and rectify source of leak, clean discs or drums, fit new pads or shoes.
	Tyre pressures unequal	Check and inflate as necessary.
	Radial ply tyres fitted at one end of the car only	Fit radial ply tyres of the same make to all four wheels.
	Brake caliper loose	Tighten backplate securing nuts and bolts.
	Brake pads or shoes fitted incorrectly	Remove and fit correct way round.
	Different type of linings fitted at each wheel	Fit the pads or shoes specified by the manufacturer all round.
	Anchorages for front suspension or rear suspension loose	Tighten front and rear suspension pick-up points including spring anchorage.
	Brake discs or drums badly worn, cracked or distorted	Fit new brake discs or drums.
Brakes tend to bind, drag or lock-on	Shoes adjusted too tightly	Slacken.
	Air in hydraulic system	Bleed system.
	Weak shoe return springs	Renew.

Chapter 10 Electrical system

Contents

Specifications

System type	12 volt negative earth
Battery	
Capacity	40 amp/hr
Alternator	
Rated voltage	14 volts
Maximum output	30 amps (430 watts)
Dynamo	
Maximum amperage	17 amps under 14 volts at 2500 rev/min
Maximum output	240 watts
Voltage regulator	
Type	3 element, contacts closed between 12.8 and 13.8 volts
Starter motor	
Type	Pre-engaged
Number of pinion teeth	9
Pinion endfloat	0.020 to 0.090 in (0.51 to 2.29 mm)
Fuses	
Rating	10 amps
Bulb ratings	
Headlamp	40/45W
Front direction indicator lamp	21W
Front parking lamp	5W
Interior lamps (front and rear)	4W (festoon)
Luggage boot lamp	4W (festoon)
Rear number plate lamp	5W
Rear stop lamp	21W
Tail lamps	5W
Rear direction indicator lamps	21W

Glove compartment lamp (1501 estate wagon) 4W

Torque wrench settings

							lb ft	kg m
Dynamo mounting bolt	...	...	...	...	...	...	35	4.8
Alternator mounting bolt	...	...	...	...	...	...	25	3.5
Starter motor bolts	...	...	...	...	...	...	16	2.2

1 General description

The electrical system is of 12 volt, negative earth type. Current is generated by a dynamo* which is belt driven from a pulley on the reverse side of the centrifugal oil filter. A voltage regulator is fitted to adjust the voltage to the battery and also to act as a cut-out to prevent the battery discharging through the dynamo when the unit is not charging.

The major units of the electrical layout may be produced by more than one manufacturer and the descriptions given in this Chapter apply to all makes, unless otherwise indicated.

Reference should be made to 'Specifications' and to the wiring diagrams for further information on the particular vehicle model circuit and components.

*_1301 and 1501 models from 1974 onwards are being fitted with either a Ducellier or Paris - Rhone alternator and the special precautions given in Section 11 must be complied with, also the servicing operations limited to those recommended._

2 Battery - removal and refitting

1 The battery is mounted on the right-hand side of the engine compartment.

2 Disconnect the two leads from the battery terminals and then unbolt the two tie bolts which secure the battery holding frame.

3 Remove the frame and lift the battery from its tray taking great care not to spill any electrolyte on the bodywork.

4 With the battery removed, take the opportunity of wire brushing any corrosion or rust from the battery tray and applying a coat of underseal or similar protective paint to it.

5 Refitting is a reversal of removal but check that the terminals are clean and the lead end fittings make a good tight connection with the terminal posts. Apply a smear of petroleum jelly to the two battery terminals to prevent corrosion.

3 Battery - maintenance and inspection

1 Keep the top of the battery clean by wiping away dirt and moisture.

2 Remove the plugs or lid from the cells and check that the electrolyte level is just above the separator plates. If the level has fallen, add only distilled water until the elctrolyte level is just above the separator plates.

3 As well as keeping the terminals clean and covered with petroleum jelly, the top of the battery should be kept clean and dry. This helps prevent corrosion and ensures that the battery does not become partially discharged by leakage through dampness and dirt.

4 Periodically, inspect the battery case for cracks. If a crack is found, clean and plug it with one of the proprietary compounds marketed by firms, such as Holts, for this purpose. If leakage through the crack has been excessive then it will be necessary to refill the appropriate cell with fresh electrolyte as detailed later. Cracks are frequently caused to the top of the battery cases by pouring in distilled water in the middle of winter _AFTER_ instead of _BEFORE_ a run. This gives the water no chance to mix with the electrolyte so the former freezes and splits the battery case.

5 If topping up the battery becomes excessive and the case has been inspected for cracks that could cause leakage, but none are found, the battery is being over-charged and the voltage regulator will have to be checked and reset (Section 12).

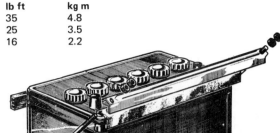

Fig 10.1 The battery and carrier

6 With the battery on the bench at the three monthly interval check, measure its specific gravity with a hydrometer to determine the state of charge and condition of the electrolyte. There should be very little variation between the different cells and if a variation in excess of 0.25 is present it will be due to either:

a) Loss of electrolyte from the battery at some time caused by spillage or a leak, resulting in a drop in the specific gravity of the electrolyte when the deficiency was replaced with distilled water instead of fresh electrolyte.

b) An internal short circuit caused by buckling of the plates or a similar malady pointing to the likelihood of total battery failure in the near future.

7 The specific gravity of the electrolyte for fully charged conditions at the electrolyte temperature indicated, is listed in Table A. The specific gravity of a fully discharged battery at different temperatures of the electrolyte is given in Table B.

TABLE A

Specific Gravity - Battery Fully Charged

1.268 at 100°F or 38°C electrolyte temperature
1.272 at 90°F or 32°C electrolyte temperature
1.276 at 80°F or 27°C electrolyte temperature
1.280 at 70°F or 21°C electrolyte temperature
1.284 at 60°F or 16°C electrolyte temperature
1.288 at 50°F or 10°C electrolyte temperature
1.292 at 40°F or   4°C electrolyte temperature
1.296 at 30°F or -1.5°C electrolyte temperature

TABLE B

Specific Gravity - Battery Fully Discharged

1.098 at 100°F or 38°C electrolyte temperature
1.102 at 90°F or 32°C electrolyte temperature
1.106 at 80°F or 27°C electrolyte temperature
1.110 at 70°F or 21°C electrolyte temperature
1.114 at 60°F or 16°C electrolyte temperature
1.118 at 50°F or 10°C electrolyte temperature
1.122 at 40°F or   4°C electrolyte temperature
1.126 at 30°F or - 1.5°C electrolyte temperature

4 Battery - electrolyte replenishment

1 If the battery is in a fully charged state and one of the cells maintains a specific gravity reading which is .025 or more lower than the others, and a check of each cell has been made with a voltage meter to check for short circuits (a four to seven second test should give a steady reading of between 1.2 to 1.8 volts), then it is likely that electrolyte has been lost from the cell with the low reading at some time.

2 Top up the cell with a solution of 1 part sulphuric acid to 2.5 parts of water. If the cell is already fully topped up draw some electrolyte out of it with a pipette. The total capacity of each cell is ¾ pint.

3 When mixing the sulphuric acid and water **never add water to sulphuric acid** - always pour the acid slowly onto the water in a glass container. **If water is added to sulphuric acid it will explode.**

4 Continue to top up the cell with the freshly made electrolyte and then recharge the battery and check the hydrometer readings.

5 Battery - charging

1 In winter time when heavy demand is placed upon the battery, such as when starting from cold, and much electrical equipment is continually in use, it is a good idea to occasionally have the battery fully charged from an external source at the rate of 3.5 or 4 amps.

2 Continue to charge the battery at this rate until no further rise in specific gravity is noted over a four hour period.

3 Alternatively, a trickle charger charging at the rate of 1.5 amps can be safely used overnight.

4 Specially rapid 'boost' charges which are claimed to restore the power of the battery in 1 to 2 hours are most dangerous as they can cause serious damage to the battery plates.

5 Where an alternator is fitted and the battery is to be charged by external means, always disconnect both leads from the battery before connecting the charger.

6 Dynamo - maintenance

1 The only regular maintenance required is to check the tension of the driving belt and adjust it if required, as described in Chapter 2.

7 Dynamo - testing in position

1 Failure of the dynamo to provide a charge may be due to a slipping or broken driving belt and this should be checked first of all.

2 Disconnect the cable which runs between the battery and the regulator unit by detaching it at the regulator end.

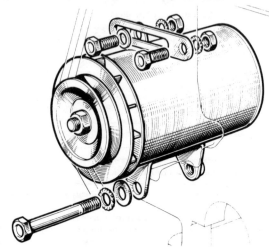

Fig 10.2 Dynamo and mounting bolts

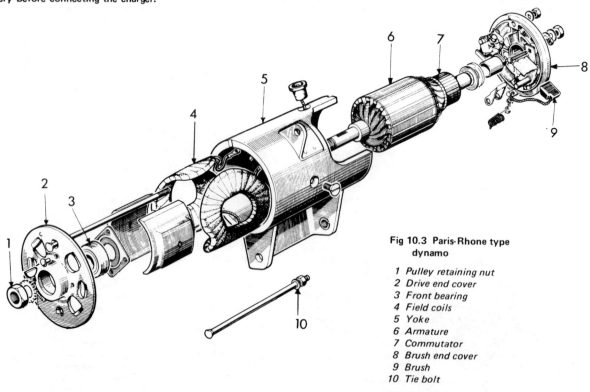

Fig 10.3 Paris-Rhone type
          dynamo

1 Pulley retaining nut
2 Drive end cover
3 Front bearing
4 Field coils
5 Yoke
6 Armature
7 Commutator
8 Brush end cover
9 Brush
10 Tie bolt

3 Connect a moving coil ammeter between the regulator terminal and the end of the cable just disconnected.
4 Start the engine and then open the throttle and observe whether the dynamo output increases progressively.
5 If the dynamo is proved to be in order, then the fault must lie in the voltage regulator and this should be renewed but first check that all leads are securely and correctly connected.
6 If the dynamo is not producing a charging current then it must be removed and serviced as described in later Sections of this Chapter.

8 Dynamo - removing and refitting

1 Identify and then remove the leads from the rear of the dynamo.
2 Unscrew and remove the bolts from the slotted adjuster strap and then slacken the mounting bolts.
3 Push the dynamo in towards the engine so that the driving belt can be slipped off the pulley.
4 Remove the mounting bolts and lift the dynamo from its location.
5 Refitting is a reversal of removal but adjust the driving belt tension as described in Chapter 2.

9 Dynamo - dismantling, servicing, reassembly

1 Unscrew the pulley securing nut and remove the lockwasher and Woodruff key. Do not grip the pulley in a vice for this operation but use an old driving belt engaged in the pulley groove and grip the two ends of the belt as close to the pulley as possible in a vice. This will hold the pulley quite still without damaging it while the nut is unscrewed.
2 Unscrew and remove the two tie bolts and then remove the drive-end cover.
3 Push the armature and brush end cover from the dynamo casing taking great care not to damage the field coils.

4 Lift the brushes against the tension of their springs and pull the brushes from their holders.
5 If the brushes are worn down to 3/8 in (9.5 mm) then they must be renewed by removing the leads.
6 If the brushes are little worn and are to be used again then ensure that they are placed in the same holders from which they were removed. When refitting brushes, either new or old, check that they move freely in their holders. If either brush sticks, clean with a petrol moistened rag and, if still stiff, lightly polish the sides of the brush with a very fine file until the brush moves quite freely in its holders.
7 Inspect the condition of the commutator. If it is blackened or burned, clean it initially with a fuel soaked rag. If necessary, polish it with a strip of glass paper (never emery cloth).
   In extreme cases of wear the commutator can be mounted in a lathe and with the lathe turning at high speed, a very fine cut may be taken off the commutator. Then polish the commutator with glass paper. If the commutator has worn so that the insulators between the segments are level with the top of the segments, then undercut the insulator to a depth of 1/32 in. (0.8 mm). The best tool to use for this purpose is half a hacksaw blade ground to a thickness of the insulator, and with the handle end of the blade covered in insulating tape to make it comfortable to hold.
8 Check the resistance of the field coils. To do this, connect an ohmmeter between the field terminal and the yoke and note the reading on the ohmmeter which should be about 6 ohms. If the ohmmeter reading is infinity this indicates an open circuit in the field winding; If the ohmmeter reading is below 5 ohms this indicates that one of the field coils is faulty.
9 In the event of the field coils being faulty or the front or rear armature shaft bearings being worn it is recommended that the dynamo be exchanged for a factory reconditioned unit.
10 Reassembly is a reversal of dismantling but apply a smear of high melting point grease to the front and rear bearings before installing the armature. The brushes must be raised in their holders so that the commutator can pass between their contact faces.

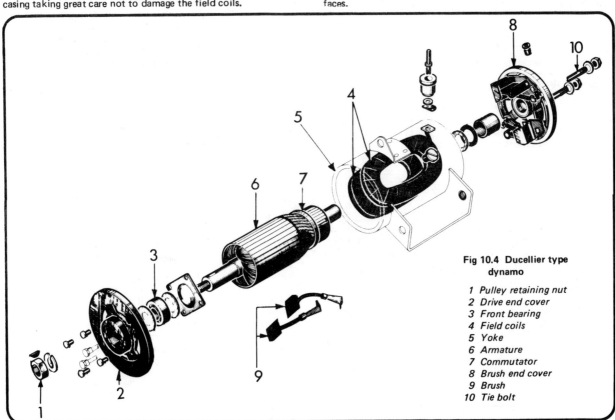

Fig 10.4 Ducellier type dynamo

1 Pulley retaining nut
2 Drive end cover
3 Front bearing
4 Field coils
5 Yoke
6 Armature
7 Commutator
8 Brush end cover
9 Brush
10 Tie bolt

10 Voltage regulator and cut-out

1 This is a sealed unit of Ducellier or Paris - Rhone manufacture.
2 It is mounted within the engine compartment and apart from checking the security of the connecting leads, no servicing or adjustment can be carried out.
3 Irregularities in the dynamo charging circuit due to malfunction of the regulator control box (see Section 7) should be checked out by a competent auto-electrician and a new unit installed if necessary.

11 Alternator - general description and precautions

1 This type of generator is installed on all later models (1974 onwards).
2 The virtue of this type of unit is that it can provide a charging current with the engine at idling speed.
3 Apart from keeping the external surfaces free from dirt and oil, and the driving belt correctly tensioned, no maintenance is required.
4 No lubrication is required as the bearings are grease sealed for life.
5 Take extreme care when making circuit connections to a vehicle fitted with an alternator and observe the following. When making connections to the alternator from a battery always match correct polarity. Before using electric-arc welding equipment to repair any part of the vehicle, disconnect the connector from the alternator and disconnect the positive battery terminal. Never start the car with a battery charger connected. Always disconnect both battery leads before using a main charger. If boosting from another battery, always connect in parallel using heavy cable. It is not recommended that testing of an alternator should be undertaken at home due to the testing equipment required and the possibility of damage occurring during testing. It is best left to automotive electrical specialists.

12 Alternator - removal and refitting

1 Loosen the alternator mounting bracket bolts and strap, push the unit towards the engine block sufficiently far to enable the fan belt to be slipped off the alternator pulley.
2 Remove the cable connectors from the alternator and withdraw the mounting bracket bolts. Lift away the alternator.
3 Replacement is a reversal of removal procedure but ensure that the connections are correctly made and that the fan belt is adjusted as described in Chapter 2.

13 Alternator (Ducellier) - servicing

1 Unscrew and remove the two screws (1) (Fig 10.7) which secure the brush holder (2) to the alternator rear casing and extract the brush holder.
2 Withdraw the earth brush from its holder.
3 Withdraw the second brush after removal of the securing screw.
4 Clean the brushes and brush holder with a rag soaked in clean fuel and check that they slide easily in their holders.
5 If the brushes are well worn, they should be renewed.
6 This should be the limit of servicing. If the rotor or stator are damaged or the front or rear bearings are worn then it is quite uneconomical to consider a repair even if the individual components were obtainable and it is recommended that a factory reconditioned unit is obtained.
7 Refitting of the brushes and brush holder is a reversal of removal.

Fig 10.5 The voltage regulator

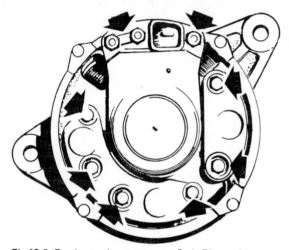

Fig 10.6 Brush securing screws on a Paris-Rhone alternator

14 Alternator (Paris - Rhone) - servicing

1 The servicing procedure is similar to that described in the preceding Section. The method of securing the brush holder should be noted. (Fig 10.6)

15 Starter motor - general description

1 The starter motor is of pre-engaged type and may be one of several different models manufactured by Ducellier or Paris - Rhone. There are detail differences in construction but operational principle and servicing procedures are similar.
2 This type of starter motor incorporates a solenoid mounted on top of the starter motor body. When the ignition switch is operated, the solenoid moves the starter drive pinion, through the medium of the shift lever, into engagement with the flywheel starter ring gear. As the solenoid reaches the end of its stroke, and with the pinion by now fully engaged with the flywheel ring gear, the fixed and moving contacts close and engage the starter motor to rotate the engine. This fractional pre-engagement of the starter drive does much to reduce the wear on the flywheel ring gear associated with inertia type starter motors.
3 On vehicles fitted with automatic transmission, only starter motors of Paris - Rhone make one fitted as there is a risk of the pinion freewheel fouling the torque convertor.

   On all manual gearbox vehicles, both makes of starter motor may be fitted and they are interchangeable.

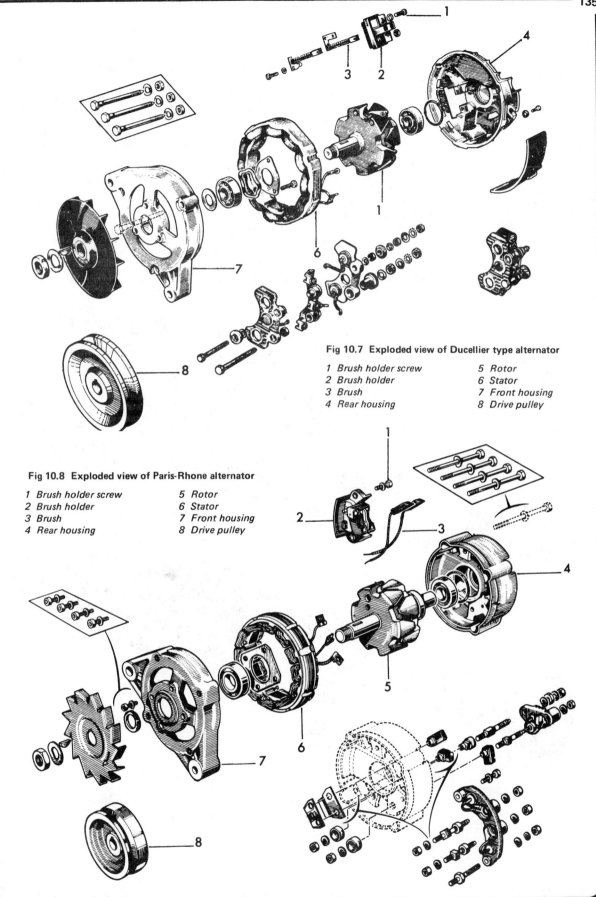

Fig 10.7 Exploded view of Ducellier type alternator

1 Brush holder screw	5 Rotor
2 Brush holder	6 Stator
3 Brush	7 Front housing
4 Rear housing	8 Drive pulley

Fig 10.8 Exploded view of Paris-Rhone alternator

1 Brush holder screw	5 Rotor
2 Brush holder	6 Stator
3 Brush	7 Front housing
4 Rear housing	8 Drive pulley

16 Starter motor - testing in vehicle

1 If unsatisfactory operation of the starter motor is experienced, check that the battery connections and the engine/transmission earth strap are secure and that the battery is charged.

2 Check the security of the cables at the terminals on the starter motor solenoid and the leads at the combined ignition/starter switch.

3 Disconnect the LT lead from the distributor to prevent the engine from firing and then connect a 0-20 voltmeter between the starter terminal and earth. Operate the starter switch and with the engine rotating, note the reading. A minimum indicated voltage of 4.5 volts proves that the cable and switch connections are satisfactory but if the motor turns only very slowly at this voltage, a fault in the starter motor is indicated.

4 Connect the voltmeter between the battery and the starter motor terminal and with the starter motor actuated, the voltage drop should not exceed more than 6 volts. If this figure is exceeded, excessive resistance in the starting circuit is indicated.

17 Starter motor - removal and refitting

1 Disconnect the negative lead from the battery.

2 Disconnect the leads from the terminals on the starter motor solenoid.

3 Unscrew and remove the bolts which secure the starter to the front face of the clutch (or torque converter - automatic transmission) bellhousing.

4 Withdraw the starter motor forward until the drive pinion clears the edges of the aperture and then lift it from the engine compartment.

5 Refitting is a reversal of removal.

18 Starter motor - dismantling, servicing, reassembly

1 Remove the end-cover.

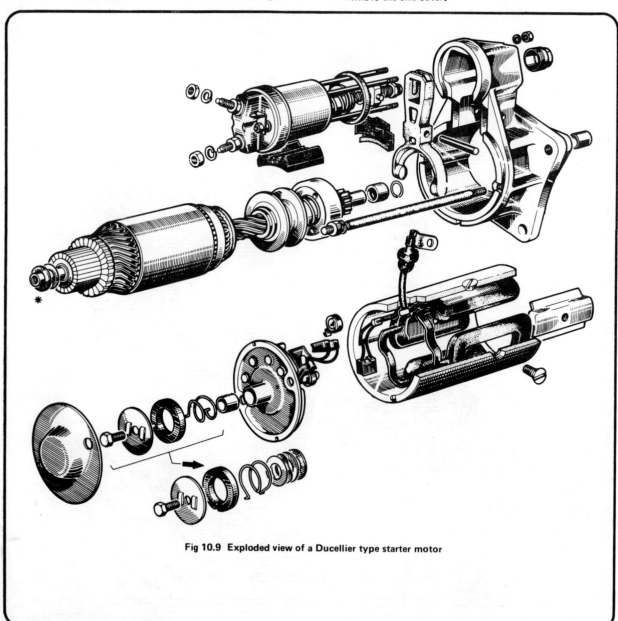

Fig 10.9 Exploded view of a Ducellier type starter motor

2 Unscrew and remove the end-bolt from the armature shaft and then withdraw the various shaft-end components and the brush holders and plate. On some earlier types of starter motor a cover band is incorporated for access to the brush gear.

3 Unscrew the nuts from the two tie bolts and draw off the body.

4 Remove the circlips from the engagement fork pivot pin and tap out the pin.

5 Withdraw the armature and disengage the fork from the pinion drive assembly.

6 The pinion drive assembly may be dismantled by driving the end collar down the armature shaft to expose the circlip which should then be removed from its groove.

7 Further dismantling should not be undertaken. Where the field coils or bearings require attention, it will be more economical to exchange the unit for a factory reconditioned one. Special tools are needed to release the pole screws and to remove and install new bearings.

19 Starter motor drive endfloat - checking and adjusting

1 Disconnect the field coil wire from the terminal on the starter solenoid.

2 Energise the solenoid by connecting a temporary lead between it and the battery (+) terminal. This will cause the pinion drive assembly to move forward into its engaged position. Press the pinion with the fingers to take up any endfloat and then using feeler blades, check the clearance between the end of the pinion and the face of the thrust collar. The clearance should be between 0.020 and 0.090 in (0.51 and 2.29 mm). If the clearance is incorrect, turn the adjuster nut which is located where the solenoid operating rod passes through the engagement fork.

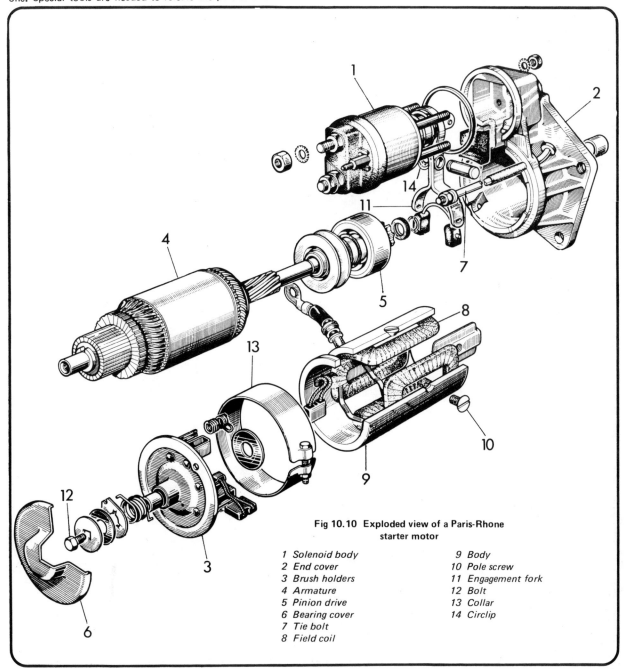

Fig 10.10 Exploded view of a Paris-Rhone
starter motor

1 Solenoid body
2 End cover
3 Brush holders
4 Armature
5 Pinion drive
6 Bearing cover
7 Tie bolt
8 Field coil
9 Body
10 Pole screw
11 Engagement fork
12 Bolt
13 Collar
14 Circlip

20 Flasher circuit - fault tracing and rectification

1   The flasher unit is a sealed container (either circular or square according to date of manufacture) located on the left-hand panel within the engine compartment. A relay which incorporates a 5 amp fuse is adjacent to the flasher unit.
2   Failure of the direction indicators may be due to a blown fuse; check this first, also the security of the connecting cables.
3   Bulb failure can be diagnosed if the flasher operating frequency is doubled compared with the speed of normal operation.
4   With the ignition switched on check that current is reaching the flasher stud by connecting a voltmeter between the '+' terminal of the unit and earth. If current is reaching the unit, bridge the other two terminals (MARKED COM and REP) and operate the direction indicator switch, still with the ignition switched on. If the flasher lamps light up at the front and rear of the vehicle (on the relevant side according to switch position) then the flasher unit itself is faulty.
5   If the lamps do not light up, check that current is reaching the COM terminal (use a test bulb) and if it is, then the direction indicator switch itself is faulty, or the relay or fuse may have failed.

21 Fuses

1   The fuse box is located on the left-hand side of the engine compartment rear bulkhead.
2   According to vehicle model and date of manufacture it may contain three or four fuses, each of 10 amp rating. (photo)
3   The three fuse type of unit protects the following circuits:
   1) wiper motor, heater motor, brake warning lamps, facia warning lamps.
   2) horn and interior light.
   3) instrument illumination, parking lamps, rear number plates lamp.

4   The four fuse type of unit protects the following circuits:
   1   (green wire) parking lamps, rear number plate, instrument illumination.
   2   (grey wire) windscreen wipers, heater motor, brake warning lamps, flasher unit, windscreen washer.
   3   (red/white wire) interior lamp, electric clock, glove compartment lamp, luggage boot lamp.
   4   (red/black wire) cigar lighter.
5   Where a heated rear window is fitted, a fusible link (10 amp) is located near the heated relay on the left-hand panel within the engine compartment.
6   Additional fuses are incorporated for the protection of head and rear lamps on some vehicles destined for operation in certain overseas territories.
7   Never renew a blown fuse more than once before identifying the source of the trouble. Always renew a fuse with one of similar rating. *never use a substitute such as a piece of wire or foil.*

22 Windscreen wiper blades and arms - removal and refitting

1   Before removing a wiper arm, turn the windscreen wiper switch on and off to ensure that the arms are in their correct 'parked' position, parallel with the bottom of the screen.
2   To remove a wiper blade, depress the 'pip' which projects through the hole in the hinged shank of the wiper blade and pull the blade from the arm. (photo)
3   To remove an arm, first pivot it away from the screen and using a small screwdriver, prise aside the small locking tongue from behind the splined driveshaft. Pull the arm from the splines of the driveshaft. (photo)
4   When refitting an arm, position it on the splines so that it is in its parked position and then press the arm home so that it is fully engaged on the driveshaft.
5   Renew the wiper blade inserts every 12000 miles (19000 km) or annually or whenever the wipers cease to wipe the glass effectively.

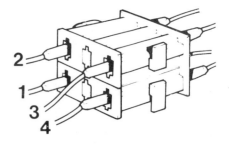

Fig 10.12 Four fuse unit (for key to circuits see text)

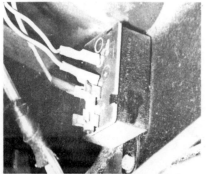

Fig 10.11 Flasher relay and fuse (right)

21.2 Three fuse unit

22.2 Removing a windscreen wiper blade

22.3 Removing a windscreen wiper arm

23 Windscreen wiper mechanism - fault diagnosis and rectification

1   Should the windscreen wipers fail, or work very slowly, then check the terminals on the motor for loss connections and make sure the insulation of all wiring has not been damaged thus causing a short circuit. If this is in order then check the current the motor is taking by connecting an ammeter in the circuit and turning on the wiper switch. Consumption should be between 2.3 and 3.1 amps.
2   If no current is passing through the motor, check that the switch is operating correctly.
3   If the wiper motor takes a very high current check the wiper blades for freedom of movement. If this is satisfactory check the gearbox cover and gear assembly for damage.
4   If the motor takes a very low current ensure that the battery is fully charged. Check the brush gear and ensure the brushes are bearing on the commutator. If not, check the brushes for freedom of movement and, if necessary, renew the tension springs. If the brushes are very worn they should be replaced with new ones. Check the armature by substitution if this part is suspect.

24 Windscreen wiper motor and linkage - removal and installation

1   One of two makes of wiper motor may be encountered, 'Bosch' or 'Marchal'. Both are of similar construction but vary in detail.
2   Within the engine compartment, disconnect the link from the crank of the wiper motor. (photo)

3   Unscrew the three mounting nuts and withdraw the wiper motor from below the facia panel. Disconnect the leads at the snap connectors.
4   The linkage may be removed after withdrawing the wiper arms and blades (Section 22) and unscrewing and removing the nuts from the splined driveshaft housings.
5   Installation is a reversal of removal but if the wiper blade arc of travel is incorrect or any new linkage components have been fitted, adjust the primary link by loosening the locknuts or pinch

24.2 Wiper motor crank and linkage

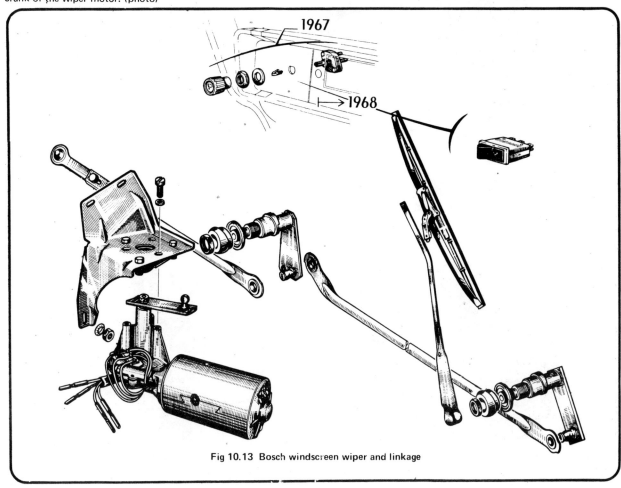

Fig 10.13 Bosch windscreen wiper and linkage

bolt according to type.

6 Any servicing of the motor should be limited to the operations described in the preceding Section otherwise the motor should be exchanged for a factory reconditioned unit.

25 Electrically operated windscreen washer

1 Fitted to later models, this device is controlled by a foot operated, three position switch to provide (i) off (ii) wipers on (iii) wipers and washers.

2 The floor mounted control is supplementary to the facia mounted wiper motor (two speed) switch which is for use in conditions of continuous rain.

3 The reservoir is located within the engine compartment and in the event of failure, check the leads and the hose connections for security otherwise the washer pump unit must be renewed as an assembly.

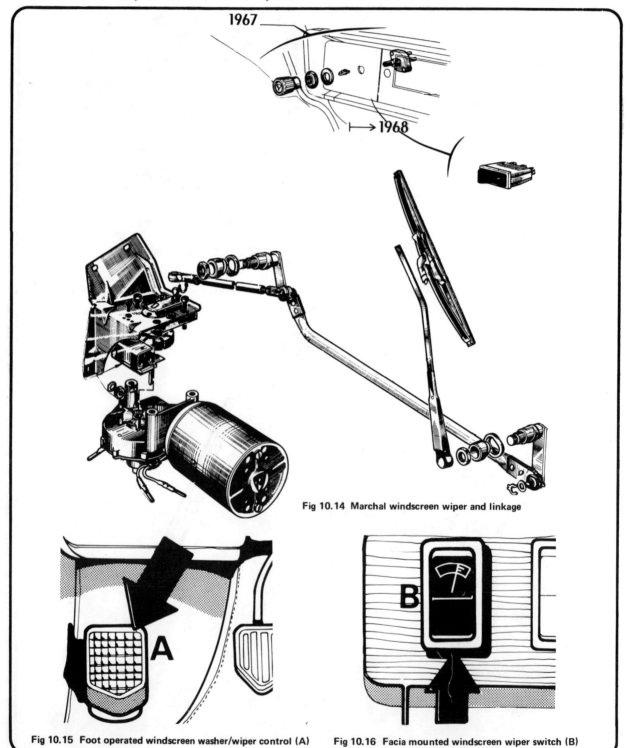

Fig 10.14 Marchal windscreen wiper and linkage

Fig 10.15 Foot operated windscreen washer/wiper control (A)   Fig 10.16 Facia mounted windscreen wiper switch (B)

26 Horns - description, fault tracing and rectification

1 According to model and date of manufacture, either a single or twin horn or air horns may be fitted. Actuation may be by central steering wheel button, horn ring or stalk type control.

2 Failure of a horn to sound may be due to broken, loose or disconnected leads or the horn mounting bolts having worked loose. Tighten and reconnect as appropriate.

3 A continuously sounding horn will probably be due to breakage of the coil spring in the steering wheel boss. Remove the steering wheel name plate and boss cover plate and renew as appropriate.

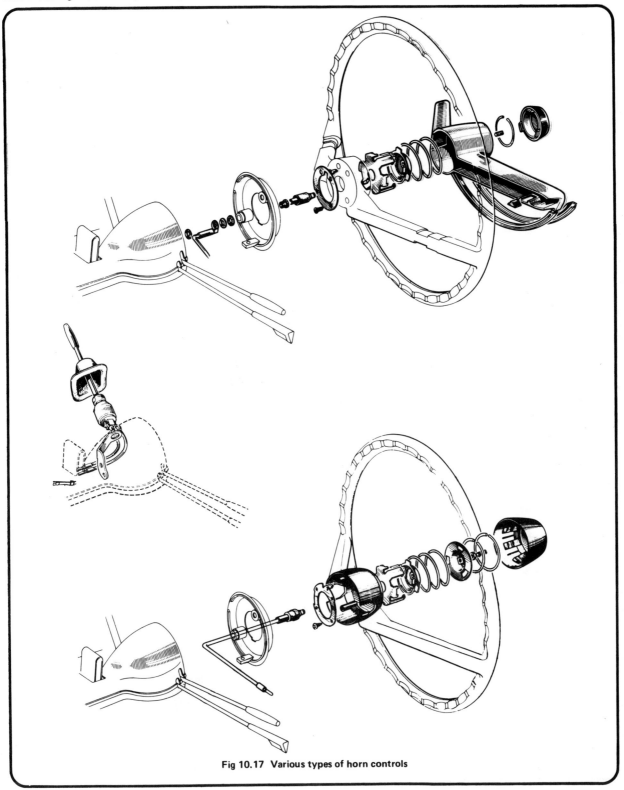

Fig 10.17 Various types of horn controls

27 Headlamp - bulb renewal

1 Insert a screwdriver at the bottom of the headlamp bezel. Lever the bezel upwards so that it disengages from the retaining tongue at its top edge. (photo)
2 A plastic ring or clip (Marchal or Cibie) will now be exposed. Pull on this while still holding the lamp unit in position. The lamp unit will now be released and can be removed from its housing. (photo)
3 On Ducellier type headlamps, after the bezel is removed, turn the lamp unit in an anti-clockwise direction to release it from the rim mounting screws.
4 Press the bulb holder retaining springs aside. (photo)
5 Withdraw the bulb holder. (photo)
6 Renew the bulb with one of the specified type and wattage.
7 Refitting is a reversal of removal.

28 Headlamp - alignment

1 It is recommended that the headlamps are aligned on optical beam setting equipment at a service station but where this is not convenient, the following procedure should be used.
2 Position the vehicle on level ground square onto a wall or screen, on which are marked the lines as shown in Fig. 10.21).
3 Check that the tyres are correctly inflated and the vehicle loaded with the equivalent of four passengers and 110 lb (50 kg) of luggage in the boot.
4 Mask each headlamp in turn and adjust each lamp unit until in the main beam position, the area of brightest illumination is concentrated at the intersection of the vertical and horizontal lines which were made on the wall.
5 In the dipped position, the measurement 'Z' must be reduced by 3 5/16 in (84.14 mm).

29 Front lamp cluster - bulb renewal

1 The lens of the front lamp cluster is secured by two screws and they should be removed to provide access to the parking lamp and direction indicator bulbs. (photo)
2 Always fit bulbs of the specified type and wattage.

30 Rear lamp cluster - bulb renewal

1 The rear lamp cluster incorporates the direction indicator, brake stop lamp, tail lamp and reversing lamp (where fitted) bulbs.
2 Access to the bulbs is obtained after removing the lens and lens securing screws. (photo)
3 Always fit bulbs of the specified type and wattage.

31 Rear number plate lamp - bulb renewal

1 Access to the rear number plate lamp is obtained by unscrewing and removing the two screws which attach the lens and body to the rear bumper. (photo)
2 Always fit a bulb of the specified type and wattage.

32 Interior lamps - bulb renewal

1 Access to the festoon type bulb in the front interior lamp is obtained after removal of the combined cover and lens (two screws)
2 The cover can be removed from the rear interior lamp by prising aside the two plastic securing tabs.

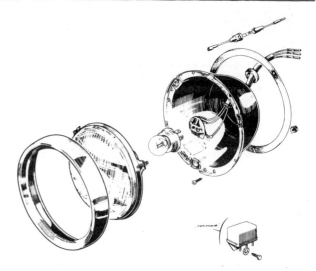

Fig 10.18 Ducellier type headlamp unit

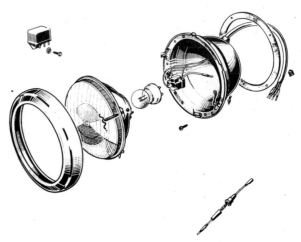

Fig 10.19 Cibie type headlamp unit

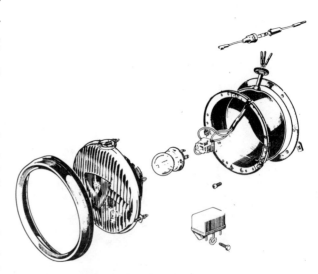

Fig 10.20 Marchal type headlamp unit

27.1 Removing a headlamp bezel

27.2 Removing a headlamp unit securing clip

27.4 Removing a bulb holder spring clip

27.5 The bulb and holder released from the headlamp unit

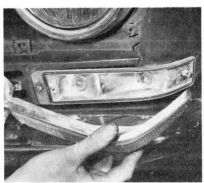

29.1 Removing a front lamp cluster lens

30.2 Removing a rear lamp cluster lens

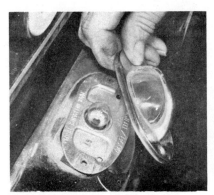

31.1 Removing the cover from the rear number plate lamp

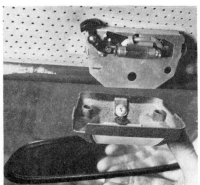

32.1 Removing the lens and cover from the interior lamp

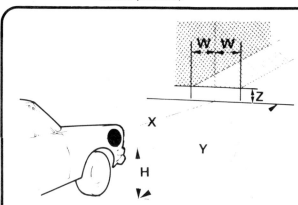

Fig 10.21 Headlamp alignment diagram

$W = 23^{5}/8$ in (0.60 m)
$Y = 32.8$ ft (10 m)
H = Distance between lowest point of headlamp and ground
Z = H with headlamp in main beam position or H minus $3^{5}/16$ in
 (84.14 mm) with headlamp in dipped position

33 Instruments - removal and refitting

1   The design of the instruments and instrument panel has undergone several changes over the years of production of this range of SIMCA vehicles

2   The earliest single dial instrument is removable after withdrawing the two screws which secure the anti-reflection hood and bezel.

3   Pull the instrument forward until the speedometer cable can be disconnected from the speedometer head and all the wires and leads removed after marking them for correct reconnection.

4   Later type instrumentation is withdrawn in the following manner.

5   Disconnect the lead from the battery negative terminal.

6   Remove the pad from the top of the instrument panel.

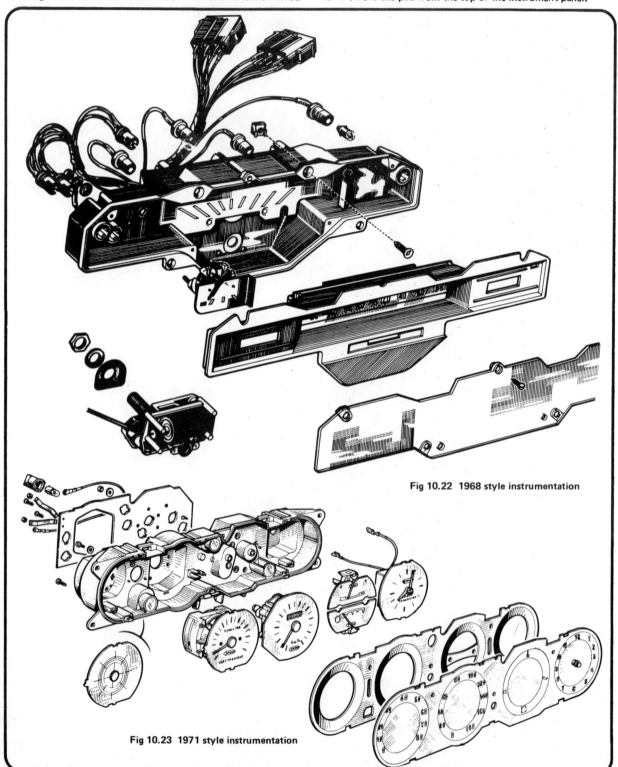

Fig 10.22 1968 style instrumentation

Fig 10.23 1971 style instrumentation

Fig 10.24 Removing the facia top panel

Fig 10.25 Instrument panel securing screws

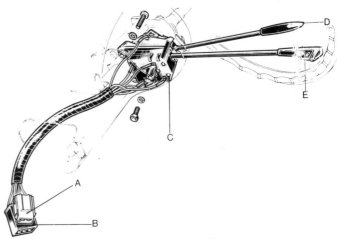

Fig 10.26 Steering column controls

A and B Harness connecting plugs
D Direction indicator
E Lighting switch

7 Remove the windscreen wiper switch control knob and lock-nut.

8 Remove the panel light rheostat switch knob and speedometer trip recorder knob.

9 Withdraw the securing screws from the instrument panel embellishment plate and remove the plate upwards from the lower pad.

10 Unscrew the four panel securing screws now exposed, and pull the panel far enough forward to enable the speedometer cable to be disconnected from the speedometer head and the electrical plugs to be disconnected; also the bulb holders to be withdrawn from the rear of the instrument panel casing.

11 The individual instruments can now be removed from the panel casing.

12 Refitting is a reversal of removal.

13 Removal and refitting of later type circular instruments is carried out in a similar manner. The bulbs of all warning, indicator and illumination lamps can be renewed by withdrawing the holders from the rear of the panels.

34 Combination switch (lighting/direction indicator) - removal and refitting

1 The lower 'stalk' on the steering column is the lighting switch and the upper one is the direction indicator control.

2 To remove the switch, the steering wheel and upper bearing bracket must be removed as described in the next Chapter.

3 Disconnect the two junction boxes 'A' and 'B' (Fig. 10.26).

4 Remove the single crosshead screw from the top of the switch and the bolt from the lower surface and lift the switch from its location.

5 Refitting is a reversal of removal but if the direction indicator cancelling ring has be withdrawn, refit it so that its tongue locates in the groove in the steering shaft.

35 Combined ignition/starter switch - testing, removal, refitting

1 The ignition switch on all models incorporates a starter position but some later models also include a steering lock arrangement.

2 To test the combined ignition/starter switch (without steering lock) note the colours and locations of the connecting leads and then detach them from their terminals.

3 Connect a battery and bulb in series with the switch, check that current flows through the switch from the red lead terminal to the grey lead terminal when the ignition switch is turned on; and from red to grey/black lead terminals when the engine start

position is selected. When the switch is in the off or 'lock' position no current should pass from any terminal to another. should pass from any terminal to another.

4 If the ignition switch proves to be faulty, remove the switch after disconnecting the terminals on the battery, and the leads to column support and remove the switch. Note that if the switch incorporates a steering lock, the switch cannot be removed unless the lock is disengaged.

5 Refitting the switch is a reversal of removal.

6 The steering lock can only be removed after drilling out the sheared retaining bolt.

36 Auxiliary lamps - guide to installation

1 The following information is presented as a guide to those contemplating the installation of fog, spot or auxiliary driving lamps.

2 Select the lamps after having assessed the available depth in front of the radiator grille and bearing in mind that the lamp lenses should be behind the leading edge of the front bumper as

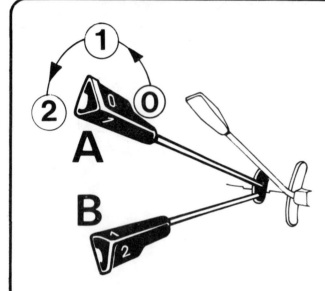

Fig 10.27 Steering column lighting switch operating diagram

O showing indicates lights out
1 showing and lever in position A — parking lamps
1 showing and lever in position B — dipped headlamps
2 showing and lever in position A — dipped headlamps
2 showing and lever in position B — main headlamp beams

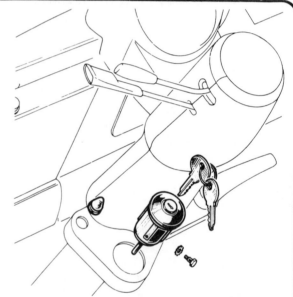

Fig 10.28 Ignition/starter switch

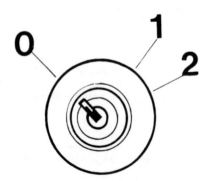

Fig 10.29 Key positions of ignition/starter switch

0 Ignition off
1 Ignition on
2 Starter motor energised

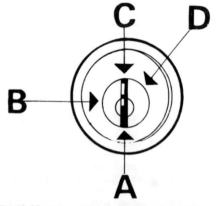

Fig 10.30 Key positions of ignition/starter/steering lock

A Ignition off and steering locked, key removable
B Ignition off, steering unlocked, key removable
C Ignition on, key cannot be removed
D Starter position, key springs back to position C when released

a protective measure.

3 Decide on the fitting position and have brackets made to ensure that the new lamps will not mask the existing ones. In accordance with UK regulations, two lamps must be fitted with their centres at least 24 inches but not more than 42 inches from the ground and at least 14 inches apart. Where these mounting conditions are not complied with, then the lamps can only be used in fog or falling snow. A single lamp is not permitted unless it is used in conjunction with a pair of headlamps or auxiliary lamps.

4 Always wire the new lamps into a fused circuit.

37 Radio - guide to installation

1 It is recommended that the receiver is installed in or below the facia panel in the position designed for it by the vehicle manufacturers.

2 If it is decided to depart from the recommended location, check that the radio will not present a source of danger in the event of the passenger being thrown forward during heavy braking.

3 Always use a fused link in the supply cable and ensure that the radio is correctly wired for a negative earth vehicle.

For 'Fault diagnosis' see next page.

4 A variety of aerials are available and the mounting position is normally on the right-hand wing just forward of the windscreen although other positions will provide satisfactory results. Always position the aerial as far away from the distributor as possible.

5 The ignition system being fully suppressed should not interfere with reception but the dynamo and windscreen wiper motor may require suppressing to overcome the result of sparking at the commutator, particularly if the units are worn.

38 Fuel gauge and transmitter unit

1 If the fuel gauge does not register, check that the fuel tank is not empty. Check the cable between the transmitter unit and the gauge to ensure that the connections are secure and that faulty insulation is not causing the cable to earth.

2 Check that the fuel gauge case is not earthing out.

3 Where the fuel gauge registers full all the time, then almost certainly, the cable between the transmitter unit and the gauge has broken or become disconnected.

4 The transmitter unit and float assembly may be removed from the fuel tank after removing the two leads and the two securing bolts from the unit which is located on the top face of the tank.

39 Fault diagnosis - electrical system

Symptom	Reason/s	Remedy
Starter motor fails to turn engine	Battery discharged	Charge battery.
	Battery defective internally	Fit new battery.
	Battery terminal leads loose or earth lead not securely attached to body	Check and tighten leads.
	Loose or broken connections in starter motor circuit	Check all connections and tighten any that are loose.
	Starter motor switch or solenoid faulty	Test and replace faulty components with new.
	Starter brushes badly worn, sticking, or brush wires loose	Examine brushes, replace as necessary, tighten down brush wires.
	Commutator dirty, worn or burnt	Clean commutator, recut if badly burnt.
	Starter motor armature faulty	Overhaul starter motor, fit new armature.
	Field coils earthed	Overhaul starter motor.
Starter motor turns engine very slowly	Battery in discharged condition	Charge battery.
	Starter brushes badly worn, sticking, or brush wires loose	Examine brushes, replace as necessary, tighten down brush wires.
	Loose wires in starter motor circuit	Check wiring and tighten as necessary.
Starter motor operates without turning engine	Starter motor pinion sticking on the screwed sleeve	Remove starter motor, clean starter motor drive.
	Pinion or flywheel gear teeth broken or worn	Fit new gear ring to flywheel, and new pinion to starter motor drive.
Starter motor noisy or excessively rough engagement	Pinion or flywheel gear teeth broken or worn	Fit new gear teeth to flywheel, or new pinion to starter motor drive.
	Starter motor retaining bolts loose	Tighten starter motor securing bolts. Fit new spring washer if necessary.
Battery will not hold charge for more than a few days	Battery defective internally	Remove and fit new battery.
	Electrolyte level too low or electrolyte too weak due to leakage	Top up electrolyte level to just above plates.
	Plate separators no longer fully effective	Remove and fit new battery.
	Battery plates severely sulphated	Remove and fit new battery.
	Generator belt slipping	Check belt for wear, replace if necessary and tighten.
	Battery terminal connections loose or corroded	Check terminals for tightness and remove all corrosion.
	Dynamo or alternator not charging properly	Take car to specialist or overhaul.
	Short in lighting circuit causing continual battery drain	Trace and rectify.
	Regulator unit not working correctly	Take car to specialist.
Ignition light fails to go out, battery runs flat in a few days	Drive belt loose and slipping or broken	Check, replace and tighten as necessary.
	Dynamo or alternator faulty	Take car to specialist or overhaul.

Failure of individual electrical equipment to function correctly is dealt with alphabetically, item by item, under the headings listed below.

Fuel gauge gives no reading	Fuel tank empty!	Fill fuel tank.
	Electric cable between tank sender unit and gauge earthed or loose	Check cable for earthing and joints for tightness.
	Fuel gauge case not earthed	Ensure case is well earthed.
	Fuel gauge supply cable interrupted	Check and replace cable if necessary.
	Fuel gauge unit broken	Replace fuel gauge.
Fuel gauge registers full all the time	Electric cable between tank unit and gauge broken or disconnected	Check over cable and repair as necessary.
Horn operates all the time	Horn push either earthed or stuck down	Disconnect battery earth. Check and rectify source of trouble.
	Horn cable to horn push earthed	Disconnect battery earth. Check and rectify source of trouble.
Horn fails to operate	Blown fuse	Check and renew if broken. Ascertain cause.
	Cable or cable connection loose, broken or disconnected	Check all connections for tightness and cables for breaks.
	Horn has an internal fault	Remove and overhaul horn.

Horn emits intermittent or unsatisfactory noise	Cable connections loose Horn incorrectly adjusted	Check and tighten all connections. Adjust horn until best note obtained.
Lights do not come on	If engine not running, battery discharged Light bulb filament burnt out or bulbs broken Wire connections loose, disconnected or broken Light switch shorting or otherwise faulty	Push-start car and charge battery (not automatics) Test bulbs in live bulb holder. Check all connections for tightness and wire cable for breaks. By-pass light switch to ascertain if fault is in switch and fit new switch as appropriate.
Lights come on but fade out	If engine not running battery discharged	Push-start car and charge battery (not automatics)
Lights give very poor illumination	Lamp glasses dirty Reflector tarnished or dirty Lamps badly out of adjustment Incorrect bulb with too low wattage fitted Existing bulbs old and badly discoloured Electrical wiring too thin not allowing full current to pass	Clean glasses. Fit new reflectors. Adjust lamps correctly. Remove bulb and replace with correct grade. Renew bulb units. Rewire lighting system.
Lights work erratically - flashing on and off, especially over bumps	Battery terminals or earth connections loose Lights not earthing properly Contacts in light switch faulty	Tighten battery terminals and earth connection. Examine and rectify. By-pass light switch to ascertain if fault is in switch and fit new switch as appropriate.
Wiper motor fails to work	Blown fuse Wire connections loose, disconnected or broken Brushes badly worn Armature worn or faulty Field coils faulty	Check and replace fuse if necessary. Check wiper wiring. Tighten loose connections. Remove and fit new brushes. If electricity at wiper motor remove and overhaul and fit replacement armature. Purchase reconditioned wiper motor.
Wiper motor works very slowly and takes excessive current	Commutator dirty, greasy or burnt Drive to spindles bent or unlubricated Wheelbox spindle binding or damaged Armature bearings dry or unaligned Armature badly worn or faulty	Clean commutator thoroughly. Examine drive and straighten out severe curvature. Lubricate Remove, overhaul or fit replacement. Replace with new bearings correctly aligned. Remove, overhaul or fit replacement armature
Wiper motor works slowly and takes little current	Brushes badly worn Commutator dirty, greasy or burnt Armature badly worn or faulty	Remove and fit new brushes. Clean commutator thoroughly. Remove and overhaul armature or fit replacement.
Wiper motor works but wiper blades remain static	Wheelbox gear and spindle damaged or worn Wiper motor gearbox parts badly worn	Examine and if faulty replace. Overhaul or fit new gearbox.

Simca 1300 Saloon wiring diagram

1963 - 1964

Key to Simca 1300 Saloon wiring diagram

Component key

A Headlights
B Front turn indicators
C Front town lights
D Rear turn indicators
E Stop lights, tail lights
F Rear licence plate lamp
G High/low pitch horn
H Battery
   Generator
   Starter motor

I Regulator
J Pressure switch
K Temperature switch
L Spark plugs
M Distributor
N Ignition coil
O Switch, stop lights
P Motor, windscreen wipers
Q Motor, heater-defroster blower
R Main timing switch

S   Fuse holder
T   Interior light
U   Switch, LH front door
UA Switch, RH front door
V   Controls on instrument panel
VA Selector switch, horn pitch
VB Switch, windscreen wipers
VC Switch, heater-defroster
W   Switch, starter motor
X   Instrument cluster

XA Warning light, turn indicators
XB Lights, instrument cluster
XC Warning light, generator charge
XD Warning light, fuel mini level
XE Fuel level gauge, instrument cluster
XF Warning light, water temp. and oil
XG Warning light, headlights beam
Y   Combined switch
YA Horn control
Z   Fuel gauge, tank unit

Wire colour key

Wire	Colour	Colour		Wire	Colour	Colour	Colour
1	Red			22T	Blue		
1A	Red			23	Blue	Yellow	
1B	Red			23A	Blue	Yellow	
1C	Red			40	Green		
3A	Red	White		41	Green	Black	
3F	Red	White		70	White	Brown	
8	Red	Yellow		70T	White		
9	Red	Green		71	White	Black	
9T	Red	Green		72	White		
10	Grey			72A	Green		Green
10A	Grey			73	White		Red
10B	Grey			73A	White		Red
10D	Grey			81	White	Green	
10F	Grey			82	White	Red	
11	Grey	Red		90A	Yellow	Black	
11A	Grey	Red		90T	Yellow	Black	
11B	Grey	Red		92	Yellow	Red	
11D	Grey	Red		93T	Yellow		
11E	Grey	Red		94A	Yellow	White	
11F	Grey	Red		94T	Yellow	White	
12	Grey	White		110	Black		
12A	Grey	Blue		110A	Black		
13	Grey	Yellow		110C	Black		
14	Grey	Black		110E	Black		
22	Blue			132	Black		
22A	Blue						

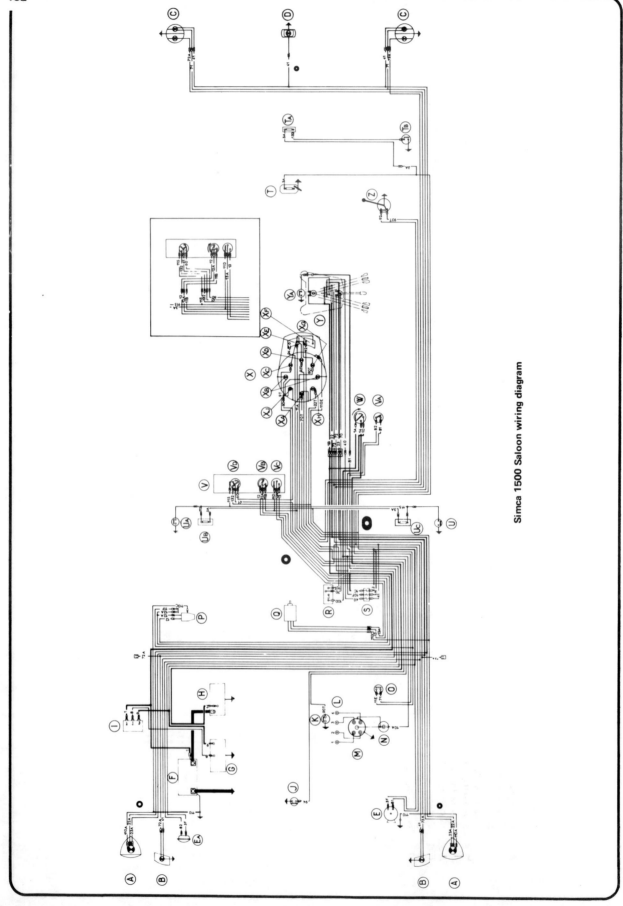

Simca 1500 Saloon wiring diagram

Key to Simca 1500 Saloon wiring diagram

Component key

A	Headlights	TB	Switch, glove compartment light
B	Front turn indicators	U	Switch, LH front door
	Front town lights	UA	Switch, RH front door
C	Rear turn indicators	UB	RH light, instrument panel
	Stop lights, tail lights	UC	LH light, instrument panel
D	Rear licence plate lamp	V	Controls, instrument panel
E	Horn, low pitch	VA	Selector switch, horn
EA	Horn, high pitch	VB	Switch, windscreen wipers
F	Battery	VC	Switch, heater-defroster
G	Generator	VD	Switch, instrum. panel lights -
H	Starter motor	W	Rheostat, instrum. cluster lights
I	Regulator		Switch, starter motor
J	Temperature switch	X	Instrument cluster
K	Pressure switch	XA	Warning light - turn indicators
L	Spark plugs	XB	Lights, instrument cluster
M	Distributor	XC	Warning light, generator charge
N	Ignition coil	XD	Warning light, fuel mini level
O	Switch, stop lights	XE	Gauge, water temperature
P	Motor, windscreen wipers	XF	Fuel level gauge, instrument cluster
Q	Motor, heater-defroster blower	XG	Warning light, oil pressure
R	Main timing switch	XH	Warning light, headlights beam
S	Fuse holder	XJ	Warning light, town lights
T	Interior light, rear	Y	Combined switch
TA	Light, glove compartment	YA	Horn control
		Z	Fuel gauge, tank unit

Wiring colour key

No.	Colour	Tracer	Tracer 2
1	Red		
1A	Red		
1B	Red		
1C	Red		
3	Red		
3A	Red	White	
3F	Red	White	
8	Red	White	Yellow
9	Red	Green	
9T	Red	Green	
10	Grey		
10A	Grey		
10D	Grey		
10F	Grey		
11	Grey	Red	
11A	Grey	Red	
11B	Grey	Red	
11D	Grey	Red	
11E	Grey	Red	
11F	Grey	Red	
12	Grey	White	
12A	Grey	Blue	
13	Grey	Yellow	
13A	Grey	Green	
14	Grey	Black	
22	Blue		

No.	Colour	Tracer	Tracer 2
22A	Blue		
22T	Blue		
23	Blue	Yellow	
23A	Blue	Yellow	
40	Green		
41	Green	Black	
60	Brown	Brown	
70	White		
70T	White	Black	
71	White		
72	White	Black	Green
72A	White		Green
73	White		Red
73A	White		Red
81	White	Green	
82	White	Red	
90T	Yellow	Black	
92	Yellow	Red	
93T	Yellow		
94	Yellow	White	
110	Black		
110A	Black		
110C	Black		
110E	Black		
115	Black	Yellow	
132	Black		

Simca 1500 Estate wiring diagram

Key to Simca 1500 Estate wiring diagram

Component key

A	Headlights	J	Temperature switch
B	Front turn indicators	K	Pressure switch
	Front town lights	L	Spark plugs
C	Rear turn indicators	M	Distributor
	Stop lights, tail lights	N	Ignition coil
D	Rear licence plate lamp	O	Switch, stop lights
E	Horn, high/low pitch	P	Motor, windscreen wipers
F	Battery	Q	Motor, heater-defroster blower
G	Generator	R	Main timing switch
H	Starter motor	S	Fuse holder
I	Regulator	T	Interior light, front

TA	Interior light, rear	XB	Lights, instrument cluster
U	Switch, LH front door	XC	Warning light, generator charge
UA	Switch, RH front door	XD	Warning light, fuel mini level
V	Controls, instrument panel	XE	Gauge, water temperature
VA	Selector switch, horn	XF	Fuel level gauge, instrument cluster
VB	Switch, windscreen wipers	XG	Warning light, oil pressure
VC	Switch, heater-defroster	XH	Warning light, turn indicators
W	Switch, starter motor	Y	Combined switch
WA	Socket, radio set	YA	Horn control
X	Instrument cluster	Z	Fuel gauge, tank unit
XA	Warning light, turn indicators		

Wiring colour key

Code	Colour 1	Colour 2	Colour 3
1	Red		
1A	Red		
1B	Red		
1C	Red		
1G	Red		
3A	Red	White	
3F	Red	White	
8	Red	Yellow	
9	Red	Green	
9T	Red	Green	
10	Grey		
10A	Grey		
10D	Grey		
10F	Grey		
11	Grey	Red	
11A	Grey	Red	
11B	Grey	Red	
11D	Grey	Red	
11E	Grey	Red	
11F	Grey	Red	
12	Grey	White	
12A	Grey	Blue	
13	Grey	Yellow	
14	Grey	Black	
22	Blue		
22A	Blue		
22T	Blue		
23	Blue		
23A	Blue	Yellow	
40	Green	Yellow	
41	Green	Black	
70	White	Brown	
70T	White		
71	White		
72	White		Green
72A	White		Green
73	White		Red
73A	White		Red
80	White	Green	
81	White	Green	
82	White	Red	
90T	Yellow	Black	
92	Yellow	Red	
93T	Yellow		
94	Yellow	White	
110	Black		
110A	Black		
110C	Black		
110E	Black		
110F	Black		
132	Black		

Simca 1500 GL Saloon wiring diagram

157

Key to Simca 1500 GL Saloon wiring diagram

Component key

A	Headlights	L	Spark plugs
B	Front turn indicators	M	Distributor
	Front town lights	N	Ignition coil
C	Rear turn indicators	O	Switch, stop lights
	Stop lights, tail lights	P	Motor, windscreen wipers
D	Rear licence plate lamp	Q	Motor, heater-defroster blower
E	Horn, low pitch	R	Main timing switch
EA	Horn, high pitch	S	Fuse holder
F	Battery	T	Interior light, rear
G	Generator	TA	Luggage compartment light
H	Starter motor	TB	Switch, luggage compart. light
I	Regulator	TC	Interior light, front
J	Temperature switch	U	Switch, LH front door
K	Pressure switch	UA	Switch, RH front door

UB	Switch, RH rear door	X	Instrument cluster
UC	Switch, LH rear door	XA	Warning light, turn indicators
UD	LH light, instrument panel	XB	Lights, instrument cluster
UE	RH light, instrument panel	XC	Warning light, generator charge
V	Controls, instrument panel	XD	Warning light, fuel mini level
VA	Selector switch, horn	XE	Gauge, water temperature
VB	Switch, windscreen wipers	XF	Fuel level gauge, instrum. cluster
VC	Switch, heater-defroster	XG	Warning light, oil pressure
VD	Switch, instrum. panel lights	XH	Warning light, headlights beam
	Rheostat, instrum. panel lights	XJ	Warning light, parking lights
W	Switch, starter motor	Y	Combined switch
WA	Socket, radio set	YA	Horn control
WB	Clock	Z	Fuel gauge, tank unit
WC	Cigar lighter		

Wiring colour key

No.	Colour	Tracer
1	Red	
1A	Red	
1B	Red	
1C	Red	
1D	Red	Blue
1E	Red	Black
1G	Red	
3	Red	White
3F	Red	White
4	Red	Blue
5	Red	Black
8	Red	Yellow
9	Red	Green
9T	Red	Green
10	Grey	
10A	Grey	
10D	Grey	
10F	Grey	
11	Grey	Red
11B	Grey	Red
11D	Grey	Red
11E	Grey	Red
11F	Grey	Red
12	Grey	White
12A	Grey	Blue
13	Grey	Yellow
13A	Grey	Green
14	Blue	Black
22	Blue	

No.	Colour	Tracer
22A	Blue	
22T	Blue	
23	Blue	Yellow
23A	Blue	Yellow
40	Green	
41	Green	Black
60	Brown	
63	Brown	Yellow
70	White	Brown
70T	White	
71	White	
72	White	Black
72A	White	
73	White	
73A	White	
80	White	Green
81	White	Green
82	White	Red
90T	Yellow	Black
92	Yellow	Red
93T	Yellow	
94	Yellow	White
110	Black	
110A	Black	
110C	Black	
110E	Black	
115	Black	Yellow
132	Black	

158

Simca 1500 GL Estate wiring diagram

Key to Simca 1500 GL Estate wiring diagram

Component key

A	Headlights
B	Front turn indicators
	Front town lights
C	Rear turn indicators
	Stop lights, tail lights
D	Rear licence plate lamp
E	Horn, low pitch
EA	Horn, high pitch
F	Battery
G	Generator
H	Starter motor
I	Regulator
J	Temperature switch
K	Pressure switch
L	Spark plugs
M	Distributor
N	Ignition coil
O	Switch, stop lights
P	Motor, windscreen wipers
Q	Motor, heater-defroster blower
R	Main timing switch
S	Fuse holder
T	Interior light, rear
TA	Interior light, front
U	Switch, LH front door
UA	Switch, RH front door
UB	Switch, RH rear door
UC	Switch, LH rear door
UD	LH light, instrument panel
UE	RH light, instrument panel
V	Controls, instrument panel
VA	Selector switch, horn
VB	Switch, windscreen wipers
VC	Switch, heater-defroster
VD	Switch, instrum. panel lights -
	Rheostat, instrum. cluster lights
W	Switch, starter motor
WA	Socket, radio set
WB	Clock
WC	Cigar lighter
X	Instrument cluster
XA	Warning light, turn indicators
XB	Lights, instrument cluster
XC	Warning light, generator charge
XD	Warning light, fuel mini level
XE	Gauge, water temperature
XF	Fuel level gauge, instrum. cluster
XG	Warning light, oil pressure
XH	Warning light, headlights beam
Y	Combined switch
YA	Horn control
Z	Fuel gauge, tank unit

Wiring colour key

No.	Colour	Tracer
1	Red	
1A	Red	
1B	Red	
1C	Red	Blue
1D	Red	Black
1E	Red	
1G	Red	
3	Red	White
3F	Red	White
4	Red	Blue
5	Red	Black
8	Red	Yellow
9	Red	Green
9T	Red	Green
10	Grey	
10A	Grey	
10D	Grey	
10F	Grey	
11	Grey	Red
11A	Grey	Red
11B	Grey	Red
11D	Grey	Red
11E	Grey	Red
11F	Grey	Red
12	Grey	White
12A	Grey	Blue
13	Grey	Yellow
13A	Grey	Green
14	Grey	Black
22	Blue	
22A	Blue	
22T	Blue	
23	Blue	Yellow
23A	Blue	Yellow
40	Green	
41	Green	Black
60	Brown	
63	Brown	Yellow
70	White	Brown
70T	White	
71	White	Black
72	White	
72A	White	
73	White	Green
73A	White	Green
80	White	Green
81	White	Green
82	White	Red
90T	Yellow	Black
92	Yellow	Red
93T	Yellow	White
94	Yellow	White
110	Black	
110A	Black	
110C	Black	
110E	Black	
110F	Black	
115	Black	Yellow
132	Black	

Simca 1301%1501 (early models) wiring diagram

Key to Simca 1301/1501 (early models) wiring diagram

Component key

A	Headlamps
B	Front turn signals
	Front town lights
C	Rear turn signals - Stop lights
	Tail lights
D	Rear licence plate lamp
E	Right high pitch horn
Ea	Left high pitch horn
F	Battery
G	Generator
H	Starter motor
I	Regulator
J	Temperature switch (water)
K	Pressure switch (oil)
L	Spark plugs
M	Distributor
N	Ignition coil
O	Switch, stop lights
P	Motor, windshield wipers
Q	Motor, heater-defroster
R	Flasher unit
S	Fuse box
T	Rear interior lamp
Ta	Luggage compartment lamp
Tb	Switch, luggage compartment lamp
Tc	Front interior lamp
U	Switch, left front door
Ua	Switch, right front door
Ub	Switch, left rear door
Uc	Switch, right rear door
Ud	Lamp, left glove box
Ue	Lamp, right glove box
W	Switch, starter motor
X	Instrument cluster
Xa	Warning light, turn signals
Xb	Switch, windshield wipers
Xc	Warning light, generator charge
Xd	Warning light, fuel mini level
Xe	Warning light, oil pressure
Xf	Warning light, headlamps high beam
Xg	Rheostat, instrument cluster lamps
Xh	Rheostat, heater-defroster control
Xj	Cigar lighter
Xk	Clock
Y	Combined switch
Ya	Control, horns
Z	Fuel gauge, tank unit

Wiring colour key

No.	Colour			No.	Colour		
1	Red			23A	Blue		
1A	Red			40	Green		
1C	Red			41	Green		
1D	Red	Black		44	Black		
1F	Red			60	Brown		
1P	Red	White		70	White	Brown	
1R	Red			70T	White		
3	Red			71	White	Violet	
3A	Red			72	White		
4	Red	White		72A	White		
5	Red	Black		73	White		
8	Red	Yellow		73A	White		Green
9	Red	Green		80	White	Blue	Red
9T	Red	Green		82	White	Green	
10	Grey			83	White	Red	
10B	Grey			90	Yellow	Black	
10C	Grey			90T	Yellow	Black	
10F	Grey			92	Yellow	Red	
11	Grey			93T	Yellow		
11B	Grey			94	Yellow	White	
11C	Grey	Red		94T	Yellow	White	
11M	Grey			110	Black		
11S	Grey			110A	Black		
12	Grey	White		110B	Black		
12A	Grey	Blue		110C	Black		
13	Grey	Yellow		110D	Black		
14	Grey	Black		110M	Black		
22	Blue			110R	Black		
22A	Blue			115	Black		
22T	Blue			132	Black		
23	Blue	Yellow					

Wiring diagram — Simca 1301 - 1501 (1969)

Key to Simca 1301/1501 (1969 models) wiring diagram

Component key

Code	Description	Models
F	Battery	
A	Dipped headlights	
A	Headlights	
AB	Long distance headlights	S & GL
UD	Headlight relay	LS
B	Front lights	S & GL
C	Rear lights	
D	Number plate light	
XD	Combined switch gear lights	
XJ	General indic. light	
in YB	Clock light	S & GL
in MA	Cigar lighter light	S
B	Front trafficators	
C	Rear trafficators	
R	Trafficator switch gear	
Xc	Trafficator indicator light	LS - GL

Code	Description	Models
XF	Batt. charge indic. light	
XE	Headlight indic. light	S & GL
XB	Oil press. indic. light	
XB	Warning light	LS
XB	Water temp. indicator	S & GL
XH	Fuel level indicator	S & GL
in XH	Fuel level indic. light	
C	Stop lights	
A	Dipped headlight signalling	
TB	Trunk courtesy light	S & GL
UE & UF	Glove box light	S
Q	Air cond. motor	
P	Windscreen wiper motor	
E	Horn blower	S
EB	Relay, horn with blower	S
ED	HF horn	

Code	Description	Models
T	Roof light, front	
TA	Roof light, rear	GL & S
C	Reverse light (except estate)	S
X	Reflectors	
X	Speedometer	S
EH	Fan electro-magnet	
H	Starter motor	
HA	Generator	
I	Regulator	
N	Coil	S
YB	Clock	S
MA	Cigar lighter	

Option

BA & BB	Side trafficator repeater

Wiring colour key

Code	Colour	Tracer
1	Red	Blue
1A	Red	Blue
1C	Red	Blue
1D	Red	Blue
1F	Red	Blue
1H	Red	Green
1J	Red	Green
1R	Red	Black
4	Red / White	Green
5	Red / Black	Brown
8	Red / Yellow	White
9	Red / Green	White
9T	Red / Green	White
10	Grey	White
10B	Grey	White
10C	Grey	White
10E	Grey	White
10F	Grey	White
11	Grey	White
11B	Grey / Red	Red
11C	Grey / Yellow	Yellow
11E	Grey / Yellow	Yellow
11F	Grey / Yellow	Yellow
11M	Grey / Red	White
11R	Grey	
11S	Grey	
12	Grey / White	
12A	Grey / Blue	
13	Grey / Yellow	
14	Grey / Black	
15	Grey / Yellow	
15A	Black	
22	Blue	
22A	Blue	
22B	Blue / Green	
22D	Blue / Green	
22R	Blue / Green	
22T	Blue	Yellow
23	Blue	Yellow
23A	Blue	
24	Blue	Blue
33	Blue	Grey
33A	Blue	Grey
40	Green	
41	Green	
44	Black	
51	Green	White
60	Brown	Brown
70	White	
70T	White	
71	White	Purple
72	White	White
72A	White	Green
73	White	White
73A	White	Red
80	White	White
85	Red	Blue
90	Yellow	Black
92	Yellow	Black
93T	Yellow	Red
94	Red / Yellow	White
110	Black	
110A	Black	
110B	White / Black	
110C	Blue / Black	Green
110D	Yellow / Black	
110E	Black / Black	
110F	Yellow / Black	Red
110H	Black	
110K	Black	
110M	Black	White
110R	Green / Black	
115	Green / Black	
132	Green / Black	

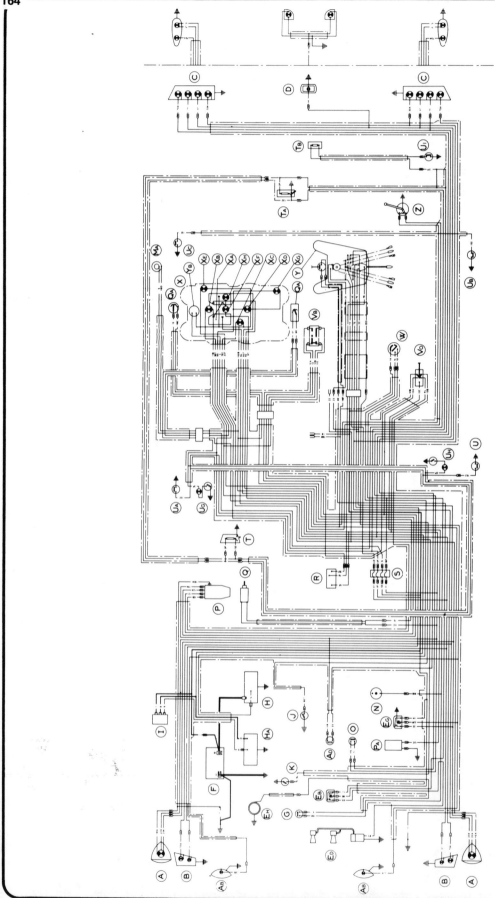

Simca 1301/1501 (1970 models) wiring diagram

Key to Simca 1301/1501 (1970 models) wiring diagram

Component key

Code	Description	Note
F	Battery	
A	Dipped beam	
A	Main beam	
EG	Main beam relay	
AB	Long range headlamp	S
B	Front side light	
C	Rear side light	
D	Registration plate light	
XD	Instrument cluster light	
XG	Side warning light	S
B	Front flasher	
C	Rear flasher	
XC	Flasher warning light	
R	Flasher unit	
C	Stop lights	
XF	Generator warning light	S
XE	Main beam warning light	
XB	Oil pressure warning light	
XH	Minimum fuel warning light	
XG	Fuel gauge	
XA	Water temperature gauge	
YB	Electric clock	S
T	Front ceiling light	
TA	Rear ceiling light	
UE & UF	Glove box light	
TB	Luggage compartment light	S & GL
P	Windscreen wiper motor	
PA	Window washer motor	
Q	Air conditioner motor	
E	Air horn compressor	
EB	Horn relay	
EH	Fan electro-magnet	
H	Starter	
HA	Generator	
I	Regulator	
N	Coil	
MA	Cigar lighter	S
C	Reflector	
C	Reversing light (except estate)	S
ED	HF horn	LS & GL

Optional

Code	Description	Note
BA & BB	Flasher side repeater	S

Wiring colour code

Code	Colour	Tracer	
1	Red		
1A	Red		
1C	Red	Black	
1D	Red	White	
1F	Red		
1H	Red		
1J	Red		
1R	Red		
3P	Red	White	
3F	Red	White	
4	Red	Black	
5	Red	Yellow	
8	Red	Green	
9	Red	Green	
9T	Red		
10	Grey		
10B	Grey		
10E	Grey		
10F	Grey		
11	Grey		
11B	Grey		
11C	Grey		
11E	Grey		
11F	Grey		
11M	Grey	Red	
11R	Grey		
11S	Grey		
12	Grey	White	
12A	Grey	Blue	
13	Grey	Yellow	
14	Grey	Black	
11L	Grey	Grey	
12B	Black	Black	
22	Blue		
22A	Blue		
22B	Blue	Green	
22D	Blue	Green	
22R	Blue	Green	
22T	Blue		
23	Blue	Yellow	
23A	Blue	Yellow	
24	Blue	Blue	Yellow
33	Blue	Grey	
33A	Blue	Grey	
40	Green		
41	Green	Yellow	
12C	Grey		
44	Black	White	
51	Green		
60	Brown	Brown	
70	White		
70T	White		
71	White	Purple	
72	White	White	
72A	White		Green
73	White	White	
73A	White		Red
80	Red	Blue	
85	Yellow	Black	
90T	Yellow	Black	
92	Yellow	Red	
93T	Yellow		
94	Yellow	White	
110	Black		
110B	Black		
110C	Black		
110D	Black		
110F	Black		
110M	Black		
110R	Black		
115	Black		

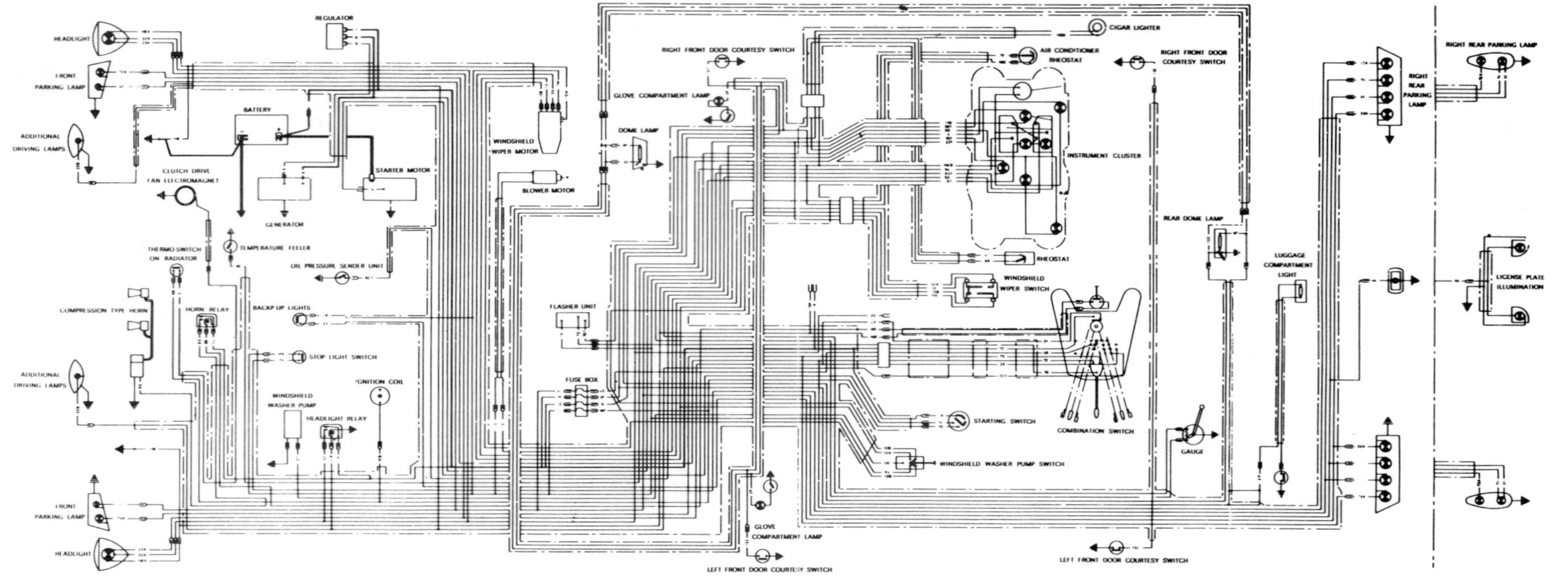

Key to Simca 1301/1501 (late models) wiring diagram

Wiring colour key

Code	Colour		Code	Colour		Code	Colour		Code	Colour
1	Red		22R	Blue		10F	Grey		73	White
1A	Red		22T	Blue		11	Grey		73A	White Blue
1C	Red Black		23	Blue		11B	Grey		80	White Black
1D	Red White		23A	Blue		11C	Grey		85	Red Black
1F	Red		24	Blue		11F	Grey Yellow		90T	Yellow Red
1H	Red		33	Blue		11M	Grey		92	Yellow
1J	Red		33A	Blue		11R	Grey Red		93T	Yellow
1R	Red		40	Green		11S	Grey		94	Yellow White
3P	Red White		41	Green		12	Grey		110	Black
3F	Red White		12C	Grey White		12A	Grey White		110A	Black
4	Red White		44	Black		13	Grey Yellow		110B	Black
5	Red Black		51	Green White		14	Grey		110C	Black
8	Red Yellow		60	Brown Brown		11L	Grey Grey		110D	Black
9	Red Green		70	White		12B	Black Black		110F	Black
9T	Red Green		70T	White Purple		22	Blue		110M	Black
10	Grey		71	White		22A	Blue		110R	Black
10B	Grey		72	White Green		22B	Blue Green		115	Black Green
10E	Grey		72A	White		22D	Blue		132	Black

Red

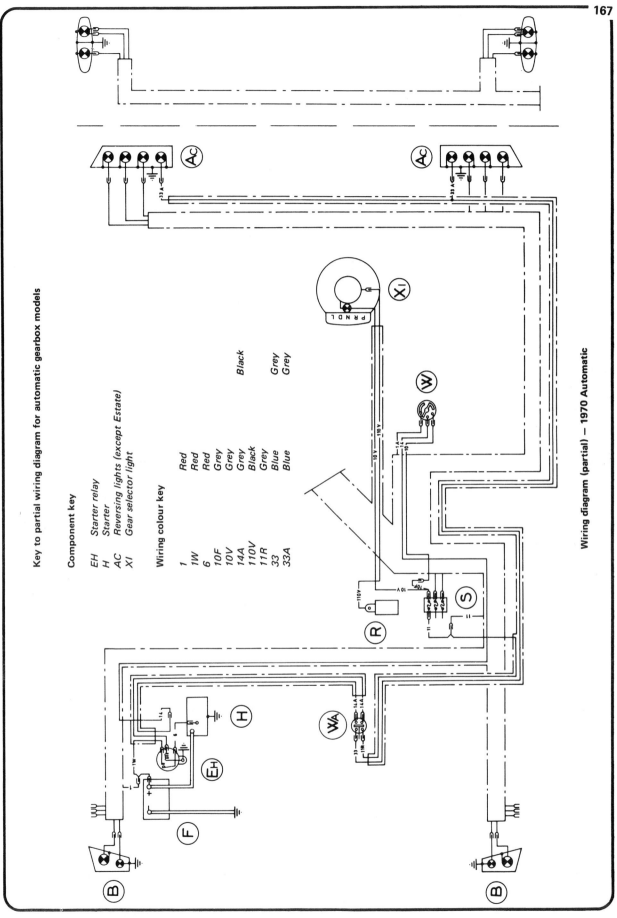

Key to partial wiring diagram for automatic gearbox models

Component key

EH   Starter relay
H   Starter
AC   Reversing lights (except Estate)
XI   Gear selector light

Wiring colour key

1	Red
1W	Red
6	Red
10F	Grey
10V	Grey
14A	Grey
110V	Black
11R	Grey
33	Blue
33A	Blue
	Black
	Grey
	Grey

Wiring diagram (partial) — 1970 Automatic

Chapter 11 Suspension and steering

Contents

Specifications

Front suspension

Type ... ...   Independent, coil springs and hydraulic telescopic dampers

Springs

	Up to body No SNL080587	Body No SNL080588 to L300646	From body No L300647	1500/1501 Estate
Free length	15.51 in (394 mm)	16.72 in (420 mm)	16.0 in (406.4 mm)	16.63 in (423.4 mm)
Coil outer diameter	4.62 in (117.4 mm) — all models			

Shock absorbers (dampers)

Type ... ...   Hydraulic, telescopic, double acting
Length extended ... ...   16.63 in (417.5 mm)
Length compressed ... ...   9.62 in (244.0 mm)

Rear suspension

Type ... ...   Coil springs, double acting hydraulic dampers. Rear axle located by upper and lower links with transverse Panhard rod.

Springs

	Up to body No SNL080587	From body No SNL080588	1500/1501 Estate
Free length	12.8 in (325.0 mm)	14.8 in (375.0 mm)	12.3 in (313.0 mm)
Coil outer diameter	4.6 in (117.4 mm)	4.8 in (123.0 mm)	4.8 in (123.0 mm)

Shock absorbers (dampers)

Type ... ...   Hydraulic, telescopic, double acting
Length extended ... ...   14.19 in (360.5 mm)
Length compressed ... ...   8.47 in (215.25 mm)

Steering

Type ... ...   Worm and roller

Camber angle ... ... 1° to 1° 45'

Castor angle ... ... 2° to 3°

Toe-in ... ...   3/64 to 1/8 in (1.2 and 3.2 mm)

Steering ratio ... ...   16.4 : 1 (overall 20.8 : 1)

Turning circle (kerb to kerb) ... ...   32 ft (9.75 m)

Wheels ... ...   4½J x 13

Tyres
     Saloon (radial) ... ...   165 x 13
     Estate (radial) ... ...   175 x 13
     Pressures:
         Saloon ... ...   Front 23 lb in^2 Rear 24 lb in^2
         Estate ... ...   Front 23 lb in^2 Rear 26 lb in^2

Clearance from ground (unladen) ... ...   9½ in (241.3 mm)

Clearance from ground (laden) ... ...   5½ in (139.7 mm)

Wheelbase ... ...   8ft 4in (2.53 m)

Front track ... ...   4ft 4in (1.31 m)

Rear track ... ...   4ft 3in (1.28 m)

Torque wrench settings	lb ft	kg m
Front damper upper mounting nuts	7	1.0
Front damper lower mounting nuts	9	1.2
Stub axle carrier lower swivel nut	58	8.0
Suspension upper arm		
Pivot to crossmember bolts	62	8.5
Pivot end nuts	60	8.2
Stub axle carrier to upper swivel nut	40	5.5
Upper swivel to suspension arm bolt	40	5.5
	lb ft	kg m
Lower suspension arm		
Arm to crossmember bolt	58	8.0
Lower ball joint to arm bolts	40	5.5
Crossmember to bodyframe bolts	34	4.7
Crossmember front support bracket bolts	16	2.2
Radius arm to suspension lower arm	44	6.0
Anti-roll bar bracket bolts	16	2.2
Radius arm clamp bolts	16	2.2
Radius arm ball joint bolts	22	3.0
Rear damper lower mounting bracket bolts	16	2.2
Rear damper upper mounting nuts	9	1.2
Rear suspension lower arm pivot to axle bolts	83	11.5
Rear suspension lower arm pivot to body	54	7.5
Rear suspension upper arm to axle bolts	83	11.5
Rear suspension upper arm to body bolts	54	7.5
Rear transverse rod to axle bolts	69	9.5
Rear transverse rod to body bolts	69	9.5
Steering box to bodyframe bolts	34	4.7
Track-rod end ball joints to steering arms	22	3.0
Track-rod locknuts or clamp bolts	16	2.2
Steering wheel nut	38	5.2
Cotter pin nut (flexible coupling)	7	1.0
Roadwheel bolts	45	6.2

1 General description

The front suspension is of independent type incorporating coil springs and telescopic hydraulic dampers. These components are mounted above the upper suspension wishbone. An anti-roll bar is fitted in front of the bolt-on type crossmember. The suspension joints are rubber bushed with the exception of the upper swivel and lower balljoint of the stub axle carrier which should be greased every 6000 miles (96000 km) by means of the nipples provided, (later models have sealed components which require no lubrication).

The rear suspension comprises coil springs and telescopic hydraulic dampers. The rear axle is positively located by upper and lower control arms and sideways movement is restricted by a transverse rod (Panhard rod).

The steering gear is of worm and roller type. A flexible coupling is incorporated in the steering shaft. An idler is fitted and a non-adjustable centre track-rod and two adjustable outer track rods.

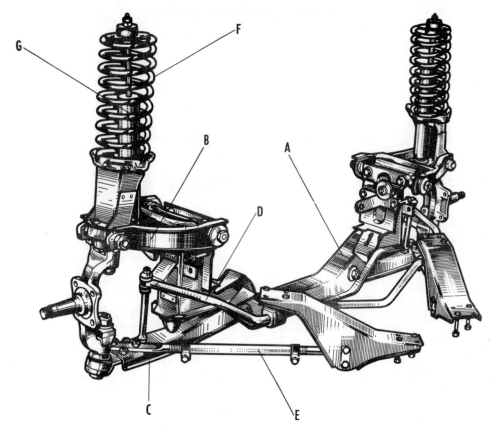

Fig 11.1 Layout of the front suspension

A Crossmember	C Suspension lower arm	E Radius arm	G Damper
B Suspension upper arm	D Anti-roll bar	F Coil road spring	

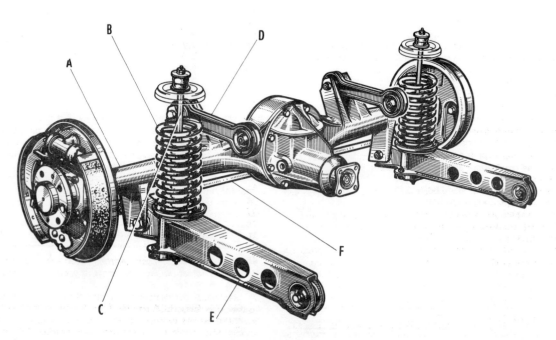

Fig 11.2 Layout of the rear suspension

A Rear axle	C Damper	E Suspension lower arm
B Coil road spring	D Suspension upper arm	F Transverse rod (Panhard rod)

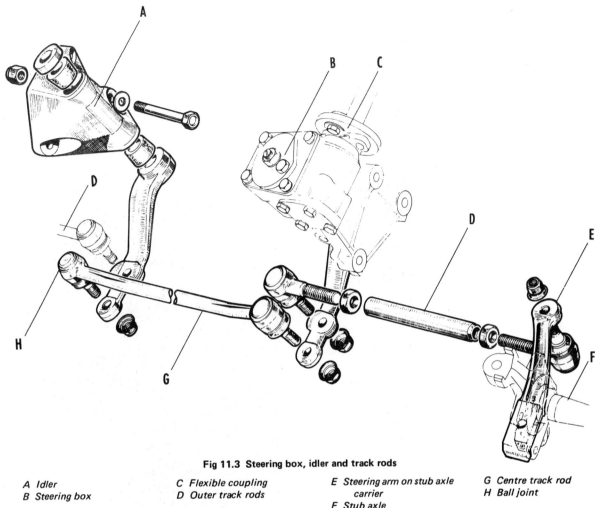

Fig 11.3 Steering box, idler and track rods

A Idler
B Steering box

C Flexible coupling
D Outer track rods

E Steering arm on stub axle
   carrier
F Stub axle

G Centre track rod
H Ball joint

2 Front hub bearings - adjustment and renewal

1 After dismantling or at regular 12000 mile (19300 km) intervals the front hub bearings should be adjusted and repacked with grease.
2 Jack-up the front of the vehicle and prise off the grease cap from the end of the stub axle.
3 Tighten the nut on the end of the stub axle, at the same time rotating the roadwheel in a forward direction until the wheel stops due to the excessive bearing preload.
4 Unscrew the nut 1/6th of a turn and check the endfloat by gripping the roadwheel and pushing and pulling it. There should be just a perceptible amount of movement at the roadwheel rim.
5 Finally, stake the collar of the nut into the groove of the stub axle, half fill the grease cap with wheel bearing grease and refit it.
6 If the bearings or grease seals are to be renewed, then proceed by jacking-up the front of the vehicle and removing the roadwheel.
7 *On 1300 models* remove the brake drum securing and road-wheel dowel bolts. Prise off the grease cap and withdraw the brake drum.
8 Unscrew and remove the stub axle nut and extract the thrust-washer. Pull the hub from the stub axle.
9 *On all other models,* the removal of the hub/disc assembly is similar to removal of the drum and hub just described except

that the caliper unit must first be unbolted and tied up out of the way. There is no need to disconnect the hydraulic circuit.
10 Reference should be made to Chapter 9 for illustrations of the front hub assemblies and to the method of removing the brake backplate or disc shield if required.
11 The bearings and grease seals should be pressed or drifted from the hub assembly and new ones fitted.
12 Apply wheel bearing grease to the bearings and adjust them as described earlier in this Section.

3 Front damper - removal, testing, refitting

1 Within the engine compartment unscrew and remove the three nuts which secure the damper upper mounting anchor plate.
2 Disconnect the damper lower mounting from its attachment to the upper suspension arm.
3 Withdraw the damper upwards from the interior of the road spring coils.
4 Examine the exterior of the damper for fluid leaks. If these are evident renew the unit.
5 Secure the damper lower mounting in a vice so that the damper is vertical. Now operate the damper to the full extent of its travel in both directions ten or twelve times. There should be a noticeable resistance in both compression and extension strokes; if otherwise the damper must be renewed.

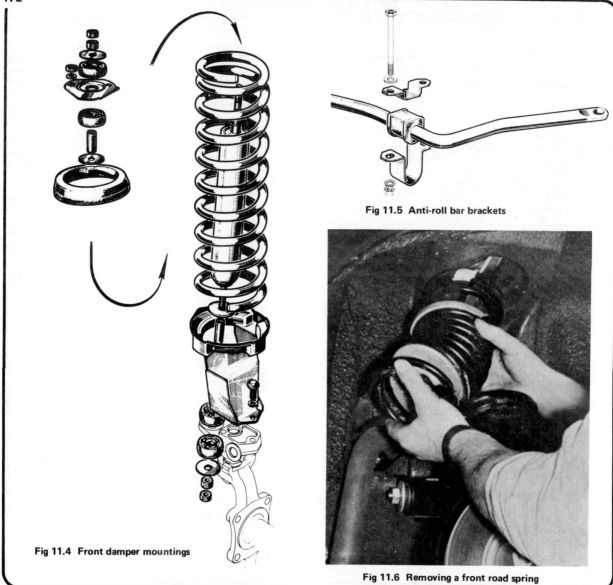

Fig 11.4 Front damper mountings

Fig 11.5 Anti-roll bar brackets

Fig 11.6 Removing a front road spring

4.2 Anti-roll bar end attachment

4.3 Unscrewing an anti-roll bar drop link from a suspension lower arm

6   Refitting is a reversal of removal but check that the mounting rubber insulators are located correctly.

4   Front anti-roll bar - removal and installation

1   Unscrew and remove the nuts which secure the anti-roll bar centre mountings to the crossmember front bracing brackets.
2   Disconnect the ends of the anti-roll bar from the drop links which are fitted to the suspension lower arm. (photo)
3   If new rubber bushes are needed on the drop links, then they can be unvolted from the suspension lower arm. (photo)
4   Remove the anti-roll bar from the vehicle.
5   Installation is a reversal of removal but do not overcompress the rubber mounting bushes at the drop links.

5   Front road springs - removal and installation

1   The front road springs may be removed using one of two methods.
2   Either use a spring compressor of the threaded rod type with nuts and retaining plates or two or three of the individual type which hook over three or four coils of the spring and are then tightened equally to compress the coils. The use of clips, after the spring has been compressed by an assistant sitting on the wing is not recommended unless the same spring is to be refitted as otherwise a compressor will still be required to remove the clips from the original spring.
3   Whichever type compressor is to be used, first remove the damper as described in Section 3 and with the spring compressed withdraw it form under the front wing having removed the road wheel beforehand.

6   Radius arm and steering lower balljoint - removal and refitting

1   Jack-up the front of the vehicle and remove the roadwheel.
2   Support the suspension lower arm with a jack or block.

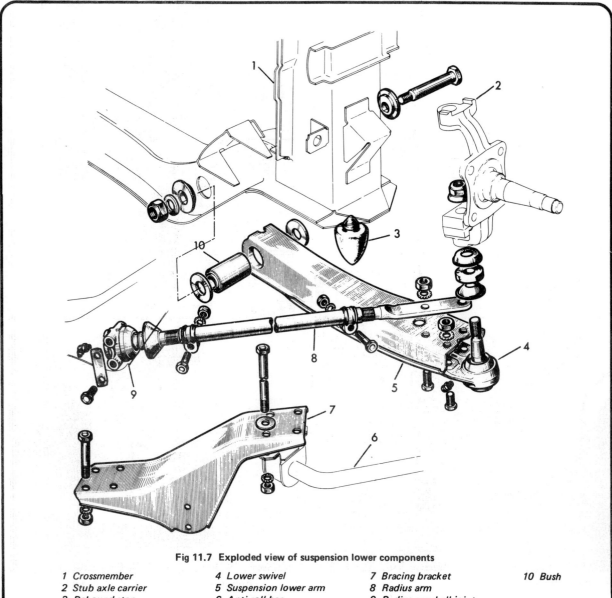

Fig 11.7 Exploded view of suspension lower components

1 Crossmember	4 Lower swivel	7 Bracing bracket	10 Bush
2 Stub axle carrier	5 Suspension lower arm	8 Radius arm	
3 Rebound stop	6 Anti-roll bar	9 Radius arm ball joint	

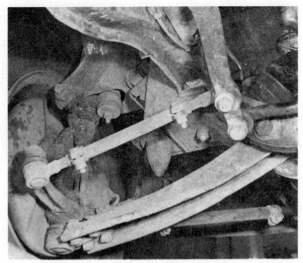

7.5 Attachment of a track-rod to steering arms

Fig 11.8 Ball joint extractor

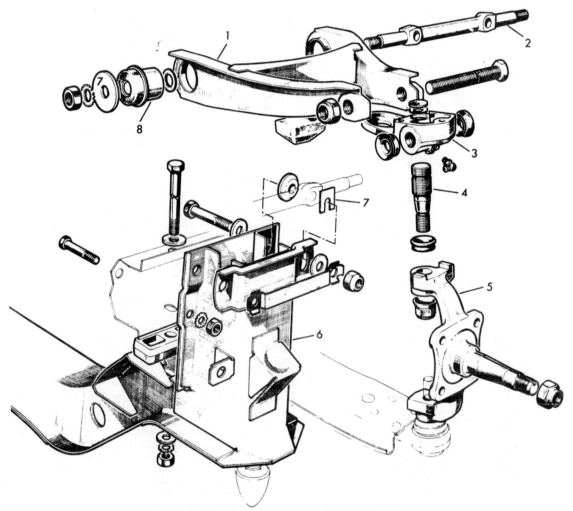

Fig 11.9 Exploded view of suspension upper components

1 Suspension upper arm	3 Swivel block	5 Stub axle carrier	7 Shim
2 Pivot	4 Swivel pin	6 Crossmember	8 Bush

3 Unscrew and remove the two bolts which secure the radius arm to the suspension lower arm. These bolts also serve to retain the lower balljoint.

4 Bend back the tabs of the locking plate which secures the bolts· at the balljoint at the opposite end of the radius arm. Unscrew these bolts which hold the balljoint to the front cross-member bracing brackets and then withdraw the radius arm.

5 Do not slacken the clamp bolts on the radius arms or the wheel alignment will be upset when the arm is refitted.

6 The lower balljoint may now be removed by removing the remaining two bolts which hold it to the suspension lower arm and then using a suitable extractor disconnecting it from the stub axle carrier.

7 Refitting is a reversal of removal but always use new lockwashers under the heads of the securing bolts and check the wheel alignment when installation is complete.

8 Early type vehicles are fitted with a grease nipple on the radius arm inner balljoint and this should be lubricated at the same intervals as the suspension upper swivel and lower balljoint.

7 Front crossmember with suspension - removal and installation

1 Remove the dampers (Section 3).

2 Remove the coil road srpings (Section 5).

3 Remove the anti-roll bar (Section 4).

4 Disconnect the radius arms from their attachment points (Section 6).

5 Disconnect the track-rod end balljoints from the steering arms of the stub axle carriers. To separate the balljoints, use wedges or an extractor. (photo)

6 Place a piece of polythene sheeting under the cap of the brake fluid reservoir and then screw on the cap. This will create a vacuum and prevent loss of fluid when the hydraulic circuit is disconnected.

7 Disconnect the rigid brake pipe (which runs from the fluid reservoir) from the 3-way connector on the crossmember. Plug the open ends of the pipe and the connector to prevent the entry of dirt.

8 Jack-up the engine under the sump (alternatively use a hoist) so that the two engine mountings can be removed from the crossmember.

9 Support the crossmember with a trolley jack and unbolt the six bolts which secure it to the bodyframe.

10 The crossmember complete with suspension may now be withdrawn from beneath the vehicle.

11 Installation is a reversal of removal but check the wheel alignment as described later in this Chapter and bleed the brakes (Chapter 9).

8 Suspension upper arm - removal and refitting

1 Jack-up the front of the vehicle, remove the roadwheel and support the suspension lower arm on a block.

2 Remove the damper and road spring as previously described in this Chapter.

3 Unscrew the nut from the taper pin of the suspension upper swivel and then, using a suitable extractor, disconnect it from the stub axle carrier.

4 Unscrew and remove the two bolts which secure the suspension arm pivot to the crossmember. Withdraw the suspension arm carefully, retaining the shims so that they will be returned exactly as originally fitted.

5 Check the movement of the swivel in its housing. If it is shaky and has sideways movement, the suspension upper swivel assembly should be renewed.

6 Check for wear in the suspension arm pivot bushes. Do not attempt to renew them without the use of a press. If the bushes are badly worn it will probably be just as economical to renew the suspension arm complete.

9.3 Lower swivel to suspension lower arm bolts (two of these bolts secure the radius arm)

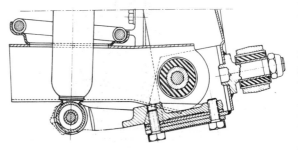

Fig 11.10 Rear damper lower (eye-bolt type) mounting

7 Refitting is a reversal of removal but check the wheel alignment as described later in this Chapter.

9 Suspension lower arm - removal and refitting

1 Jack-up the front of the vehicle and remove the roadwheel.

2 Compress the road spring but it need not be removed.

3 Disconnect the anti-roll bar drop link from the suspension lower arm and then unscrew and remove the four nuts from the bolts which connect the radius arm and the lower balljoint to the suspension lower arm. (photo)

4 Unscrew and remove the pivot bolt which connects the suspension lower arm to the crossmember and then carefully withdraw the suspension arm noting the sequence of washers and particularly the location of shims.

5 If the pivot bush requires renewal then it will have to be removed and installed using a press.

6 Refitting is a reversal of removal but check the wheel alignment on completion, as described later in this Chapter.

10 Rear damper - removal, testing, refitting

1 Unscrew the locknut and nut from the upper mounting. These are accessible within the luggage boot on saloon models and covered by small domes in the luggage platform of estate wagon versions.

2 Unscrew the two bolts which secure the damper lower mounting plate and then withdraw the damper through the coil spring and suspension arm in a downward direction. Later model dampers have an eye-bolt type lower mounting. (photo)

3 Testing is carried out in a similar manner to that described

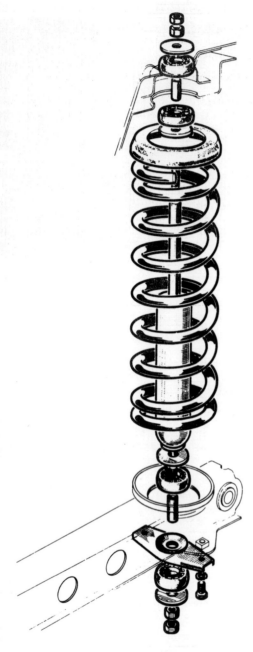

Fig 11.11 Rear damper mountings

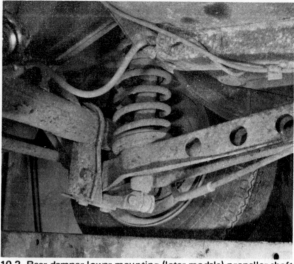

10.2 Rear damper lower mounting (later models) propeller shaft removed in the interest of clarity

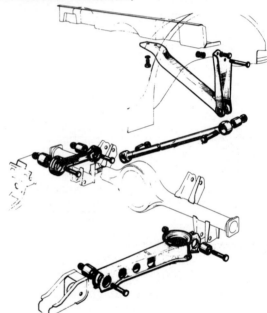

Fig 11.12 Exploded view of rear suspension arms and transverse rod

Fig 11.13 Steering box external components

    A Flexible coupling
    B Top cover plate
    C Drop arm

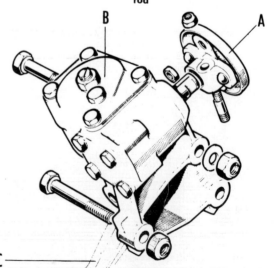

C

for the front dampers in Section 3.

4 Refitting is a reversal, of removal but do not over compress the rubber insulators.

11 Rear road spring - removal and refitting

1 Jack-up the rear of the vehicle and support the body side-members on axle stands. Remove the roadwheel.
2 Remove the telescopic damper as described in the preceding Section.
3 Release the nut (a turn or two) on the suspension lower arm front pivot bolt.
4 Support the rear end of the lower suspension arm on a jack and remove the rear pivot bolt.
5 Slowly lower the jack until the road spring can be withdrawn from its pans.
6 Refitting is a reversal of removal but tighten the pivot bolts when the weight of the vehicle is on the suspension with all jacks and axle stands removed. Tighten the front pivot bolt to a torque of 54 lb/ft (7.5 kg/m) and the rear one to 83 lb/ft (11.5 kg/m).

12 Rear suspension lower arm - removal and refitting

1 Raise the rear of the vehicle and support the body side-members and also place jacks under the rear axle.
2 Remove the roadwheel.
3 Remove the damper (Section 10).
4 Remove the roadspring (Section 11).
5 Remove the two pivot bolts from the suspension arm and detach the handbrake cable guide before lifting the arm from the attachment points.
6 If the bonded rubber bushes are worn they must be renewed by pressing them out on a press.
7 Refitting is a reversal of removal, but tighten the pivot bolts to the specified torque when the weight of the vehicle is on the suspension and the jacks have been removed.

13 Rear suspension upper control arm - removal and refitting

1 The upper control arm may be removed by withdrawing the two pivot bolts.
2 Where new bushes are required then the old ones should be extracted and the new ones installed using a press.
3 Refitting the arm is a reversal of removal but tighten the rear pivot bolt to a torque of 83 lb/ft (11.5 kg/m) and the front one to 54 lb/ft (7.5 kg/m).

14 Rear transverse rod (Panhard rod) - removal and refitting

1 Mark the rod before removing it so that it can be refitted the same way round.
2 Unscrew and remove the pivot bolt from each end of the rod and remove it from the rear axle casing and the body support brackets.
3 Renewal of the bonded rubber bushes should be carried out using a press.
4 Refitting is a reversal of removal but tighten the pivot bolts to a torque of 69 lb/ft (9.5 kg/m) with the normal weight of the vehicle on the suspension.

15 Steering gear and linkage - inspection

1 Commence inspection by first eliminating any possible wear or movement in the suspension arm bushes, the radius arm-end fittings and the front crossmember securing bolts.
2 Check that the front hubs are correctly adjusted (Section 2).

3 Check that the bolts which secure the steering box, the idler assembly and the steering arms to the stub axle carrier are all tight.
4 Lost motion between the steering wheel and the roadwheels must now be due to wear in the steering box, idler, balljoints or steering shaft flexible couplings.
5 Test each of these components by gripping it, and the adjacent parts firmly and testing for movement or play in all directions.
wheel alignment whenever any part of the steering or front suspension has been dismantled or reassembled.

16 Steering box - adjustment

1 Provision is made for taking up play in the steering box which occurs between the worm and roller. This must not be confused with wear in the steering linkage or other components which should always be checked as described in the preceding Section.
2 Jack-up the front of the vehicle and support it on stands so that the roadwheels are clear of the ground and can be turned from lock-to-lock.
3 Set the roadwheels in the straight ahead position with the steering wheel centered.
4 Turn the steering wheel one ¼ turn to the left and then grip the steering drop arm and test it for free movement by moving it in both rotational directions.
5 Repeat the test at the ½ turn and ¾ turn positions of the steering wheel and then repeat the three checks on the opposite lock.
6 If free-movement can be detected only when the steering wheel is turned not more than one ¼ turn from the centered position then slacken the locknut on the adjuster screw which is located on the top cover plate of the steering box and screw the adjuster screw in a fraction of a turn at a time until by turning the steering wheel through 90° in both directions of lock, the free movement is just eliminated.
7 Hold the adjuster screw still and tighten the locknut.
8 If looseness in the drop arm can be detected when the steering wheel is moved to the ½ and ¾ turn positions then it is probably that the steering box components are worn and must be renewed.

17 Steering box - removal and installation

1 Within the engine compartment, disconnect the steering column flexible coupling from the wormshaft by removing the cotter pin.
2 On models fitted with steering column gearchange, remove the spring clips from the selector rod pivot and withdraw the pivot from the bracket on the steering box (Fig. 11.14).
3 Unscrew the nuts from the two track rod end taper pins which are located in the eyes of the drop arm. Using a suitable extractor or forked wedges, disconnect the track rod end ball-joints from the drop arm.
4 Unscrew and remove the six bolts which secure the steering box to the bodyframe and bulkhead support.
5 Withdraw the steering box downwards to disengage it from the flexible coupling.
6 Installation is a reversal of removal but centre the steering wheel and check that the marks on the worm shaft and the steering box are in alignment before inserting the cotter pin (Fig. 11.15).
7 Tighten all bolts to the torque wrench settings given in 'Specifications'.

18 Steering box - dismantling, servicing, reassembly

1 Clean all dirt and oil from the external surfaces of the unit.
2 Bend back the tab washer and unscrew and remove the nut

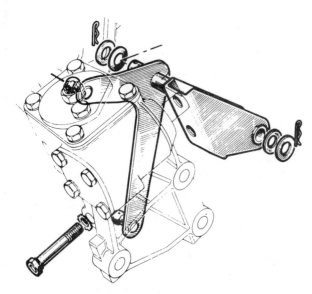

Fig 11.14 Steering column gearchange linkage attachment to steering box

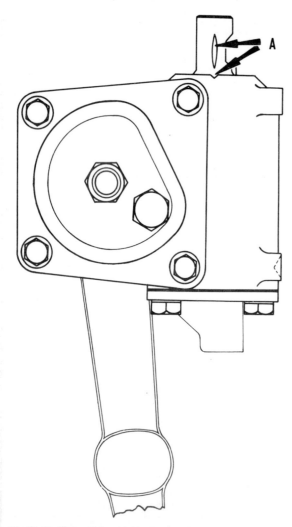

Fig 11.15 Wormshaft and steering box alignment marks (A)

which secures the steering drop arm. Scribe a mark across the end of the roller shaft and the drop arm so that the drop arm can be refitted to the splines in its original position and then using a suitable extractor, pull the drop arm from the shaft.

3   Unscrew the locknut from the adjuster screw on the steering box cover plate and then unbolt and remove the cover plate and gasket. Drain the oil from the housing and then withdraw the roller shaft upwards.

4   From the front of the steering box, remove the cover plate (four bolts) retaining the shims and gaskets.

5   Withdraw the worm shaft complete with bearings.

6   Clean all components and examine for wear, scoring or chipping.

7   New bearings may be fitted after pressing out the old outer tracks and pressing in the new.

8   Renew the oil seals as a matter of routine.

9   Reassembly is a reversal of dismantling. Use the original end-cover shim pack if the original bearings are retained, otherwise adjust the thickness of the shim pack to eliminate all endfloat of the wormshaft when the end-cover is bolted up.

10 Adjust the screw on the top cover plate (Section 16) and refill the unit with oil.

19 Steering wheel - removal and installation

1   Disconnect the leads from the battery.

2   On models having a central horn button, prise off the cap from the steering wheel hub. Extract the circlip and centre retaining screw and locknut and remove the horn switch components, (see Chapter 10).

3   On vehicles fitted with a horn ring, prise off the cap from the steering wheel hub. Extract the circlip and pull off the horn ring assembly from the steering wheel spokes. Remove the horn switch components now exposed (see Chapter 10).

4   With all models, the centre steering wheel retaining nut should now be unscrewed and removed and the wheel pulled off the steering shaft splines. If it is stuck, try striking the rear of the spokes with the palms of the hands otherwise use a two or three legged extractor but protect the steering wheel hub and spokes from damage.

5   Installation is a reversal of removal but first check that the roadwheels are in the straight-ahead position before locating the steering wheel, in its correct attitude, on the steering shaft splines.

20 Steering column - removal and installation

1   Disconnect the lead from the battery negative terminal.

2   Withdraw the cotter pin which connects the steering column shaft to the wormshaft of the steering box at the flexible coupling.

3   Disconnect the brake lines from the master cylinders which control the brake and clutch hydraulic circuits. Plug the lines to prevent loss of fluid or dirt entering.

4   Disconnect the brake stop lamp switch leads.

5   Disconnect the accelerator cable from the carburettor.

6   Disconnect the gearshift idler arm (steering column gearchange only) from its support. Retain the shims carefully.

7   Also on vehicles fitted with steering column change, disconnect the rod from the control lever at the bottom of the gearchange control tube.

8   Unscrew and remove the four nuts which secure the steering column support baseplate.

9   Disconnect the handbrake primary cable at the relay lever (see Chapter 9).

10 Disconnect the two wiring harness junction boxes located at the side of the steering column.

11 Disconnect the leads from the starter/ignition switch.

12 Disconnect the accelerator cable from the accelerator pedal.

13 Peel back the floor mat from around the steering column.

14 Unbolt the steering column bracket from the facia panel.

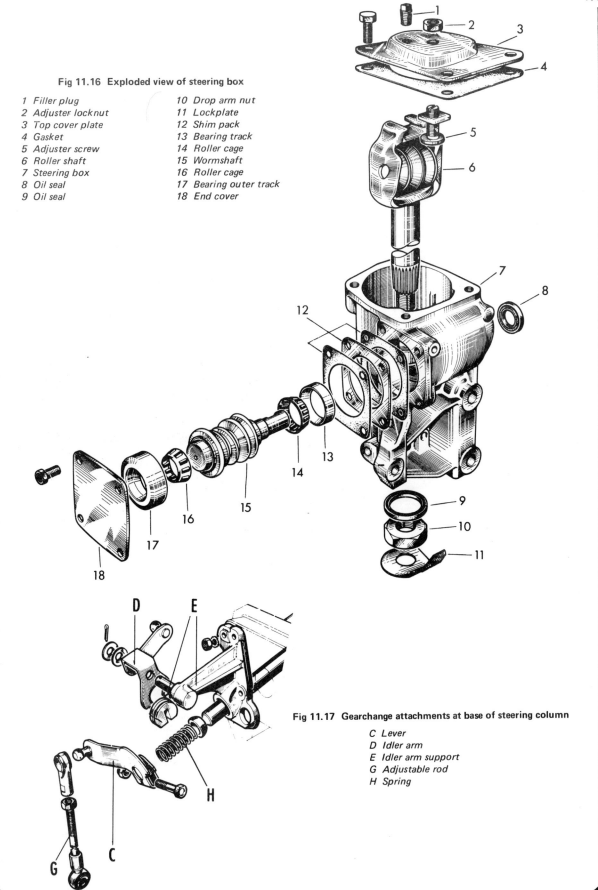

Fig 11.16 Exploded view of steering box

1 Filler plug
2 Adjuster locknut
3 Top cover plate
4 Gasket
5 Adjuster screw
6 Roller shaft
7 Steering box
8 Oil seal
9 Oil seal

10 Drop arm nut
11 Lockplate
12 Shim pack
13 Bearing track
14 Roller cage
15 Wormshaft
16 Roller cage
17 Bearing outer track
18 End cover

Fig 11.17 Gearchange attachments at base of steering column

C Lever
D Idler arm
E Idler arm support
G Adjustable rod
H Spring

15 The steering column can now be withdrawn into the interior of the vehicle complete with steering wheel.

16 Installation is a reversal of removal but observe the following points.

17 Align the marks on the flexible coupling and the wormshaft and then centre the steering wheel before inserting the cotter pin which secures the flexible coupling to the wormshaft. Do not tighten the cotter pin nut at this stage.

18 Insert the steering column to facia support bracket bolts only finger tight; also the four nuts at the steering column base support plate.

19 Move the steering column up or down so that there is a clearance between the lower face of the steering wheel hub and the upper rim of the steering column shroud of 5/64 in (2.0 mm).

20 Tighten the cotter pin nut of the flexible coupling, the upper bracket bolt and the base support plate nuts.

21 Should the steering column gearchange linkage require adjustment as the result of removing and installation of the steering column, refer to Chapter 6.

21 Steering column upper bearing - renewal

1 Should the steering column upper bearing become worn, causing movement in the shaft, it must be renewed. Similarly, removal of the combination lighting switch (if fitted) can only be removed after the upper bearing bracket is withdrawn from the steering column.

2 Disconnect the lead from the battery negative terminal.

3 Remove the steering wheel (Section 19).

4 Remove the collar (B) (Fig. 11.18) and the two half sections of the shroud (C and D).

5 Remove the upper bearing bracket (E) complete with retaining cup (F) and the bearing (G).

6 Prise up the crimped edges of the retaining cup and remove the cup and bearing from the upper bearing bracket.

7 Fit a new bearing and a new retaining cup and crimp the cup to secure it and the bearing to the upper bearing bracket. The bearing is self-lubricating and requires no additional lubrication.

8 Refitting is a reversal of dismantling but make sure that the

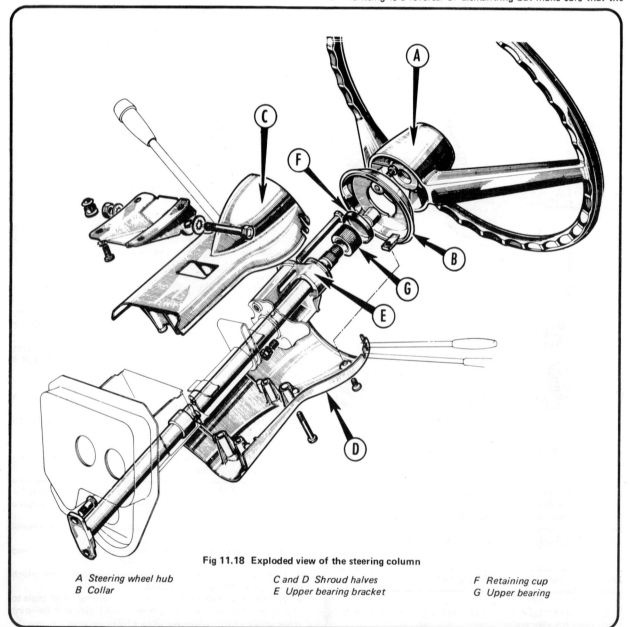

Fig 11.18 Exploded view of the steering column

A Steering wheel hub   C and D Shroud halves   F Retaining cup
B Collar   E Upper bearing bracket   G Upper bearing

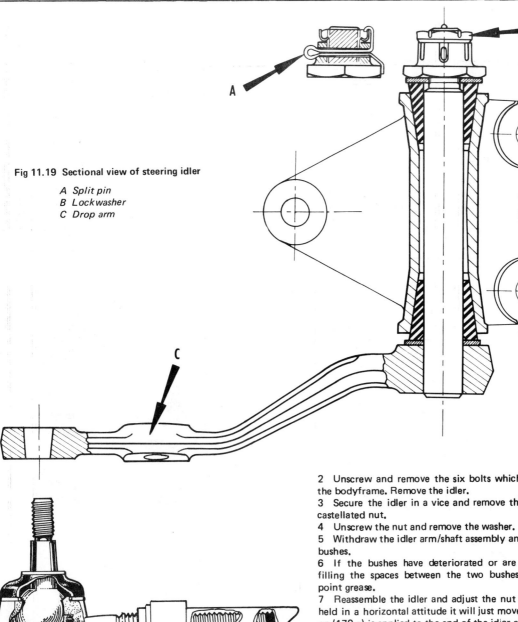

Fig 11.19 Sectional view of steering idler

A Split pin
B Lockwasher
C Drop arm

Fig 11.20 Cross sectional view of track-rod with clamp type
fixing

2   Unscrew and remove the six bolts which secure the idler to
the bodyframe. Remove the idler.
3   Secure the idler in a vice and remove the split pin from the
castellated nut.
4   Unscrew the nut and remove the washer.
5   Withdraw the idler arm/shaft assembly and extract the rubber
bushes.
6   If the bushes have deteriorated or are worn, renew them,
filling the spaces between the two bushes with high melting
point grease.
7   Reassemble the idler and adjust the nut so that with the arm
held in a horizontal attitude it will just move when a weight of 6
oz (170 g) is applied to the end of the idler arm.
8   Fit a new split pin.
9   Fit the idler to the bodyframe, tightening the bolts to a
torque of 34 lb/ft (4.7 kg/m).
10 Reconnect the balljoints to the steering idler arm and tighten
the taper pin nuts to a torque of 22 lb/ft. (3.0 kg/m).

23 Track-rods and balljoints

1   Early type balljoints and swivel joints have grease nipples for
regular lubrication. Later components are sealed and require
no maintenance.
2   Any wear in either type of balljoint will necessitate renewal
as no adjustment is possible.
3   On early models, the outer track-rods are adjustable and
secured by locknuts on the track-rod ends.
4   Later models are also adjustable and have track-rods which
incorporate clamps and pinch bolts.
5   It is imperative that the track-rod ends are set at an angle to
engage with the steering arm eyes and thus locate each balljoint
at the centre of its arc of travel (Fig. 11.21).

steering wheel is centered and fitted to the shaft splines while the
roadwheels are in the straight-ahead position.
9 Fit the half sections of the shroud so that there is a gap
between the lower face of the steering wheel hub and the upper
rim of the steering column shroud of 5/16 in (2.0 mm).

22 Steering idler - removal, servicing, refitting

1   Using forked wedges or an extractor, disconnect the two balljoints from the idler arm.

24 Front wheel alignment and steering angles

1   Accurate front wheel alignment is essential for good steering and tyre wear. Before considering the steering angle, check that the tyres are correctly inflated, that the front wheels are not buckled, the hub bearings are not worn or incorrectly adjusted and that the steering linkage is in good order, without slackness or wear at the joints.
2   Wheel alignment consists of four factors:

Camber, which is the angle at which the front wheels are set from the vertical when viewed from the front of the car. Positive

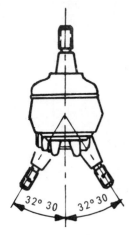

Fig 11.21 Track-rod ball joint setting diagram

camber is the amount (in degrees) that the wheels are tilted outwards at the top from the vertical.

Castor is the angle between the steering axis and a vertical line when viewed from each side of the car. Positive caster is when the steering axis is inclined rearward.

Steering axis inclination is the angle, when viewed from the front of the car, between the vertical and an imaginary line drawn between the upper and lower suspension leg pivots.

Toe in is the amount by which the distance between the front inside edges of the road wheels (measured at hub height) is less than the diametrically opposite distance measured between the rear inside edges of the front road wheels.
3   It is recommended that all steering angles are checked and set by a service station which has modern alignment equipment and where the necessary gauges are available or can be made up then carry out the following procedure:
4   **Camber angle** This is adjusted by slackening the nuts (E) (Fig. 11.24) and turning the eccentric washers. The correct camber angle is between 1° and 1° 45' (positive). It is possible to make up a gauge with a plumb line to check this setting by holding it against the wheel rims. Tighten the nuts on the lower suspension arm, when adjustment is complete, to a torque of 58 lb/ft (8.0 kg/m).
5   **Castor angle** is adjustable after slackening the two bolts which secure the radius arm to the suspension lower arm; also the two bolts which secure the suspension upper arm pivot to the crossmember. Release the clamps on the radius arms and adjust their lengths. Shortening the radius arms increases the caster angle and lengthening the radius arms descrease the castor angle. The correct castor angle is between 2° and 3° positive and it must not vary more than 0° 30' between left and right-hand sides.
6   **Toe-in.** Place the vehicle on level ground with the wheels in

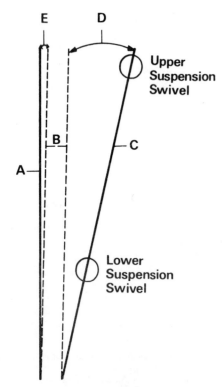

Fig 11.22 Steering angles viewed from the
front of vehicle (LH side)

A Roadwheel centre line   D Angle of inclination
B Vertical datum lines   E Camber angle (positive)
C Steering angle inclination

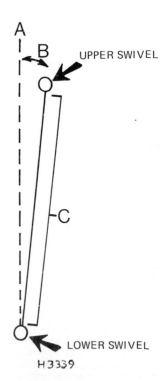

Fig 11.23 Typical castor angle diagram (positive)
viewed from side of vehicle

A Vertical datum line   C Steering axis
B Castor angle

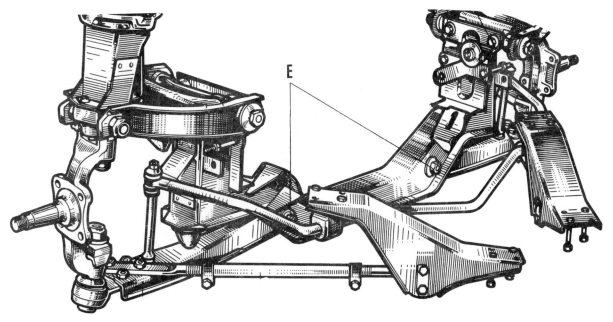

Fig 11.24 Camber angle adjusters (E)

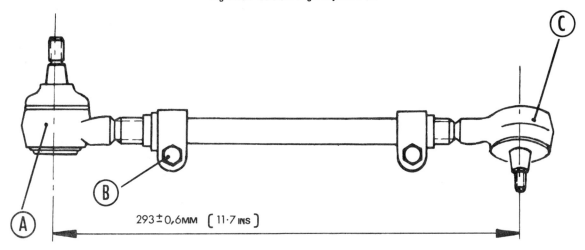

293±0,6мм [11·7 ins]

Fig 11.25 Outer track-rod basic setting diagram

A Ball joint nearest road wheel   B Pinch bolt   C Ball joint at centre track-rod connection

the straight ahead position.

7   Obtain or make a toe-in gauge. One may be easily made from tubing, cranked to clear the sump and bellhousing, having an adjustable nut and setscrew at one end. With the gauge, measure the distance between the two inner wheel rims at hub height at the front of the wheel.

8   Rotate the road wheel through 180° (half a turn) and measure the distance between the inner wheel rims at hub height at the rear of the wheel. This measurement should be greater by between 3/64 and 1/8 inch (1.2 and 3.2 mm).

This represents the correct toe-in of the front wheels.

9   Where the toe-in is found to be incorrect, slacken the lock-nuts (clamps on the later models) on each outer track rod and rotate each track rod an equal amount until the correct toe-in is obtained. Tighten the locknuts ensuring that the balljoints are held in the centre of their arc of travel during tightening. If new track rods or balljoints have been fitted, a starting point for adjusting the front wheel alignment is to set each outer track rod so that the distance measured between the balljoint centres (located one at each end of the track rod) is 11.7 in (293.0 mm).

25 Roadwheels and tyres

1   To avoid undue tyre wear and to maintain good roadholding and cornering, the tyre pressures should be checked and the tyres inflated if necessary, at weekly intervals.

2   Periodically remove each road wheel and pick out any stones from the tread. If the wheels have been balanced off the vehicle, they should be moved round the vehicle to equalise tyre wear. With radial tyres however, the wheels should be inter-changed between front and back on the same side and not from side to side in order to maintain the same direction of rotation. Where the wheels have been balanced on the vehicle the wheels should not be moved round the vehicle and if a wheel is removed its position on the hub should be marked so that it can be refitted as originally located to avoid upsetting the balance.

3   Check for wear or elongation of the roadwheel bolt holes and renew the wheel if evident.

4   Check the tyre tread depth. Where this is 1 mm or less in thickness then the tyre must be renewed.

26 Fault diagnosis - suspension and steering

Symptom	Reason/s	Remedy
Steering vague, car wanders and 'floats' at speed	Tyre pressures uneven	Check pressures and adjust as necessary.
	Dampers worn	Test, and replace if worn.
	Steering gear ball joints badly worn	Fit new ball joints.
	Suspension geometry incorrect	Check and rectify.
	Steering mechanism free play excessive	Adjust or overhaul steering mechanism.
	Front suspension and rear suspension pick-up points out of alignment or badly worn	Normally caused by poor repair work after a serious accident. Extensive rebuilding necessary.
	Front suspension lacking grease	Check condition and grease or replace worn parts according to type.
Stiff and heavy steering	Tyre pressures too low	Check pressures and inflate tyres.
	No oil in steering box	Top up steering box.
	No grease in steering ball joints	Replace or grease according to type.
	Front wheel toe-in incorrect	Check and reset toe-in.
	Suspension geometry incorrect	Check and rectify.
	Steering gear incorrectly adjusted too tightly	Check and re-adjust steering gear.
	Steering column badly misaligned	Determine cause and rectify (usually due to bad repair after severe accident damage and difficult to correct).
Wheel wobble and vibration	Wheel nuts loose	Check and tighten as necessary.
	Front wheels and tyres out of balance	Balance wheels and tyres.
	Steering ball joints badly worn	Replace steering gear ball joints.
	Hub bearings badly worn	Remove and fit new hub bearings.
	Steering gear free play excessive	Adjust and overhaul steering gear.

Chapter 12 Body and fittings

Contents

Specifications

	1300/1301 Saloon	1300/1301 Estate wagon	1500/1501 Saloon	1500/1501 Estate wagon
Unladen kerb weight	2227 lb (1010 kg)	2381 lb (1080 kg)	2249 lb (1020 kg)	2403 lb (1090 kg)
Gross laden weight	3152 lb (1429 kg)	3483 lb (1580 kg)	3175 lb (1440 kg)	3483 lb (1580 kg)

	Saloon	Estate wagon
Overall length	14ft 7½in (4.4 m)	14ft 1½in (4.2 m)
Overall width	5ft 2in (1.5 m)	5ft 2in (1.5 m)
Overall height (unladen - all models)	4ft 7in (139.7 cm)	
Overall height (laden - all models)	4ft 3in (129.54 cm)	

Luggage capacity
Saloon ... ... $15ft^3$ ($0.424 m^3$)
Estate wagon ... ... $56.5 ft^3$ ($1.599 m^3$)

1 General description

The body and underframe is of unitary, all-welded steel construction on all models within the range.

The front wings are bolted in position for ease of replacement in the event of damage.

The bonnet is locked from the interior of the vehicle, the doors are all hinged at their leading edges and are fitted with anti-burst type locks.

2 Maintenance - bodywork and underframe

1 The general condition of the car's bodywork is the one thing that significantly affects its value. Maintenance is easy but needs to be regular and particular. Neglect, particularly after minor damage, can lead quickly to further deterioration and costly repair bills. It is important also to keep watch on those parts of the car not immediately visible, for instance the underside, inside all the wheel arches and the lower part of the engine compartment.

2 The basic maintenance routine for the bodywork is washing preferably with a lot of water, from a hose. This will remove all the loose-solids which may have stuck to the car. It is important to flush these off in such a way as to prevent grit from scratching the finish.

The wheel arches and underbody need washing in the same way to remove any accumulated mud which will retain moisture and tend to encourage rust. Paradoxically enough, the best time to clean the underbody and wheel arches is in wet weather when the mud is thoroughly wet and soft. In very wet weather the underbody is usually cleaned of large accumulations automatically and this is a good time for inspection.

3 Periodically it is a good idea to have the whole of the underside of the car steam cleaned, engine compartment included, so that a thorough inspection can be carried out to see what minor repairs and renovations are necessary. Steam cleaning is available at many garages and is necessary for removal of accumulation of oily grime which sometimes is allowed to cake thick in certain areas near the engine, gearbox and back axle. If steam facilities are not available, there are one or two excellent grease solvents available which can be brush applied. The dirt can then be simply hosed off.

4   After washing paintwork, wipe off with a chamois leather to give an unspotted clear finish. A coat of clear protective wax polish will give added protection against chemical pollutants in the air. If the paintwork sheen has dulled or oxidised, use a cleaner/polisher combination to restore the brilliance of the shine. This requires a little effort, but is usually caused because regular washing has been neglected. Always check that the door and ventilator opening drain holes and pipes are completely clear so that water can drain out. Bright work should be treated the same way as paintwork. Windscreen and windows can be kept clear of the smeary film which often appears, if a little ammonia is added to the water. If they are sractched, a good rub with a proprietary metal polish will often clear them. Never use any form of wax or other body or chromium polish on glass.

3   Maintenance - upholstery and carpets

1   Mats and carpets should be brushed or vacuum cleaned regularly to keep them free of grit. If they are badly stained remove them from the car for scrubbing or sponging and make quite sure they are dry before replacement. Seats and interior trim panels can be kept clean by a wipe over with a damp cloth. If they do become stained (which can be more apparent on light coloured upholstery) use a little liquid detergent and a soft nail brush to scour the grime out of the grain of the material. Do not forget to keep the head lining clean in the same way as the upholstery. When using liquid cleaners inside the car do not over-wet the surfaces being cleaned. Excessive damp could get into the seams and padded interior causing stains, offensive odours or even rot. If the inside of the car gets wet accidentally it is worthwhile taking some trouble to dry it out properly, particularly where carpets are involved. Do NOT leave oil or electric heaters inside the car for this purpose.

4   Minor body damage - repair

See also photo sequences on pages 187, 188 and 189
Repair of minor scratches in the car's bodywork
If the scratch is very superficial, and does not penetrate to the metal of the bodywork repair is very simple. Lightly rub the areas of the scratch with a paintwork renovator (eg 'Top-Cut'), or a very fine cutting paste, to remove loose paint from the scratch and to clear the surrounding bodywork of wax polish. Rinse the area with clean water.

Apply touch-up paint to the scratch using a thin paint brush; continue to apply thin layers of paint until the surface of the paint in the scratch is level with surrounding paintwork. Allow the new paint at least two weeks to harden; then, blend it into the surrounding paintwork by rubbing the paint in the scratch area with a paintwork renovator (eg. 'Top-Cut'), or a very fine cutting paste. Finally apply wax polish.

An alternative to painting over the scratch is to use Holts 'Scratch-Patch'. Use the same preparation for the affected area; then simply, pick a patch of suitable size to cover the scratch completely. Hold the patch against the scratch and burnish its backing paper; the patch will adhere to the paintwork, freeing itself from the backing paper at the same time. Polish the affected area to blend the patch into the surrounding paintwork.

Where a scratch has penetrated, right through to the metal of the bodywork, causing the metal to rust, a different repair technique is required. Remove any loose rust from the bottom of the scratch with a penknife, then apply rust inhibiting paint (eg. 'Kurust') to prevent the formation of rust in the future. Using a rubber or nylon applicator fill the scratch with body-stopper paste. If required, this paste can be mixed with cellulose thinners to provide a very thin paste which is ideal for filling narrow scratches. Before the stopper-paste in the scratch hardens, wrap a piece of smooth cotton rag around the tip of a finger. Dip the finger in cellulose thinners and then quickly sweep it across the surface of the stopper-paste in the scratch;

this will ensure that the surface of the stopper-paste is slightly hollowed. The scratch can now be painted over as described earlier in this Section.

Repair of dents in the car's bodywork
When deep denting of the car's bodywork has taken place the first task is to pull the dent out, until the affected bodywork almost attains its original shape. There is little point in trying to restore the original shape completely, as the metal in the damaged area will have stretched on impact and cannot be re-shaped fully to its original contour. It is better to bring the level of the dent up to a point which is about 1/8 inch (3 mm) below the level of the surrounding bodywork. In cases where the dent is very shallow anyway, it is not worth trying to pull it out at all.

If the underside of the dent is accessible, it can be hammered out gently from behind, using a mallet with a wooden or plastic head. Whilst doing this, hold a suitable block of wood firmly against the outside of the dent. This block will thus prevent a large area of bodywork from being 'belled-out'.

Should the dent be in a section of the bodywork which has a double skin or some other factor making it inaccessible from behind, a different technique is called for. Drill several small holes through the metal inside the dent area - particularly in the deeper sections. Then screw long self-tapping screws into the holes just sufficiently for them to gain a good purchase in the metal. Now the dent can be pulled out by pulling on the protruding heads of the screws with a pair of pliers.

The next stage of the repair is the removal of the paint from the damaged area, and from an inch or so of the surrounding 'sound' bodywork. This is accomplished most easily by using a wire brush or abrasive pad on a power drill, although it can be done just as effectively by hand using sheets of abrasive paper. To complete the preparations for filling, score the surface of the bare metal with a screwdriver or the tang of a file, or alternatively, drill small holes in the affected area. This will provide a really good 'key' for the filler paste.

To complete the repair see the Section on filling and re-spraying.

Repair of rust holes or gashes in the car's bodywork
Remove all paint from the affected area and from an inch or so of the surrounding 'sound' bodywork, using an abrasive pad or a wire brush on a power drill. If these are not available a few sheets of abrasive paper will do the job just as effectively. With the paint removed you will be able to gauge the severity of the corrosion and therefore decide whether to replace the whole panel (if this is possible) or to repair the affected area. Replacement body panels are not as expensive as most people think and it is often quicker and more satisfactory to fit a new panel than to attempt to repair large areas of corrosion.

Remove all fittings from the affected area, except those which will act as a guide to the original shape of the damaged body-work (eg. headlamp shells etc.,). Then, using tin snips or a hack-saw blade, remove all loose metal and any other metal badly affected by corrosion. Hammer the edges of the hole inwards in order to create a slight depression for the filler paste.

Wire brush the affected area to remove the powdery rust from the surface of the remaining metal. Paint the affected area with rust inhibiting paint (eg. 'Kurust'); if the back of the rusted area is accessible treat this also.

Before filling can take place it will be necessary to block the hole in some way. This can be achieved by the use of one of the following materials: Zinc gauze, Aluminium tape or Poly-urethane foam.

Zinc gauze is probably the best material to use for a large hole. Cut a piece to the approximate size and shape of the hole to be filled, then position it in the hole so that its edges are below the level of the surrounding bodywork. It can be retained in position by several blobs of filler paste around its periphery.

Aluminium tape should be used for small or very narrow holes. Pull a piece off the roll and trim it to the approximate size and shape required, then pull off the backing paper (if used) and stick the tape over the hole; it can be overlapped if the thickness

Preparation for filling
Typical example of rust damage to a body panel. Before starting ensure that you have all of the materials required to hand. The first task is to ...

... remove body fittings from the affected area, except those which can act as a guide to the original shape of the damaged bodywork - the headlamp shell in this case.

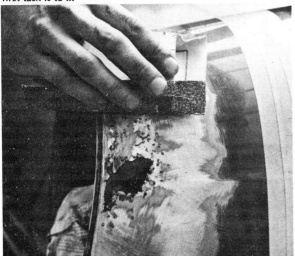

Remove all paint from the rusted area and from an inch or so of the adjoining 'sound' bodywork - use coarse abrasive paper or a power drill fitted with a wire brush or abrasive pad. Gently hammer in the edges of the hole to provide a hollow for the filler.

Before filling, the larger holes must be blocked off. Adhesive aluminium tape is one method; cut the tape to the required shape and size, peel off the backing strip (where used), position the tape over the hole and burnish to ensure adhesion.

Alternatively, zinc gauze can be used. Cut a piece of the gauze to the required shape and size; position it in the hole below the level of the surrounding bodywork; then ...

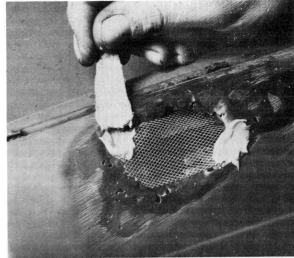

... secure in position by placing a few blobs of filler paste around its periphery. Alternatively, pop rivets or self-tapping screws can be used. Preparation for filling is now complete.

Filling and shaping
Mix filler and hardener according to manufacturer's instructions -
avoid using too much hardener otherwise the filler will harden
before you have a chance to work it.

Apply the filler to the affected area with a flexible applicator -
this will ensure a smooth finish. Apply thin layers of filler at 20
minute intervals, until the surface of the filler is just 'proud' of
the surrounding bodywork. Then ...

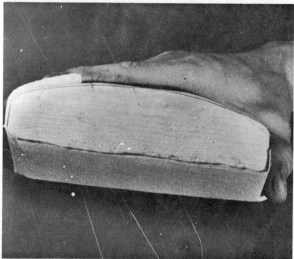

... remove excess filler and start shaping with a Surform plane or
a dreadnought file. Once an approximate contour has been
obtained and the surface is relatively smooth, start using ...

... abrasive paper. The paper should be wrapped around a flat
wood, cork or rubber block - this will ensure that it imparts a
smooth surface to the filler.

40 grit production paper is best to start with, then use progressively finer abrasive paper, finishing with 400 grade 'wet-and-dry'
When using 'wet-and-dry' paper, periodically rinse it in water
ensuring also, that the work area is kept wet continuously.

Rubbing-down is complete when the surface of the filler is
really smooth and flat, and the edges of the surrounding paintwork are finely 'feathered'. Wash the area thoroughly with clean
water and allow to dry before commencing re-spray.

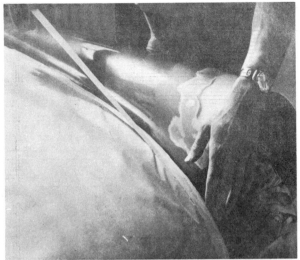

Masking and spraying
Firstly, mask off all adjoining panels and the fittings in the spray area. Ensure that the area to be sprayed is completely free of dust. Practice using an aerosol on a piece of waste metal sheet until the technique is mastered.

Spray the affected area with primer - apply several thin coats rather than one thick one. Start spraying in the centre of the repair area and then work outwards using a circular motion - in this way the paint will be evenly distributed.

When the primer has dried inspect its surface for imperfections. Holes can be filled with filler paste or body-stopper, and lumps can be sanded smooth. Apply a further coat of primer, then 'flat' its surface with 400 grade 'wet-and-dry' paper.

Spray on the top coat, again building up the thickness with several thin coats of paint. Overspray onto the surrounding original paintwork to a depth of about five inches, applying a very thin coat at the outer edges.

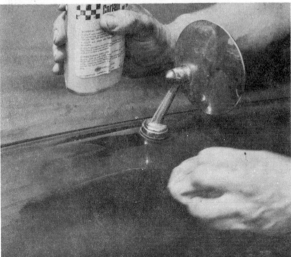

Allow the new paint two weeks, at least, to harden fully, then blend it into the surrounding original paintwork with a paint restorative compound or very fine cutting paste. Use wax polish to finish off.

The finished job should look like this. Remember, the quality of the completed work is directly proportional to the amount of time and effort expended at each stage of the preparation.

of one piece is insufficient. Burnish down the edges of the tape with the handle of a screwdriver or similar, to ensure that the tape is securely attached to the metal underneath.

Polyurethane foam is best used where the holes are situated in a section of bodywork of complex shape, backed by a small box section (eg. where the sill panel meets the rear wheel arch - most cars). The usual mixing procedure for this foam is as follows: Put equal amounts of fluid from each of the two cans provided in the kit, into one container. Stir until the mixture begins to thicken, then quickly pour this mixture into the hole, and hold a piece of cardboard over the larger apertures. Almost immediately the polyurethane will begin to expand, gushing frantically out of any small holes left unblocked. When the foam hardens it can be cut back to just below the level of the surrounding bodywork with a hacksaw blade.

Having blocked off the hole the affected area must now be filled and sprayed - see Section on bodywork filling and re-spraying.

Bodywork repairs - filling and re-spraying

Before using this Section, see the Sections on dent, deep scratch, rust hole, and gash repairs.

Many types of bodyfiller are available, but generally speaking those proprietary kits which contain a tin of filler paste and a tube of resin hardener (eg "Holts Cataloy") are best for this type of repair. A wide, flexible plastic or nylon applicator will be found invaluable for imparting a smooth and well contoured finish to the surface of the filler.

Mix up a little filler on a clean piece of card or board - use the hardener sparingly (follow the maker's instructions on the packet), otherwise the filler will set very rapidly.

Using the applicator, apply the filler paste to the prepared area; draw the applicator across the surface of the filler to achieve the correct contour and to level the filler surface. As soon as a contour that approximates to the correct one is achieved, stop working the paste; if you carry on too long the paste will become sticky and begin to 'pick-up' on the applicator. Continue to add thin layers of filler paste at twenty-minute intervals until the level of the filler is just 'proud' of the surrounding bodywork.

Once the filler has hardened, excess can be removed using a Surform plane or Dreadnought file. From then on, progressively finer grades of abrasive paper should be used, starting with a 40 grade production paper and finishing with 400 grade 'wet-and-dry' paper. Always wrap the abrasive paper around a flat rubber, cork, or wooden block - otherwise the surface of the filler will not be completely flat. During the smoothing of the filler surface the 'wet-and-dry' paper should be periodically rinsed in water; this will ensure that a very smooth finish is imparted to the filler at the final stage.

At this stage the 'dent' should be surrounded by a ring of bare metal, which in turn should be encircled by a finely 'feathered' edge of the good paintwork. Rinse the repair area with clean water, until all of the dust produced by the rubbing-down operation is gone.

Spray the whole repair area with a light coat of grey primer - this will show up any imperfections in the surface of the filler. Repair these imperfections with fresh filler paste or body-stopper, and once more smooth the surface with abrasive paper. If bodystopper is used, it can be mixed with cellulose thinners to form a really thin paste which is ideal for filling small holes. Repeat this spray and repair procedure until you are satisfied that the surface of the filler, and the feathered edge of the paintwork are perfect. Clean the repair area with clean water and allow to dry fully.

The repair area is now ready for spraying. Paint spraying must be carried out in a warm, dry, windless and dust free atmosphere. This condition can be created artifically if you have access to a large indoor working area, but if you are forced to work in the open, you will have to pick your day very carefully. If you are working indoors, dousing the floor in the work area with water will 'lay' the dust which would otherwise be in the atmosphere. If the repair area is confined to one body panel,

mask off the surrounding panels; this will help to minimise the effects of a slight mis-match in paint colours. Bodywork fittings (eg chrome strips, door handles etc) will also need to be masked off. Use genuine masking tape and several thicknesses of newspaper for the masking operation.

Before commencing to spray, agitate the aerosol can thoroughly, then spray a test area (an old tin, or similar) until the technique is mastered. Cover the repair area with a thick coat of primer; the thickness should be built up using several thin layers of paint rather than one thick one. Using 400 grade 'wet-and-dry' paper, rub down the surface of the primer until it is really smooth. While doing this, the work area should be thoroughly doused with water, and the wet-and-dry paper periodically rinsed in water. Allow to dry before spraying on more paint.

Spray on the top coat, again building up the thickness by using several thin layers of paint. Start spraying in the centre of the repair area and then, using a circular motion, work outwards until the whole repair area and about 2 inches of the surrounding original paintwork is covered. Remove all masking material 10 to 15 minutes after spraying on the final coat of paint.

Allow the new paint at least 2 weeks to harden fully; then, using a paintwork renovator (eg "Top-Cut") or a very fine cutting paste, blend the edges of the new paint into the existing paintwork. Finally, apply wax polish.

---

5   Major body damage - repair

Where serious damage has occurred or large areas need renewal due to neglect, it means certainly that completely new sections or panels will need welding in and this is best left to professionals. If the damage is due to impact it will also be necessary to completely check the alignment of the body shell structure. Due to the principle of construction the strength and shape of the whole can be affected by damage to a part. In such instances the services of a SIMCA agent with specialist checking jigs are essential. If a body is left misaligned it is first of all dangerous as the car will not handle properly and secondly uneven stresses will be imposed on the steering, engine and transmission, causing abnormal wear or complete failure. Tyre wear may also be excessive.

---

6   Maintenance - hinges and locks

1   Oil the hinges of the bonnet, boot and doors with a drop or two of light oil periodically. A good time is after the car has been washed.
2   Oil the bonnet release catch pivot pin and the safety catch pivot pin periodically.
3   Do not over lubricate door latches and strikers. Normally a little oil on the rotary cam spindle alone is sufficient.

---

7   Doors - tracing rattles and their rectification

1   Check first that the door is not loose at the hinges and that the latch is holding the door firmly in position. Check also that the door lines up with the aperture in the body.
2   If the hinges are loose or the door is out of alignment it will be necessary to reset the hinge positions, as described in Section 15.
3   If the latch is holding the door properly it should hold the door tightly when fully latched and the door should line up with the body. If it is out of alignment it needs adjustment as described in Section 15. If loose, some part of the lock mechanism must be worn out and requiring renewal.
4   Other rattles from the door would be caused by wear or looseness in the window winder, the glass channels and sill strips or the door buttons and interior latch release mechanism.

8 Front wing - removal and refitting

1   Jack-up the front of the vehicle and support the body frame securely on axle stands or blocks.
2   Remove the roadwheel.
3   Unbolt the front bumper assembly.

4   Remove the rear shield (A.3 screws), from under the wing.
5   From the inside of the lower rear section of the wing remove the nut which secures the sill bright trim.
6   Unscrew and remove all the wing flange securing screws, two at the leading edge (B), four at the rear blanking plate (C), one at the rear bottom edge (D) and five (E) along the top edge which

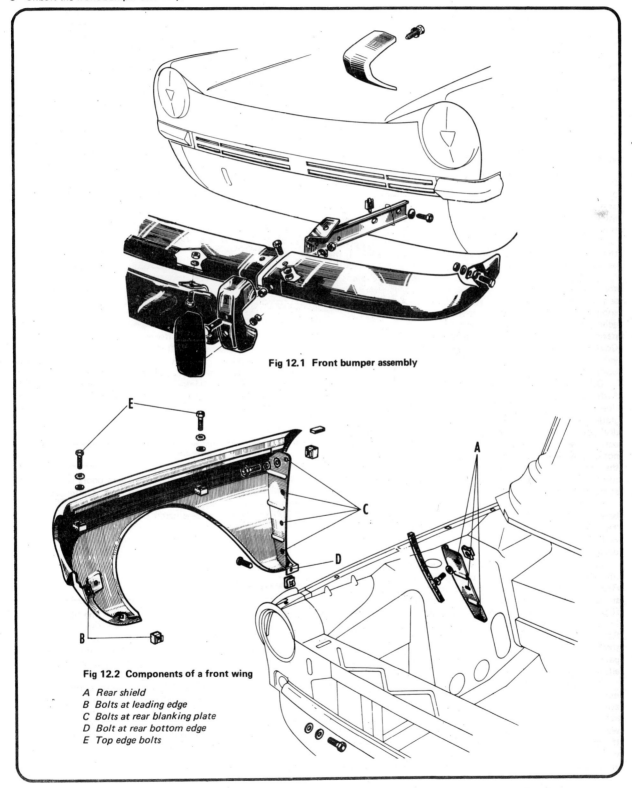

Fig 12.1 Front bumper assembly

Fig 12.2 Components of a front wing

A Rear shield
B Bolts at leading edge
C Bolts at rear blanking plate
D Bolt at rear bottom edge
E Top edge bolts

lie in the bonnet drain channel.

7   Installation is a reversal of removal but a bead of suitable sealant or mastic must be laid on the mating flanges of the body before the wing is offered into position.

8   When the wing is fitted it should be given a coat of under-body protection on its lower surface and sprayed on the outside to match the body colour.

9   Windscreen glass - removal and installation

1   Where a windscreen is to be replaced then if it is due to shattering, the facia demister vents should be covered before attempting removal. Adhesive sheeting is useful to stick to the outside of the glass to enable large areas of crystallised glass to be removed.

2   Where the screen is to be removed intact then an assistant will be required. First release the rubber surround from the bodywork by running a blunt, small screwdriver around and under the rubber weatherstrip both inside and outside the car. This operation will break the adhesive of the sealer originally used. Take care not to damage the paintwork or cut the rubber surround with the screwdriver. Remove the windscreen wiper arms and interior mirror and place a protective cover on the bonnet.

3   Have your assistant push the inner lip of the rubber surround off the flange of windscreen body aperture. Once the rubber surround starts to peel off the flange, the screen may be forced gently outwards by careful hand pressure. The second person should support and remove the screen complete with rubber surround and metal beading as it comes out.

4   Remove the beading from the rubber surround.

5   Before fitting a windscreen, ensure that the rubber surround is completely free from old sealant and glass fragments, and has not hardened or cracked. Fit the rubber surround to the glass and apply a bead of suitable sealant between the glass outer edge and the rubber.

6   Refit the bright moulding to the rubber surround.

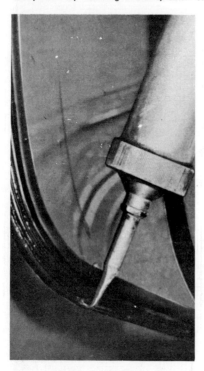

Fig 12.3 Applying sealant to windscreen rubber surround

10.1A Door interior handle showing spring retaining clip

10.1B Removing a window regulator handle

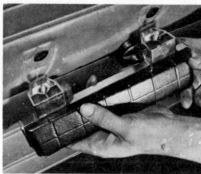

10.2 Removing an arm rest from the door panel

10.3 Removing the door interior trim panel

10.6 Front door lock mechanism and glass channel

10.7 Lock striker plate on door edge

10.11 Location of door lock plunger

7 Cut a piece of strong cord greater in length than the periphery of the glass and insert it into the body flange locating channel of the rubber surround.

8 Apply a thin bead of sealant to the face of the rubber channel which will eventually mate with the body.

9 Offer the windscreen to the body aperture and pass the ends of the cord, previously fitted and located at bottom centre into the vehicle interior.

10 Press the windscreen into place, at the same time have an assistant pulling the cords to engage the lip of the rubber channel over the body flange.

11 Remove any excess sealant with a paraffin soaked rag.

10 Door locks - removal and refitting

1 Remove the door interior handle and the window regulator handle. These handles are retained by spring clips which engage in a groove in the operating shank and they can be removed by inserting a hooked piece of wire between the handle and the escutcheon plate. (photos)

2 Unscrew and remove the two screws from the arm rest on the door panel and remove it. (photo)

3 Remove the door interior trim panel. To do this, insert the fingers under the lower edge and carefully prise it from its securing clips. (photo)

4 Peel away the waterproof sheeting without tearing it.

5 On left-hand front doors which are fitted with the cylinder type lock, extract the forked retaining plate (A) (Fig 12.4) from the lock barrel (B) and remove the barrel.

6 On front doors only, the glass channel bracket at the bottom of the channel must be released before the lock mechanism, within the door cavity, can be removed. (photo)

7 Unscrew and remove the lock striker plate (C) from the edge

of the door.

8 Remove the two securing screws from the remote control mounting plate (D).

9 Remove the remote control rod insulator (E).

10 Remove the bellcrank securing bolt and disconnect it from the lock mechanism. On rear doors only, washers are incorporated in the bellcrank pivot.

11 Remove the door lock plunger (F) which is located on the sill of the door, by unscrewing it. (photo)

12 Withdraw the lock and remote control assembly from within the door cavity.

13 Refitting is a reversal of removal.

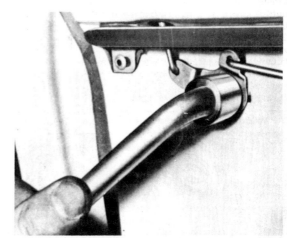

Fig 12.5 Removing bellcrank from door interior

Fig 12.4 Exploded view of a front door (early type without opening quarterlight ventilator)

A Forked retaining plate
B Lock barrel
C Lock striker plate
D Remote control mounting plate
E Remote control rod insulator
F Door lock plunger
G Plunger connecting rod

11 Front door glass and regulator - removal and refitting

1 Remove the door interior handles and trim as described in the preceding Section.
2 Temporarily refit the window regulator handle and wind the window down to its fullest extent.
3 Remove the weather strips by prising the securing clips upwards.
4 Remove the adjuster bolt which secures the lower run of the central channel guide assembly.
5 Remove the glass bracket guide.
6 Raise the glass and release the glass channel lower bracket.
7 Now lower the glass until with the regulator mechanism securing screws removed, the arms and rollers can be extracted from the slide at the bottom of the glass.
8 Prop the window glass while the regulator mechanism is withdrawn through the door aperture.
9 Lower the glass fully and remove it from its guide channels. The glass can then be withdrawn upwards after turning it through 90°.
10 Refitting is a reversal of removal.

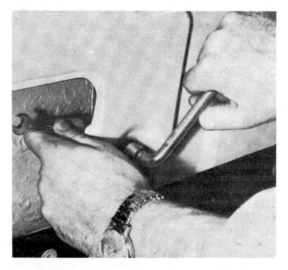

Fig 12.6 Removing central channel guide adjuster bolt

12 Rear door glass and regulator - removal and refitting

1 Remove the door interior handles and trim as previously described.
2 Remove the weather strip by prising off the securing clips.
3 Temporarily refit the regulator handle and wind the window fully up. Support the glass with a prop.
4 Unscrew and remove the four securing screws from the window regulator mechanism and push it towards the front of the vehicle to release the rollers from the slide at the bottom of the glass.
5 Withdraw the window regulator through the aperture in the door inner panel.
6 Unscrew and remove the two screws which are located under the weatherstrip at the top of the doorframe.
7 Remove the adjuster bolt which secures the lower run of the central channel guide assembly.
8 Remove the prop and lower the glass fully.
9 Press on the central channel guide to separate it from the glass upper channel.
10 Tilt the central channel towards the front of the vehicle and then withdraw it complete with quarter light from the door cavity.
11 The main window glass may now be withdrawn.
12 Refitting is a reversal of removal.

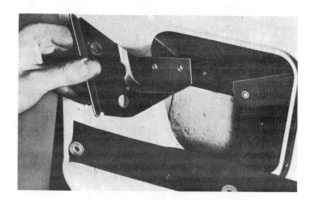

Fig 12.7 Removing the glass bracket guide

13 Front door quarterlight ventilators - removal and refitting

1 Remove the door interior trim as described in Section 10.
2 Prise out the weather strips and retaining clips adjacent to the central channel guide.
3 Prise the glass channel from the central guide.
4 Unscrew and remove all the screws which are located under the weather strip and secure the ventilator frame to the door frame.
5 Unscrew and remove the adjuster bolt which secures the lower run of the central channel guide assembly. Extract the glass channel.
6 Temporarily refit the window regulator handle and wind the window fully down then pull the central channel guide to the rear disengaging it from the door frame.
7 Turn the ventilator assembly through 90° and withdraw it from the door.
8 Refitting is a reversal of removal. Adjustment can be carried out to provide easier or stiffer opening of the ventilator by screwing in or releasing the bolt located at the clamp on its lower swivel. This bolt can be reached from within the door cavity when the quarterlight ventilator is still in position.

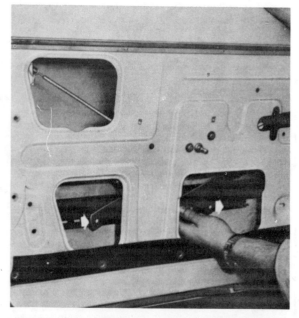

Fig 12.8 Disconnecting window regulator rollers from slide

Fig 12.9 Withdrawing the window regulator mechanism

Fig 12.10 Removing the front door glass

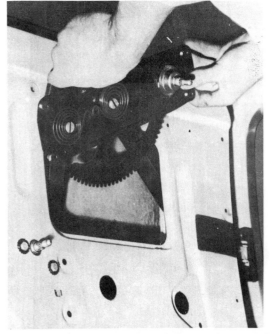

Fig 12.11 Withdrawing a rear door window regulator assembly

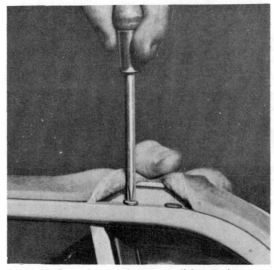

Fig 12.12 Removing rear door quarterlight securing screws

Fig 12.13 Removing front door quarterlight ventilator securing screws

Fig 12.14 Removing quarterlight ventilator from a front door

14 Rear door fixed quarterlight - removal and refitting

1   The procedure is described in Section 12 paragraphs 1 to 9 in conjunction with removal of the main glass. However, it is not necessary to remove the channel guide assembly but just to withdraw the glass and weatherstrip from the door frame, once the adjuster bolt has been released at the base of the central channel guide and the guide pushed aside.

15 Door - removal and installation

1   Open the door wide and prise out the rubber grommet from around the check strap.
2   Grind or file off the peened end of the securing pin and drive it from the check strap.
3   Support the lower edge of the door on jacks or blocks, using a cloth pad or blanket to protect the paintwork.
4   Drive out the hinge pins using a suitable drift.
5   If the hinge plates are worn, their holes can be carefully drilled out and oversize pins fitted. Where this does not prove satisfactory, the hinge plate bolts will have to be removed and new ones fitted.
6   Installation is a reversal of removal but check that the gap round the doorframe is equal at all points. Slight adjustment of the door within the frame can be made by moving the hinge plates on the door pillar or the door edge or by the inclusion of shims under them.
7   Test the door closure and adjust the position of the striker plate on the door pillar as necessary.

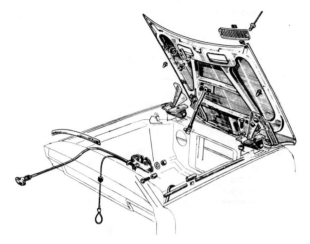

Fig 12.15 Bonnet and release mechanism

16 Bonnet - removal and installation

1   Raise the bonnet and prop it open.
2   Scribe round the hinge plates so that they can be located in their original positions.
3   With the help of an assistant, support the bonnet and unscrew the bolts which attach the hinge plates to the body. Lift the bonnet from the vehicle.
4   In the event of the internal bonnet release breaking, an emergency pull is located beneath the facia panel.

17 Luggage boot lid - removal and refitting

1   Open the lid and support it in the fully open position using a prop.
2   Place rags between the rear edge of the lid and the bodywork to prevent damage to the paint during removal.
3   Scribe round the hinge plates so that they can be refitted in their original positions.
4   Unscrew the bolt from the central retaining clip which anchors the ends of the counterbalance torsion bars.
5   With the help of an assistant, unscrew the bolts from the hinge plates and remove the lid.
6   Refitting is a reversal of removal. Check the positioning of the lid within the bodywork and adjust the location of the hinge plates if necessary.
7   Test the closure of the lid and adjust the position of the striker plate if required.

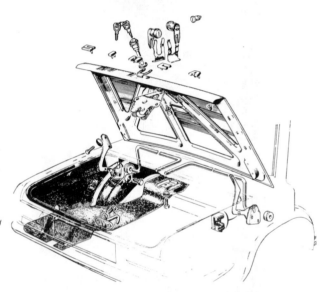

Fig 12.16 Luggage boot lid components

18 Estate wagon tailgate - removal and installation

1   Close the tailgate and lower the window.
2   Remove the retaining clips from the hinge pins.
3   With an assistant holding the tailgate in position, drive out the hinge pins using a thin drift.
4   Release the tailgate locks and unbolt the tailgate check straps. Lift the tailgate from the bodyframe but if it is to be withdrawn more than a few inches, the leads to the rear number

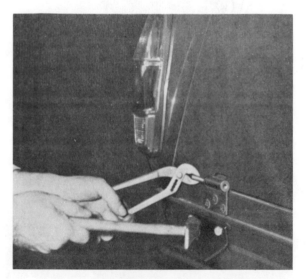

Fig 12.17 Driving out a tailgate hinge pin

plate will have to be disconnected. Installation is a reversal of removal.

19 Tailgate - dismantling and reassembly

1   Lower the window and open the tailgate.
2   Unscrew and remove the tailgate inner panel and peel off the waterproof sheet.
3   Unclip the weather strip and the window glass horizontal guide (A). (Fig 12.18)
4   Remove the tailgate lock handle (B).
5   Wind up the tailgate window and remove the four screws which secure the regulator mechanism within the tailgate cavity. Remove the regulator assembly after disengaging it from the drive grooves and the roller slide.
6   Draw the window glass upwards from the tailgate and remove it.
7   Remove the side locks and the striker plates from the edges of the tailgate and detach the remote control assembly.
8   The window regulator handle and cylinder lock, located on the outside of the tailgate may be removed by first unscrewing the large locknut sited within the tailgate cavity. Extract the circlip and the ring nut.
9   Depress the plunger in the barrel and withdraw the lock cylinder by means of its key. The window regulator and lock can be removed after lifting the tailgate trim panel without dismantling any other components but take care not to crack the glass or distort the regulator mechanism during the operation.
10 Reassembly is a reversal of dismantling.

Fig 12.18 Tailgate weatherstrip and glass guide (A) and lock handle (B)

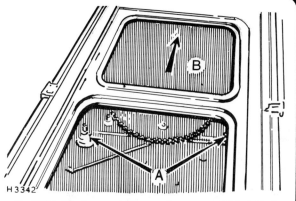

Fig 12.19 Window regulator securing screws within tailgate cavity (A) (B) Direction of removal of window regulator mechanism

Fig 12.20 Detaching the tailgate remote control assembly

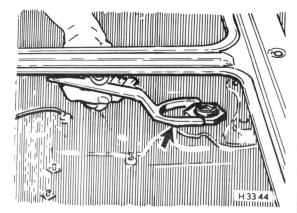

Fig 12.21 Unscrewing tailgate window regulator locknut

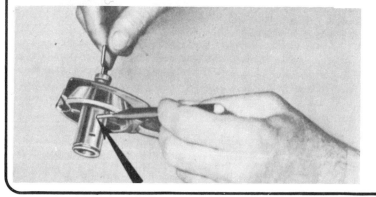

Fig 12.22 Depressing the plunger in the tailgate lock to withdraw the lock cylinder

20 Radiator grille - removal and refitting

1   The grille is held in position by a combination of clips and self-tapping screws.

2   On later models fitted with auxiliary driving lamps, these will first have to be disconnected if the inner grille is to be withdrawn.

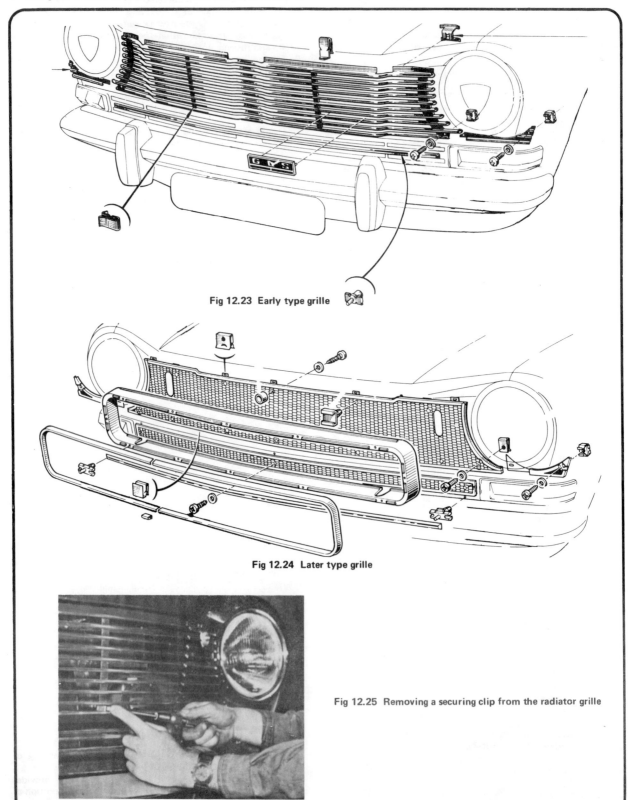

Fig 12.23 Early type grille

Fig 12.24 Later type grille

Fig 12.25 Removing a securing clip from the radiator grille

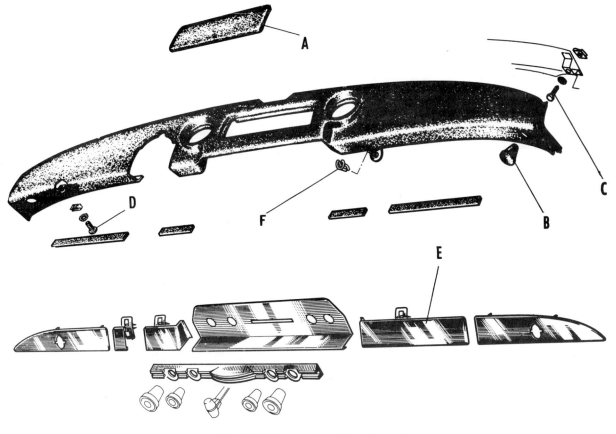

Fig 12.26 Components of the facia panel

A Cover plate
B Rubber plugs

C End screws
D Vertical retaining screws

E Embellisher
F Hook

21 Facia panel - removal and refitting

1   The upper section of the fascia panel is removable but the lower section is welded up to the bodyframe.
2   Disconnect the lead from the battery negative terminal.
3   Prise out the cover plate (A) (Fig 12.26) located on the top face of the facia panel.
4   Remove the instrument panel according to type as described in Chapter 10. Disconnect the speedometer cable.
5   Remove the instrument panel support plate (two screws) from the facia panel.
6   Pull out the two rubber plugs (B) one from each end of the facia panel.
7   Remove the two end screws (C) from the facia panel.
8   Remove the two screws (D) which are accessible from within the glove compartments.
9   Detach the embellisher (E) and the hook (F).
10 Withdraw the facia panel horizontally so that it is eased from the two brackets located at the base of the windscreen. With the facia panel withdrawn a few inches, disconnect each of the demister hoses.
11 Refitting is a reversal of removal.

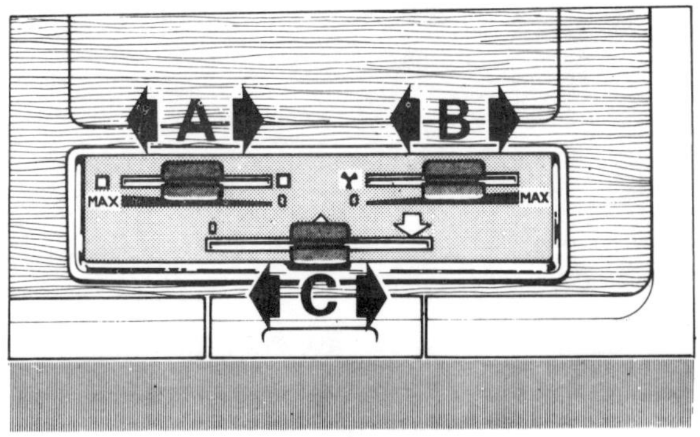

22 Heating and ventilation unit - general description

The heater unit is located on the engine compartment rear bulkhead. It operates from water circulated by the engine cooling system and incorporates a blower fan to supplement air flow through the heater matrix which is normally drawn through

Fig 12.27 Heater/ventilation control

A Heat control lever
B Blower (fan) control lever
C Air intake valve flap lever

two air intake grilles located just forward of the lower edge of the windscreen when the vehicle is in motion.

A control panel is located on the facia which provides variable heat control, adjusts the air intake and the proportion of air flow supplied to screen or vehicle interior.

23 Heater - removal and refitting

1 Disconnect the lead from the battery negative terminal.
2 Drain the cooling system. Place the heater control in the 'maximum' position and retain the coolant if it is required for further use.
3 Disconnect the leads from the heater motor.
4 Disconnect the speedometer cable from its securing clip on the heater air intake casing on the rear engine bulkhead.
5 Unscrew and remove the two lower securing hooks from the heater air intake casing.
6 Remove the securing nut and clip from the top of the heater air intake casing and draw it forward slightly and then upwards.
7 Disconnect the heater hoses from the nozzles on the matrix (B) (Fig 12.28) and the thermostatic valve, taking care not to wrench them off if stuck. It is better to cut them from the matrix and have to buy new hoses than crack a soldered joint

which can be very expensive to repair.
8 Disconnect the control cable from the lever on the thermostatic valve of the matrix. Disconnect the bypass hose from the thermostatic valve and remove the valve bracket screws.
9 Remove the two matrix securing screws and remove the matrix.
10 Disconnect the control cable from the flap valve (C).
11 Remove the securing screw from the deflector (D) and then withdraw the deflector carefully so that the retaining clips are left on the flap valve (C).
12 Unscrew and remove the four securing screws from the flap valve and remove it.
13 Refitting is a reversal of removal but check that the control rods are correctly connected to give smooth and complete operation between the closed and open positions.
14 Refill the cooling system.
15 Always check that the rubber outlet valves at the base of the heater air intake casing are operating correctly and are not

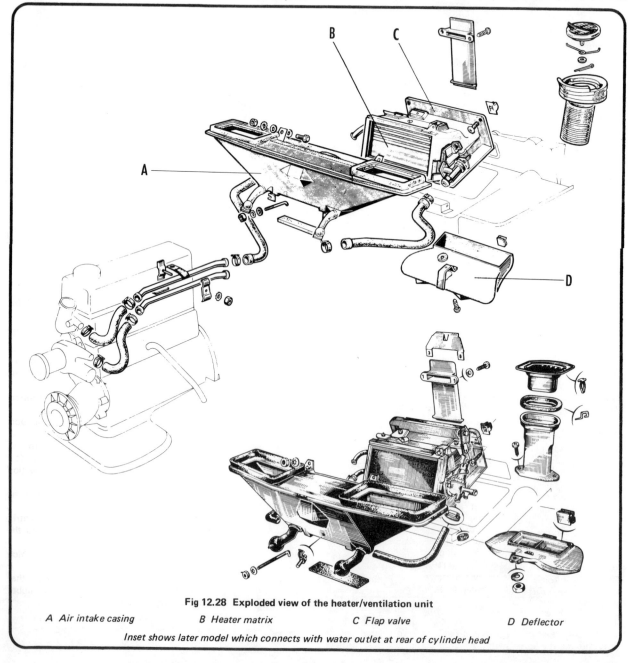

Fig 12.28 Exploded view of the heater/ventilation unit

A Air intake casing   B Heater matrix   C Flap valve   D Deflector

Inset shows later model which connects with water outlet at rear of cylinder head

Fig 12.29 Drilling out the heater motor resis[ ]securing rivet

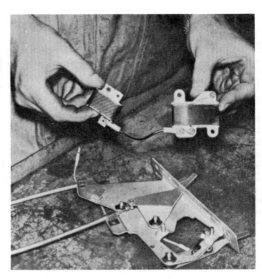

Fig 12.30 Removing the heater motor rheostat and resistor

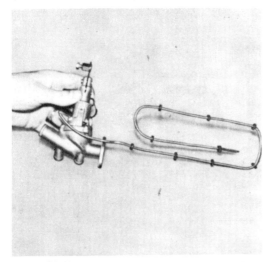

Fig 12.31 Heater thermostatic valve and sensor tube

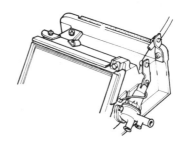

Fig 12.32 Heater matrix with thermostatic valve and sensor tube
correctly located

choked, otherwise rainwater will collect in the casing and either rust it or water will enter the vehicle interior.

24 Heater - servicing

1 Always ensure that the electrical leads to the heater motor are secure, also the coolant hoses.
2 Failure of the heater to warm up will probably be due to a clogged matrix, in which case, the heater flow and return hoses should be disconnected and a cold water hose connected to reverse flush it.
3 It is not recommended that radiator cleansers are used as they are likely to dislodge scale and other impurities from the cooling system generally which will only aggravate the condition by blocking the fine tubes of the matrix.
4 A leaking matrix should be removed and either repaired professionally or exchanged for a reconditioned unit. It is seldom that home soldering proves successful due to the need for localising any heat used in order to avoid opening up a seam elsewhere.

5 Should the heater motor rheostat fail, this can be renewed by first withdrawing the control panel from the facia panel and disconnecting the leads from the rheostat.
6 Drill out the rivet which secures the resistor to the support plate.
7 Unscrew the nuts which secure the rheostat to the support plate and remove both the resistor and the rheostat.
8 Installation of the two components is a reversal of removal.
9 Renewal of the thermostat valve can be carried out after removing the matrix and valve assembly as described in Section 23, paragraphs 1 to 9.
10 Disconnect the matrix to thermostatic valve hose from the valve end.
11 Remove the valve sensor tube from the face of the matrix and then remove the two screws which hold the valve to the matrix.
12 Withdraw the valve complete with sensor tube which cannot be separated.
13 Refitting the valve is a reversal of removal but ensure that the sensor tube is arranged as indicated and the little rubber insulating rings are fitted to prevent vibration.

Metric conversion tables

Inches	Decimals	Millimetres	Millimetres to Inches		Inches to Millimetres	
			mm	Inches	Inches	mm
1/64	0.015625	0.3969	0.01	0.00039	0.001	0.0254
1/32	0.03125	0.7937	0.02	0.00079	0.002	0.0508
3/64	0.046875	1.1906	0.03	0.00118	0.003	0.0762
1/16	0.0625	1.5875	0.04	0.00157	0.004	0.1016
5/64	0.078125	1.9844	0.05	0.00197	0.005	0.1270
3/32	0.09375	2.3812	0.06	0.00236	0.006	0.1524
7/64	0.109375	2.7781	0.07	0.00276	0.007	0.1778
1/8	0.125	3.1750	0.08	0.00315	0.008	0.2032
9/64	0.140625	3.5719	0.09	0.00354	0.009	0.2286
5/32	0.15625	3.9687	0.1	0.00394	0.01	0.254
11/64	0.171875	4.3656	0.2	0.00787	0.02	0.508
3/16	0.1875	4.7625	0.3	0.01181	0.03	0.762
13/64	0.203125	5.1594	0.4	0.01575	0.04	1.016
7/32	0.21875	5.5562	0.5	0.01969	0.05	1.270
15/64	0.234375	5.9531	0.6	0.02362	0.06	1.524
1/4	0.25	6.3500	0.7	0.02756	0.07	1.778
17/64	0.265625	6.7469	0.8	0.03150	0.08	2.032
9/32	0.28125	7.1437	0.9	0.03543	0.09	2.286
19/64	0.296875	7.5406	1	0.03937	0.1	2.54
5, 16	0.3125	7.9375	2	0.07874	0.2	5.08
21/64	0.328125	8.3344	3	0.11811	0.3	7.62
11/32	0.34375	8.7312	4	0.15748	0.4	10.16
23/64	0.359375	9.1281	5	0.19685	0.5	12.70
3/8	0.375	9.5250	6	0.23622	0.6	15.24
25/64	0.390625	9.9219	7	0.27559	0.7	17.78
13/32	0.40625	10.3187	8	0.31496	0.8	20.32
27/64	0.421875	10.7156	9	0.35433	0.9	22.86
7/16	0.4375	11.1125	10	0.39370	1	25.4
29/64	0.453125	11.5094	11	0.43307	2	50.8
15/32	0.46875	11.9062	12	0.47244	3	76.2
31/64	0.484375	12.3031	13	0.51181	4	101.6
1/2	0.5	12.7000	14	0.55118	5	127.0
33/64	0.515625	13.0969	15	0.59055	6	152.4
17/32	0.53125	13.4937	16	0.62992	7	177.8
35/64	0.546875	13.8906	17	0.66929	8	203.2
9/16	0.5625	14.2875	18	0.70866	9	228.6
37/64	0.578125	14.6844	19	0.74803	10	254.0
19/32	0.59375	15.0812	20	0.78740	11	279.4
39/64	0.609375	15.4781	21	0.82677	12	304.8
5/8	0.625	15.8750	22	0.86614	13	330.2
41/64	0.640625	16.2719	23	0.90551	14	355.6
21/32	0.65625	16.6687	24	0.94488	15	381.0
43/64	0.671875	17.0656	25	0.98425	16	406.4
11/16	0.6875	17.4625	26	1.02362	17	431.8
45/64	0.703125	17.8594	27	1.06299	18	457.2
23/32	0.71875	18.2562	28	1.10236	19	482.6
47/64	0.734375	18.6531	29	1.14173	20	508.0
3/4	0.75	19.0500	30	1.18110	21	533.4
49/64	0.765625	19.4469	31	1.22047	22	558.8
25/32	0.78125	19.8437	32	1.25984	23	584.2
51/64	0.796875	20.2406	33	1.29921	24	609.6
13/16	0.8125	20.6375	34	1.33858	25	635.0
53/64	0.828125	21.0344	35	1.37795	26	660.4
27/32	0.84375	21.4312	36	1.41732	27	685.8
55/64	0.859375	21.8281	37	1.4567	28	711.2
7/8	0.875	22.2250	38	1.4961	29	736.6
57/64	0.890625	22.6219	39	1.5354	30	762.0
29/32	0.90625	23.0187	40	1.5748	31	787.4
59/64	0.921875	23.4156	41	1.6142	32	812.8
15/16	0.9375	23.8125	42	1.6535	33	838.2
61/64	0.953125	24.2094	43	1.6929	34	863.6
31/32	0.96875	24.6062	44	1.7323	35	889.0
63/64	0.984375	25.0031	45	1.7717	36	914.4

1   Imperial gallon = 8 Imp pints = 1.16 US gallons = 277.42 cu in = 4.5459 litres

1   US gallon = 4 US quarts = 0.862 Imp gallon = 231 cu in = 3.785 litres

1   Litre = 0.2199 Imp gallon = 0.2642 US gallon = 61.0253 cu in = 1000 cc

Miles to Kilometres		Kilometres to Miles	
1	1.61	1	0.62
2	3.22	2	1.24
3	4.83	3	1.86
4	6.44	4	2.49
5	8.05	5	3.11
6	9.66	6	3.73
7	11.27	7	4.35
8	12.88	8	4.97
9	14.48	9	5.59
10	16.09	10	6.21
20	32.19	20	12.43
30	48.28	30	18.64
40	64.37	40	24.85
50	80.47	50	31.07
60	96.56	60	37.28
70	112.65	70	43.50
80	128.75	80	49.71
90	144.84	90	55.92
100	160.93	100	62.14

lb f ft to Kg f m		Kg f m to lb f ft		lb f/in^2 : Kg f/cm^2		Kg f/cm^2 : lb f/in^2	
1	0.138	1	7.233	1	0.07	1	14.22
2	0.276	2	14.466	2	0.14	2	28.50
3	0.414	3	21.699	3	0.21	3	42.67
4	0.553	4	28.932	4	0.28	4	56.89
5	0.691	5	36.165	5	0.35	5	71.12
6	0.829	6	43.398	6	0.42	6	85.34
7	0.967	7	50.631	7	0.49	7	99.56
8	1.106	8	57.864	8	0.56	8	113.79
9	1.244	9	65.097	9	0.63	9	128.00
10	1.382	10	72.330	10	0.70	10	142.23
20	2.765	20	144.660	20	1.41	20	284.47
30	4.147	30	216.990	30	2.11	30	426.70

List of illustrations

Index